STONES OF EMPIRE

Inside the Gateway of India, Bombay, which was built in 1927 to commemorate a visit, sixteen years before, of the then King-Emperor, George V. A Mr G. Wittet designed this fanciful mixture of Arc de Triomphe and Moorish palace in yellow basalt. It was the last monument to Empire built in India, and, appropriately, it was the site from which the last soldiers of the Raj left India after Independence in 1947.

STONES OF EMPIRE

The Buildings of the Raj

TEXT BY
JAN MORRIS

PHOTOGRAPHS AND CAPTIONS BY
SIMON WINCHESTER

Oxford   New York

OXFORD UNIVERSITY PRESS

1983

Oxford University Press, Walton Street, Oxford OX2 6DP

London Glasgow New York Toronto
Delhi Bombay Calcutta Madras Karachi
Kuala Lumpur Singapore Hong Kong Tokyo
Nairobi Dar es Salaam Cape Town
Melbourne Auckland
and associates in
Beirut Berlin Ibadan Mexico City Nicosia

Oxford is a trade mark of Oxford University Press

British Library Cataloguing in Publication Data
Morris, Jan
Stones of Empire.
1. Architecture—India—History—Pictorial works
I. Title   II. Winchester, Simon
722'.4   NA1501
ISBN 0-19-211449-2

Library of Congress Cataloging in Publication Data
Morris, Jan, 1926–
Stones of empire.
Bibliography: p.
Includes index.
1. Architecture—India—British influences.
2. India—History—British occupation, 1765–1947.
I. Winchester, Simon.   II. Title.
NA1502.M67 1983   722'.44   83-2424
ISBN 0-19-211449-2

Set by Rowland Phototypesetting Ltd
Printed in Hong Kong

CONTENTS

ACKNOWLEDGEMENTS

The authors wish to thank the following for giving their permission to reproduce the photographs on the pages listed:

British Architectural Library/RIBA, London, pp. 78 (bottom), 79, 170 (top).
The British Library, pp. 28 (bottom), 34 (bottom), 43 (bottom), 48 (all), 53 (bottom), 66 (both), 73 (bottom), 75 (bottom), 87 (bottom), 108, 116 (both), 129 (bottom), 132 (both), 156, 184 (bottom), 208 (top), 213 (bottom), 221 (top).
Country Life, pp. 100, 170 (bottom).
Denis Thorpe, p. 12.

A NOTE ABOUT THE TEXT

When this book speaks of 'India', it means India before the partition of 1947.

When it speaks of 'Anglo-Indian', it uses the phrase in its original sense – appertaining, that is, to the British in India.

The structures it describes were all built in Indian territories under direct British sovereignty, except for a few built by the British for their own use within the territories of independent Indian rulers.

1 · Introductory

A brutal virtue

Like it or not, there was virtue in the Greek sense to the idea of empire, the assumption that one tribe, race, or nation might, by the brutal privilege of *force majeure*, legitimately lord it over another. The idea is disguised nowadays in economic device or political euphemism, but in its days of climax it was creatively explicit. If it was born out of petty squabbles around cave or cromlech, it developed into majestic movements of men and beliefs, so that the whole world is still shaped by its progressions and layered with its deposits. Every empire wanes in the end – 'one with Nineveh and Tyre' – but all our lives have been affected, sometimes directed, by the long march of imperialism.

The most potent legacies of empires are immaterial things: religions, languages, frames of mind, systems of law, manners and pastimes, conventions, traditions, so that to this day (for instance) the Christianity of Spain blazes on in Mexico or Peru, the language of France finds speakers of exquisite cadence in Chad or Guadeloupe, they are still playing cricket in Papua New Guinea (fifty-nine players a side), and the legacy of Roman order survives sporadically over most of western Europe, ending recognizably even now at the point where the Roman Empire ended, on the shores of the Irish Sea.

Grand animate effects also testify to the godlike presumptions of imperialism. American potatoes sprout in Nepal. English rabbits multiply in Queensland. Spanish horses roam the pampas of Argentina. The human race itself was physically mutated by the imperial experience. On the one hand new kinds of person were created – mulattos and mestizos, Eurasians, Coloureds, Creoles. On the other old kinds were altered by unaccustomed climes and landscapes. If empire was a sterilization in some respects, it was a fertilization in others. It was like an unreliable gene, productive alike of cretins, thugs, saints and geniuses.

But more than most political abstractions, imperialism expressed itself directly in material objects too. Every conqueror dreamed up his own monuments, every empire liked to emblemize itself in marble. Architects were always ready to oblige, from the Pharoah's Imhotep to the Führer's Albert Speer, and they have left their tributes everywhere: mile upon mile of ceremonial highway, labyrinths of imperial offices, mountains of obelisk and triumphal arch – heroic catafalques and lapidary texts – effigies of emperors, generals, law-makers – sun-lions of Persia, winged lions of Venice, eagle-heads of Russia or Austria, serpents of Egypt, cocks of France, wolves of Italy – 'Look on these works, ye mighty, and despair!'

The British way of empire

It says something for the British Empire, the greatest of the conventional empires and possibly the last, that it built relatively few of these self-glorifying prodigies. Though at its apogee it ruled a quarter of the earth's land surface and nearly a quarter of its people, though the sun then really did never set upon all its scattered possessions at the same time, still hubris was not its habitual style. This was hardly a matter of modesty, but was perhaps because this particular empire never really possessed an ideology – was temperamentally opposed, indeed, to political rules, theories and generalizations. It was the most powerful political organism of its time, yet it was seldom altogether sure of itself or its cause. Except in brief periods of special activity, or among specific groups of activists, it lacked the fanatic fire.

For one thing its ruling people, the British themselves, were traditionally dedicated to the liberty of subjects, which made the practice of British imperialism an anomaly from the start, and meant that its purposes were never unanimous. A united ruling class, it used to be said, was necessary to inspire a nation into imperial causes, but the members of the English land-owning hierarchy, far from being united in the excitement of empire-building, were more often than not profoundly bored by it, being perfectly content with their own lovely houses and magnificent countryside. As Lord Melbourne once asked, how could a gentleman possibly be interested in a country like Canada, where a salmon would not even rise to a fly? Or as an Indian Maharajah observed when visiting a country house in Derbyshire, how could an Englishman bring himself to go out to the discomforts of the East, when he could stay at home in such a place playing the flute and watching the rabbits?

Then again, the fundamental purpose of British imperialism was commercial, the pursuit of profit by a nation of merchants and manufacturers. Its political, strategic and improving activities were ancillary to the making of money, the securing of raw materials and markets, the manipulation of prices. The Flag went forth so that Trade could follow, and very often, in point of fact, the order was reversed. Of course the empire-builders often liked to claim loftier intentions, and by the nature of things the British Empire, having seized responsibility for the lives of such multitudes across the world, developed into something far greater than a mere economic agency: but still the establishment of law and order, the

Victoria, Queen-Empress: in canopied magnificence outside Chisholm's Indo-Saracenic University of Madras; and dusty and forgotten in a back corridor of the Memorial Hall, Udaipur.

The Victoria Memorial, Calcutta – Britain's answer to the Taj Mahal. The Prince of Wales laid the foundation stone of Sir William Emerson's white marble monument in 1906. It took fifteen years to finish, with the ornamental statuary fashioned in Italy. It is guarded by the police of Independent India with considerable zeal, so frequently has it been a target for Calcutta's enthusiastic demonstrators.

alleged enlightenment of the heathen, the reform of stagnant systems, the policing of the world, the glory and the sacrifice – all these were subject *au fond* to the exigencies of trade.

Except among a minority of zealots or visionaries, British imperialism was never its own cause. Parliament, always the supreme arbiter of the Empire, was seldom altogether seduced by the imperial idea, so that public money was begrudgingly spent, and every excess was questioned. No flamboyant satraps were let loose upon the far frontiers to commemorate themselves in pillars or temples: when in the 1850s the Governor of Bombay was rash enough to build himself a new house, it was criticized in the House of Commons as 'a typical instance of extravagance and insubordination'. Workaday railroads, not triumphal highways, were the mark of this *imperium*. Even the effigies of Queen Victoria which, in the heyday of the British Empire, arose like so many idols wherever the British ruled or settled – even these were subject to votes in municipal councils, reluctantly allowed for in departmental estimates, or paid for by church fêtes.

The Raj

There were really two British Empires. The first was a settlement empire, a western extension of Britain itself, and was lost to the Crown when, in 1778, the settlers of the Thirteen Colonies obeyed their manifest destiny and threw off the authority of London. The second was empire in the classic kind, empire by guile or conquest: though it too contained several great settler colonies – in Canada, Australasia, South Africa and the West Indies – it chiefly consisted of vast undeveloped tracts of tropical territory from which the British could extract the substances they needed for their industries, and into which, in highly profitable converse, they could pour their manufactured goods. This was essentially the Victorian Empire, Kipling's Empire, the Empire of the White Man's Burden, of the Zulus and the Fuzzy-Wuzzies, of the memsahib, the sundowner, General Gordon, Kitchener, Rorke's Drift, the Great Game – the empire which was to go into myth, like the American West, engendering its own images down the generations, and firing its own fancies.

Its centre-piece was always India. In the climactic years of British imperialism, the last decades of the nineteenth century, five-sixths of the Empire's subjects lived there. It was the possession of India that made Britian a great world power. The material resources of the place seemed illimitable, its markets were insatiable, its reserves of manpower were enormous, the prestige of its possession was incalculable, and around this colossal source of strength, wealth and authority much of the rest of the Empire was assembled. In many British minds indeed India *was* the Empire. It was only of India that, in 1877, Victoria was proclaimed

Uncompromising reminders of British dominion. New Writers' Buildings, Calcutta, where a thousand 'baboos' clerked to keep the rickety machine of the Bengal Civil Service in something approaching working order. The gateway gives entrance to the British Residency in Hyderabad – its Resident was charged with Viceregal powers, and his mansion was accordingly splendid, the better to treat with the fiefdom's rulers.

Queen-Empress, and all the wildest hyperboles of imperialist propaganda were reserved for the Jewel of the East, the Gem of the Imperial Diadem. Such art as came out of the British imperial experience came chiefly out of India: most of the nostalgia which, into our own times, has attached itself to the imperial idea is concerned with what has become known sentimentally to the British as the Raj (though the Hindi word simply means 'sovereignty' – *any* sovereignty).

India became part of the British national consciousness like no other possession. Whole families devoted themselves to the Indian connection, their members going out decade after decade as soldiers, governors or merchants. There were never more than a thousand British members of the covenanted Indian Civil Service, the administrative corps which ran the country, but many thousands of businessmen and their families lived in India, and thousands of planters, missionaries, foresters, railwaymen, river pilots, physicians or newspapermen. The powerful Indian Army was officered by Britons, and regiments of the British Army, too, regularly served in the country. In the 1830s there were some 41,000 Britons in India; in the 1860s about 126,000; in the 1930s about 165,000, half of them soldiers. So constant was the flow of traffic between the two countries, the ships of the Peninsular and Oriental or the British India lines, the lumbering biplanes and flying-boats of Imperial Airways, that the association came to seem, in British eyes, virtually indestructible. India was part of the British way of things. Without India, people used to say, Britain herself (or England, as they generally preferred it) would never be the same again.

First to last

The British had first established themselves in India, as speculative traders, at the beginning of the seventeenth century, when the paramount force in the country was the Muslim Empire of the Moguls, based in the north. The Portuguese had possessed colonies at Goa and Bombay for a century already, and Dutch, French, Swedish and Danish merchants were also active, so that at first the traders of the British East India Company were scarcely more than rival beachcombers upon the shore. In 1639, though, the Company acquired governmental rights in Madras, on the eastern coast, and thirty years later it came into possession of Bombay, in the west, which had been passed to Charles II as part of his dowry from the Portuguese Catharine of Braganza. Thereafter the Company became more than just a trading organization, but a Power. As the authority of the Moguls weakened, and India fell apart in war and rivalry, so the Company developed the appurtenances of a State, armies, fleets, administrators, tax-collectors, minting its own money, imposing its own laws. By the end of the century it was in effect the sovereign authority in the three principal ports of India – Bombay, Calcutta and Madras – all virtually established by the British themselves, and henceforth known as the Presidency towns.

Gradually, by diplomacy, skulduggery, and force of arms, the Company's power then spread across India, defeating foreign rivals and recalcitrant indigenes alike; by the 1850s almost the whole subcontinent was, in one way or another, under its control. A British Governor-General ruled the roost, with his headquarters in Calcutta. The Mogul Emperor was a mere puppet, the lesser Indian princelings were all vassals, the Portuguese, French, Danes, Dutchmen, and Swedes had either been expelled, or were confined to infinitesimal holdings that posed no threat. The Indian Mutiny, which broke out in 1857 in a savage explosion of native resentment and foreboding, only strengthened the British hold on India in the end, while the astonishing hurling of railways across the land, in the most formidable of all the technical achievements of the British, gave their command a new strategic, commercial and even cultural cohesion.

In 1858 the Company formally handed over power to the British Crown, and India became an empire in itself, with a Queen-Empress in London, and a Viceroy to represent her in Calcutta. The splendour of it all was terrific, the assurance supreme, but even so within half a century it began to fade. Wars, nationalist protests, lagging vitality, economic falter at home, criticism abroad, moral doubts and intellectual arguments, all weakened the state of British India. The hold was relaxed, the confidence evaporated, until in the middle of the twentieth century the British more or less voluntarily abandoned their vast and ancient estates in India, and the last of the conquering soldiers sailed away to mingled tears, hurrahs and catcalls.

Imperial masonries

It had lasted, from the first landfall to the last embarkation, more than 300 years, but it had never really succeeded in reducing India. The British were proud that they had given the entire subcontinent, perhaps for the first time, political cohesion, binding it all together under their efficient aegis, and ensuring in the end almost a century of unbroken peace. But they never homogenized it, or subdued it to a single style or loyalty.

It was much too unwieldy for that. It spanned twenty-five degrees of latitude, from the Himalayan frontiers of China, Russia and Tibet in the north to Cape Cormorin in the south, and thirty degrees of longitude, marching in the west with Iran and Afghanistan, in the east with Burma (itself part of the Indian Empire until 1937, when it was made a separate British Dominion). Within these borders it displayed most of the earth's geographical kinds – tremendous mountains, wide and barren plains, lush pasture-lands, rain forests, marshlands, palmy beaches, bogs, grassy uplands like English downs, paddy-fields like China, orchards like

The whimsical side of the Raj. The somewhat weathered statues adorn the skyline of New Writers' Buildings, Calcutta — Science, Commerce, Justice and Agriculture preside a hundred feet above the bustle of Dalhousie Square. Three miles away the cherub, his cheek brushed bright by a million hopeful visitors, floats in a marble cloud at the Victoria Memorial.

Italy. It contained, by the end of British rule, more than 400 million people, speaking 800 languages, multiplying at a dizzy rate and exerting the energies of many religions and uncountable traditions. What was more, even in the most grandiose days of Empire, some 600 Indian princes retained the sovereignty of their own Native States under British protection and supervision, ranging from potentates like the Nizam of Hyderabad or the Maharajah of Mysore to country squires or even village notables, and powerfully contributing to the variety and unpredictability of everything. In books of statistics or imperial publicity India might seem a manageable entity, brought to order by British method: on the ground, first to last, it was a pungent, virile and gigantic muddle, kept in hand by British bluff.

Such was the unimaginable prize which the British had grasped for themselves in the East by their greed, courage and originality, and it dictated the nature of their imperialism at large. In India the British Empire found all its truest expressions, in its mixture of the opportunist and the self-righteous, the admirable and the inexcusable, the benevolent and the insufferable, the charming and the arrogant, the imaginative and the insensitive. The British were deeply and permanently influenced by their long stay in India, and the effects were felt not merely among the imperialists on the spot, but more diffusely among people at home too; so that like heliographs, across three centuries, India and England flashed their messages one to another, each simultaneously instructing and obeying.

All this the British transmuted, often unintentionally, into the buildings they erected in India. There was more stylish architecture to be found elsewhere in their Empire. The colonial structures of North America and the Caribbean, the exquisite Georgian streets of Dublin, the fine stone country houses of Tasmania were better than almost anything they built in India. But the range of their Indian construction was unrivalled. Not since the Romans, it is probably safe to say, had an imperial people erected such a grand range of structures in a subject land. They expressed the will of a people not simply to rule, evangelize, or exploit another, but to adapt itself to utterly alien circumstances, landscapes altogether unlike its own, a climate unfamiliar and demanding, against which it must compete both for imperial effect and for its own survival, and for which it evolved specific new vernaculars – tropical adaptations of the Georgian terrace, orientalized railway stations, or seaside villas, whisked from Paignton or Weymouth, that were inventively adjusted to Himalayan conditions.

Built into their masonries we may detect the mingled emotions of British imperialism, at once so arrogant and so homesick, and they provide an index to its techniques and aspirations: how it worked, what it wanted, what it thought itself to be. If the British anywhere left stones of empire in a generic sense, then India is the place to find them.

Figures representing the dignity of rural life, carved above one of the entrances to the Crawford Market, Bombay. The bas-reliefs were carved by Rudyard Kipling's father.

2 · *Theoretical*

Modes and origins

It is said that, even when British rule ended in 1947, millions of Indians had never set eyes upon a Briton. Nevertheless there were few villages in India where the empire-builders did not leave some physical sign of their passing. It might only be a water-pump, or a post-box, or a level crossing gate, or just the long line of telegraph-poles stretching away to the dun horizon, but still it was unmistakably theirs. These were technical imperialists. Gasworks or water-towers were at least as characteristic of their dominion as courts of justice or gubernatorial mansions.

It was because of their mastery of technique that the British had an empire in India at all. They were the first harnessers of steam, and the first to take the radical new systems of the machine age into the simpler places of the earth. The great period of their ascendancy in India coincided almost exactly with their industrial pre-eminence in the world at large, and the buildings they constructed in India were the direct reflection of their achievements at home. But there was a time-lag – not just the gap that always separates architecture from political and social events, but also the gap that separated happenings in Britain from reactions in India.

On one level there was the sheer physical delay. It was 11,000 miles from London to Bombay, until the cutting of the Suez Canal, and in the days before steamships and cables it took six months to get a letter home, and another six months to receive a reply. Fashions were always out of date in India – Paris modes from the season before last, archaic cuts of shoes or saddlery, instalments of *Pickwick* or *Vanity Fair* long since absorbed at home, or bound up definitively into volumes. As late as the 1930s visitors found life among the Anglo-Indians curiously echo-like: 'Oxford bags!' they used irritatingly to exclaim, 'Good God, haven't seen them for years', or, 'My dear, you're not *still* reading *If Winter Comes* . . .?' Anachronism was part of the ambience: only the arrival of American troops during the Second World War convinced imperial officialdom that the unremitting wearing of topis was not after all absolutely essential to survival in the Indian climate.

Lutyens in New Delhi. A red sandstone cupola provides relief from the new capital's summer sun.

On a deeper level there were delays in taste and attitude because of imperialism's innate conservatism. Boldly innovative in its first stages, imperialism generally became almost immobile in the end, and in the later British Empire, as in most others, new ideas were prima facie suspect. They wanted no new-fangled nonsense from Europe. Not only did they know best what suited themselves in their own colonial environment, but they had always at the backs of their minds what was modern in England when they left it – ten, twenty, fifty years before. The Viceroys of India, who were political appointees from home and normally served a five-year term of office, were often regarded by the Anglo-Indian Establishment as meddling radicals, until the old machinery tamed and slowed them – 'like the diurnal revolution of the earth', wrote the exasperated Lord Curzon, 'went the files, steady, solemn, sure and slow'. British India, so swift off the mark in its youth, was terribly lumbering in its maturity.

So the architectural modes of England, too, all reached India, but rather late. The age of the Raj spanned several architectural periods. When the British first became a Power in India, the Palladian and the Baroque were the dominant styles in England – the British established themselves in Bombay during the construction of St. Paul's Cathedral in London. Georgian neo-classicism was all the fashion in the years when they were developing the Presidency towns, and by the time they had made themselves paramount throughout India the Gothic Revival was in full flair. The eclectic flamboyance of High Victorian coincided with the imperial apogee; during the decades that followed, when the British gradually lost their convictions of grand destiny in India, English architecture degenerated into a mishmash of compromise and half measure, generally lacking either swank or tenderness, and toying only timidly with the new modernism coming out of Germany and America.

Sooner or later, as we shall see, all these styles found their mirror images in India. The connection was constant from Wren to Lutyens.

Mutations

But they were all, like the empire-builders themselves, slightly mutated *en voyage*. The men and women got browner, louder, thinner, or sometimes thicker. The architectural styles got cruder, looser, wider and very often larger. They were making the sea change from a highly advanced Western country, whose art stood in the direct line of descent from Greece, Rome, the Gothic master-masons and the Renaissance, to a country whose educated architecture sprang from different roots altogether, and whose vernacular styles were evolved to meet the demands of extreme poverty and simplicity of material.

Throughout the long building period of British India the constructions were, so to speak, roughened by their setting. It was inevitable. The profligacy of the

Comfortable Bombay, classical Calcutta. The High Victorian splendour of Elphinstone Circle, Bombay (*left*), built in the 1860s after the style of Tunbridge Wells, or Leamington Spa. It is currently named Horniman Circle, after an anti-Raj editor who once lived there. India's former British capital, though, is more severely classical, as in the Doric columns of St. Andrew's Church, seen against the Gothic redbrick pile of New Writers' Buildings (*right*).

country, the inexorable pressure of population, hardly made for daintiness, and few buildings could remain altogether immune to the environment. The poor jostled about the garden gates, the supplicants spat their betel juice up the office stairs, the thousands upon thousands of clerks sat awash in paper in departments of State, the indomitable millions of India deposited themselves like nomads, surrounded by bundles and bedding, crowded about by numberless children, in the proudest alcoves of railway stations.

And if it was not people, it was birds, beasts, or insects. We must imagine early Anglo-Indian buildings aswarm with animal life, dogs, horses, flying-foxes, goats, bats, snakes, camels sometimes, even elephants or buffaloes, not to speak of flapping crows and mynas, circling kites, lizards, rats, flies and multitudinous termites. The patter of monkeys' paws on roofs was one of the essential sounds of Simla, the summer capital of the British Empire in India. The adjutant cranes which habitually sat about the parapet of the Viceroy's Palace in Calcutta were so much a part of the place that in old prints they look like artificial ornaments. Jackals and peacocks competitively yelled and squawked around Government House, Allahabad, and Lady Canning, the first Vicereine, reported that during the monsoon her dinner-table in Calcutta was 'covered with creatures as thickly as a drawer of them in a museum'. When in 1916 a funeral service was held for Sir Alexander Pinhey, British Resident in Hyderabad, the swarm of bees which nested beneath the roof of the Residency portico were so angry to be awoken by the strains of the harmonium that they sent the gun-carriage horses bolting down the drive.

Imperial social arrangements further elided the lines of architecture. Nothing was simple in Anglo-India. The most modest British household employed half a dozen servants, the grandest, the Viceroy's, employed in 1939 some 6,000, fifty being engaged solely in scaring the birds off the palace gardens. Each grade of domestic was separated from the others not just by seniority or importance, but probably by caste too, so that elaborate expedients must be devised to prevent mutual defilements; the kitchen quarters of an Anglo-Indian household often looked like a fairly shambled hamlet of its own, and needed stern supervision by the memsahib. As *The Complete Indian Housekeeper and Cook* observed severely in 1892, 'an Indian household can no more be governed peacefully, without dignity and prestige, than an Indian Empire'.

The climate was an architectural complication, too. Most kinds of climate were represented somewhere in India, but the mean was extremely trying, being terribly hot and dry at one time of the year, horribly wet and humid at others. Even the Grecian styles of building, though they looked fine in the brilliant light of India, could not cope with the climate unadapted – it was one thing to stand high in the limpid purity of scented Attic hills, quite another to resist temperatures of up to 120 degrees Fahrenheit, together with fearful dust-storms, violent

Bombay's Trafalgar Square – the wonderfully ornate Flora Fountain, built in honour of Sir Bartle Frere, Governor of Bombay Presidency. All distances to and from Bombay are measured from the Fountain, and many riots begin beside it.

monsoon rains, the ravages of insects and scavenging birds, months of unbroken winter snow in the north, unremitting tropical damp in the south, all conspiring to rot and fret a building, warp its pillars and flake its mouldings.

Anglo-Indian architecture of all styles was accordingly cluttered with devices against the weather. Rattan screens blocked its porticoes and verandahs. Shutters, hoods, lattice-work or venetian blinds shaded its windows. Proportions had to be adjusted, layouts adapted, in response to the heat and the blazing light: the more subtle Anglo-Indian designers learnt, like the Moguls before them, to make vivid use of shade and shadow, but the less skilled merely shoved on an extra verandah here, projecting eaves there, giving their work, all too often, an air of slightly hangdog makeshift.

'Cutcha'

Makeshift too, in the early years, were the materials they used. At first they followed common Indian practices, and built their houses of bamboo, or reeds plastered with earth and cowdung, or mud bricks. The bricks were generally sun-dried and called *cutcha*, a word which consequentially went into Anglo-Indian jargon as a synonym for the second-rate or the half-baked – we learn for example from *Hobson-Jobson*, the nineteenth-century dictionary of the dialect compiled by Henry Yule and A. C. Burnell, that a *cutcha* scoundrel was 'a limp and fatuous knave'.

Pitched roofs were thatched at first, or tiled in rough clay; flat roofs were often made of wood covered with tightly compacted layers of dried leaves and earth. Ceilings were of whitewashed hessian, giving rooms a limp and temporary air, balustrades were frequently of terracotta, and in the absence of glass, oyster shells in wooden frames were sometimes used as windows.

All these compromises the builders did their best to disguise. The façade was everything! They covered their shoddy brick and woodwork with lime plaster, to make it look like stone: in particular the Madras variety of stucco, made of burnt sea shells and known as *chunam*, they learnt to polish with marvellous effect, giving it a convincing look of marble. They dressed up their buildings with sham domes, fake pillars, and misleading substances. The early nineteenth-century Government House at Calcutta was modelled upon Kedleston House in Derbyshire, but as was rhymingly quipped by Lord Curzon, incumbent of both houses at one time or another, the pillars of one were alabaster, the pillars of the other lath and plaster.

Often enough bad materials led to precarious construction, and the annals of early Anglo-Indian construction are full of collapses. The brick pillars of Calcutta houses, a resident complained in 1798, were apt to crumble away before the rest of the house was even finished, and after a few days' rain, he said, their roofs 'drop and leak all over'. Even Calcutta Town Hall fell down during its construction in 1809, while six years later its ballroom floor began to jump disconcertingly about; though its architect rebuilt it at his own expense, for years people were chary of waltzing on it, and Sir Charles D'Oyley, an eminent local humorist, went into verse about it:

> When pillars bulged, and their foundations gave,
> And the great builder (not to be disgraced)
> Commenced anew, folks still were heard to rave,
> And shunned its tottering walls, as one would shun the grave . . .

No wonder good building materials were much in demand. If sun-dried bricks stood for the mediocre, properly kiln-fired bricks came to represent the Real Thing (*pukka* bricks they were called, and so we have the pukka sahib, the pukka appointment, or – *Hobson-Jobson* again – the pukka scoundrel, 'one whose motto is "Thorough" '). Sometimes the imperial builders had to import their materials – marble from China, teak from Burma, gravel from Bayswater for Calcutta in the 1800s, flagstones from Caithness for Bombay in the 1860s. Sometimes they looted it: wood from the palace of Tipu, Sultan of Mysore, defeated in battle in 1799, went into many a British building. So rare was the use of stone, in the early days of the Empire, that the church of St. John's in Calcutta was simply called The Stone Church, and the first house at Ootacamund was called Stone House. The granite used for the mausoleum of Job Charnock, the seventeenth-century founder of Calcutta, actually went into the geological language as 'charnockite', while the thirty-two black granite columns that stood in ceremonial display outside the British fort at Madras were thought so precious that they became an objective of war during the eighteenth-century conflicts with the French – the French raided Madras and shipped them away to their own colony of Pondicherry, the British raided Pondicherry and shipped them back again.

Later stone replaced brick as the prime material of British buildings in India; slate, machine-made tiles, and steel girders came in, galvanized iron revolutionized the Anglo-Indian roof, and gave the Simla monkeys something more sonorous to drum their feet upon. Even as late as 1911, though, when they were planning a new Viceroy's palace at Delhi, it was urged that for economy's sake the building ought to be plaster-fronted, and somehow the British in India generally failed to achieve that sense of rootedness which is a hallmark of most good architecture. Perhaps it was the debilitating climate, which gave so many of their buildings a tentative feel; perhaps it was the nature of empire itself; whatever the reason, one often senses of their villas, palaces and temples, however ambitious of scale or ostentatious of design, that their foundations are shallow and their walls flimsy – rather like those little prairie towns of western America which look, with their false fronts and rickety brickwork, as though the next strong wind will blow them, along with the tumble-weed, helter-skelter down the street.

The amateurs

Most of the constructions of British India were anonymous. Though English bricklayers made an early appearance in the Presidency towns, and the Company had its own resident architects, from first to last only a handful of eminent practitioners ever designed a building for the Raj. The stones of this empire were mostly put together by amateurs, by soldiers who had learnt the building trade perfunctorily during their military education in England, or in later years by employees of the Public Works Department, established in 1854.

A carpenter was the probable designer of the first Writers' Buildings, the East India Company's residential quarters in Calcutta, and Britons of many other callings boldly undertook architectural work around the place. Administrators who were responsible for the safety, welfare and discipline of millions of people were undaunted by the challenge of building a house or office; as late as the 1860s Mr H. Rohde of the Madras Civil Service not only designed his own house, The Cedars, but made all its doors and woodwork with his own hands. Their work was not invariably admired, though. 'It is the misfortune of Calcutta', wrote the architectural historian James Fergusson in 1862, 'that her Architecture is done by amateurs – generally military engineers – who have never thought of the subject till called upon to act, and who fancy that a few hours' thought and a couple of days' drawing is sufficient . . .'. 'If one was told the monkeys had built it all', said the architect Edwin Lutyens upon first seeing the British buildings of Simla in 1912, 'one could only say, "What wonderful monkeys – they must be shot in case they do it again!" '

Often they relied upon handbooks of architecture, very popular in the eighteenth and nineteenth centuries. There was Colin Campbell's *Vitruvius Britannicus* (1725) which translated into English idioms the precepts both of the Roman Vitruvius and of Palladio his interpreter: many of the grander early buildings of the Presidency towns owe their genesis to this useful text. There was James Gibbs's *Book of Architecture*, published in 1728 by the architect of St. Martin-in-the-Fields in London; the chief result of this publication was a positive rash of emulative St. Martins throughout the British possessions, North America to Oceana. James Paine, one of the architects of Kedleston, facilitated the construction of Calcutta's Government House by publishing his designs for the original in *Plans, Elevations and Sections of Noblemen's and Gentlemen's Houses*. John Wood the Younger, one of the presiding geniuses of Georgian Bath, published his *Plans for Cottages* in 1781. John Soane, architect of the Bank of England, brought out his *Plans for Buildings* in 1788, and in the 1830s appeared the invaluable works of John Loudon, whose several encyclopaedic textbooks offered models for almost every kind of building, and probably had a greater influence than any others on the architecture of British India.

Stairways: (*left*) at the Viceregal Summer Lodge in Simla, designed in English High Renaissance style by Henry Irwin and Captain H. H. Cole of the Royal Engineers; and (*right*) at the Victorian Gujerat Government College in Ahmedabad.

The gateway to Victoria Gardens,
Bombay (*top*), designed in Corinthian style, has a turnstile from a
foundry in Bear Lane, Southwark,
and terracotta ornamental panels
from Blashfield's factory in Lancashire. The heavy iron gateway to
the Victoria Memorial, Calcutta
(*middle*), runs on rollers, still lovingly oiled. Even the gate of a private
bungalow in Poona (*bottom*) has a
stolid quality about it, as though its
owner knew it would become a
memorial in time.

The London magazine called *The Builder* was always handy source material for amateur architects far away. *The Ecclesiologist* laid down guide-lines for proper Anglican design, such as a Christian Empire needed. All the successive sages of the architectural art in England, the Pugins, the Ruskins, the Morrises, the Geddes, had their eager disciples in India, and occasionally plans by well-known practitioners were sent out for implementation east of Suez: John Rennie was the designer of the prefabricated iron bridge over the River Gumti at Lucknow; Isambard Brunel, as adviser in England to the Great East Indian Railway, told them how to build Calcutta's Sealdah Station; J. D. Sedding and G. F. Bodley restored and enlarged buildings from afar; ideas about the interior of the Afghan Memorial Church, Bombay, were provided at a comfortable distance by William Butterfield, architect of Keble College, Oxford; Sir Gilbert Scott, the great Gothicist, planned Bombay University from his London offices.

Alternatively actual buildings could be more or less reproduced – St. Martin-in-the-Fields, of course, and Kedleston Hall, but also Ypres Cloth Hall and the Parthenon – and all over British India architectural enthusiasts would be visited by blurred sensations of *déjà vu*. Wasn't that Hereford Cathedral, incongruous among the Ambala bazaars? Could that be Bell Harry from Canterbury, rising above the *maidan* at Calcutta? The New Louvre in Paris, built by L. T. J. Visconti at the time of the Indian Mutiny, had a visible effect on Anglo-Indian institutional designers; so did Queen Victoria's country house at Osborne in the Isle of Wight, completed in 1851, if only because one of its architects was the Prince Consort himself; Hampstead Garden Suburb was clearly related, architecturally if not socially, to the new imperial capital laid out at Delhi in the twentieth century; the tiered patterns of the hill-stations, disposed along their Himalayan ridges, comfortably suggested the archetypal pleasure-terraces of Georgian England – dimly remembered, perhaps, by their subaltern planners from boyhood visits to Uncle Alfred in Hove, or tea and scones in Cheltenham.

We know a little about some of the early engineer-designers. Lieutenant James Agg, for instance, who designed St. John's, Calcutta, is immortalized in the diaries of William Hickey, for the two had sailed to India together in 1779: he was a modest and ingenious fellow, Hickey says, and though he rose no higher than Captain in the Company's service, he prospered so handsomely on the side that he went home rich, and was able to decline the Company's subsequent invitation to become Lieutenant-Governor of St. Helena. Charles Wyatt, Bengal Engineers, who designed Government House, Calcutta, at the end of the eighteenth century, was a member of a famous English architectural family who went on to become a Member of Parliament. His contemporary, Samuel Russell, who built the British Residency in Hyderabad, the one with all the bees, was the son of a well-known painter, John Russell, RA. Lieutenant Sankey, Madras Engineers, who designed Nagpur Cathedral in 1851, ended life as Sir R. H. Sankey, KCB. Two of the engineer-colonels who built Victorian Bombay, H. St. Clair Wilkins and J. A. Fuller, went on to become generals.

Mostly, though, even their names are forgotten. Not necessarily lost, all the same, for they loved to commemorate themselves on their own buildings. Never-to-be-promoted captains, majors otherwise obscure, are remembered on tablets in musty churches and dingy offices of their conception, and often, we may feel, frustrated artists found their only true fulfilment in these distant constructions under the sun.

The professionals

Later the amateurism left the Empire, and the soldier-designers and engineers gave way to professional architects. In 1902 the Government of India appointed its first Consulting Architect, James Ransome; in 1919 Robert Tor Russell was appointed the first Chief Architect to the Government of India. Some British architects set up private practices in India, and the names of the engineers and the Indian contractors, to be found engraved on most big Anglo-Indian buildings, were supplemented now by those of Associates of the Royal Institute of British Architects, or even occasionally Fellows. This development was not universally welcomed: some people thought that India, under British guidance, should be moving back to the tradition of the indigenous master-builder, rather than importing expensive talent from abroad.

But in any case few very distinguished British architects were tempted out to these uncomfortable fields of profit. Sir William Emerson, President of the RIBA, spent some years in India, his *chefs-d'oeuvre* being the cathedral at Allahabad, begun in 1871, and the Victoria Memorial Museum in Calcutta, begun in 1906. Vincent Esch, a Calcutta-based architect, helped him with that museum and built many ambitious buildings of his own in the Native State of Hyderabad. H. V. Lanchester, who died in 1953, was an eminent architectural planner with a flourishing Indian connection. Sir Swinton Jacob of the Public Works Department, who died in 1917, was a virtuoso of the hybrid styles. In the nineteenth century Walter Granville, F. W. Stevens and Robert Chisholm, in the twentieth century George Wittet, John Begg and H. A. N. Medd were all Anglo-Indian architects of distinguished talent. And when it came to the supreme commission of all, the design of the new capital of New Delhi in the first decades of the twentieth century, the job was entrusted to the two most famous British practitioners of the day, Edwin Lutyens and Herbert Baker. It was an irony, but not perhaps a surprise, that they presently quarrelled over the task, and left the great work, the noblest attempted in the architectural history of the British Empire, sadly indecisive in the end.

Classical devices

The first recognizable styles of British India were, in one sort or another, classical: this was the chosen mode of the East India Company until its dissolution, and it was altogether deliberate. The British in India were evolving from traders to rulers, and they welcomed a style that would so graphically express their cool superiority and their historical antecedents.

The eighteenth-century victories in the field that led to British supremacy in India powerfully boosted this lofty self-image. As the artist Thomas Daniell wrote in 1810, 'the splendour of the British Arms produced a sudden change . . . the bamboo roof suddenly vanished; the marble column took the place of brick walls . . .'. Visitors to Madras or Calcutta around the turn of the nineteenth century found themselves, like travellers to St. Petersburg at the same period, entering brand new cities of white classical silhouette. Against those blazing blue skies, those ominous monsoon clouds, the buildings of Empire seemed to stand majestically untroubled, reincarnations of the antique – an appearance, suggested the painter William Hodges, approaching Madras in 1781, 'similar to what we may conceive of a Grecian city in the age of Alexander'. This was the triumph of reason over barbarism, and the elegant order of the classical styles was used in pointed antithesis to the riotous tangle of Hindu architecture, with its delight in excess and grotesquerie. The British buildings of Calcutta and Madras seemed to speak of a civilization self-sufficient and unshakeable, whose inhabitants must surely be as contemptuous of corruption as of climate, sipping their heavy claret there in handsome shuttered dining-rooms, or puffing contentedly at their hookahs. 'I thought I was no longer in the world I had left in the east', remarked an awestruck Malay visiting Calcutta at this time, and that was just the impression he was supposed to get.

The imperial architecture was meant to emphasize a lesson. For most of their time in India the British were profoundly contemptuous of the indigenous cultures – 'astronomy which would move laughter in the girls at an English boarding-school', Thomas Macaulay sneered, 'history abounding with kings thirty feet high and reigns thirty thousand years long'. The British were determined to demonstrate the superiority of their own ways, both for their own security and for the attention of the natives, and they did so brazenly. Just as they heedlessly appropriated Indian sacred buildings for their own secular use – they once thought of demolishing the Taj Mahal for the sake of its materials – so they built into their own structures implications of timeless infallibility and strength. When they took Delhi in 1803 they commandeered a fine local palace, built in the Mogul style, to be their Residency in the city: hardly had the smoke of battle died away before they had affixed to its façade a grand colonnade of Ionic columns, setting their style and stamp upon it for all to see.

Many a classical device contributed to these ends – triumphal arches, toga'd statues, trophy halls, and Pantheons – and the traditional orders, Corinthian, Ionic, Tuscan and Doric, provided the early British architects with useful allegories. Their grammar, to be sure, was sometimes less than impeccable. Bishop Heber, in 1823, declared St. John's Church, Calcutta, to be 'full of architectural blunders, but . . . in other respects handsome'. Mrs Martha Graham, visiting Calcutta fourteen years before, thought the lavish use of the orders gave the place a general appearance of grandeur all right, but complained that they were seldom used 'according to the strict rules of art', while James Fergusson wrote that many of the buildings had been arranged 'in such a manner as to be as unlike a truly Grecian design as was possible with such correct details'. But the symbolism was the thing, and anyway few of those who saw these buildings, whether indigenes or imperialists, really knew a pilaster from an architrave.

Besides, there was an inner meaning to this architecture which was impervious to pedantry. Early British India was a community of tradesmen, but it aspired to grander things. Empire itself, the sudden acquisition of new wealth and grandeur, was a species of *nouvelle richesse*, and every Briton automatically went up in the world, when he sailed out to the lands of serfs and subjects. Nothing represented this sensation better, at the end of the eighteenth century, than the neo-classical mansions British businessmen built for themselves, in the more congenial suburbs of the Presidency towns, where they stood encouched in wide gardens as to the manner born – distant reflections of the country houses of the English aristocracy at home (into whose ranks many of the astuter nabobs were, in their rich old age, eventually to be admitted).

Gothic trends

Presently the Gothic crept in. Ruskin was heeded, and in Anglo-India the forms of neo-classicism went out of fashion. The first signs of Gothic indeed, stemming from the romantic Strawberry Hill kind, were to be seen in Madras and Calcutta at the end of the eighteenth century – a Gothic chapel, with pepper-pot turrets and flying buttresses, was surprisingly provided for Calcutta's Fort William in 1784; but the approach of true Victorian Gothic was most clearly announced by the design of Calcutta Cathedral, the metropolitan church of British India, which was completed in 1847 in a significant mixture of the medieval and the antique specified by its Bishop as being 'the Gothic or rather Christian style of architecture'.

For by then evangelical religion had added a fervent new impulse to the energies of Empire. The early merchant-adventurers, though generally practising Christians, had certainly not been Christian militants. Their relations with

Classical relics. (*Top left.*) Lieutenant Charles Wyatt's Government House, Calcutta, built in 1799, after the design of Kedleston Hall, Derbyshire. The metope, architrave and capitals of Russell's Corinthian-style Residency in Hyderabad (*bottom*), showing the acanthus leaves carved by patient Indian workmen in 1803, and the bees' nest created nearly two centuries later. And a detail from the old Residency in Bangalore (*top right*).

The Imperial masters liked grand entrances: the British Residency in Hyderabad is approached via Doric columns, goats' heads and the Royal Arms; Government House, Calcutta, shows a lion, its forepaw resting, appropriately, on the globe which he largely controlled.

Indians were generally easy-going and often lascivious, when they were not murderous, and even when they developed convictions of cultural supremacy, religiosity was not part of it. The Victorian empire-builders, though, had different ideas. They believed passionately in Christian duty and divine providence, and soon many of the Empire's fiercest activists were Christians of fundamentalist zeal.

Gothic became their idiom above all others. For one thing it was cheaper to build than classical, so that you could have two evangelistic churches for the price of one; for another it possessed none of the heathen implications of classical forms; and for a third it had the imprimatur of all the best authorities at home, the Church Commissioners, the Camden Society, *The Ecclesiologist*, Ruskin and Pugin. The Anglo-Indian church designers quickly got the point. Not another St. Martin-in-the-Fields was built, and when in 1865 they wanted to extend the eighteenth-century classical cathedral at Bombay, without a second thought they tacked an Early English chancel on the end of it. Before long Indian Christians had learnt to call the Gothic pointed arch 'the praying arch', because it was supposed to possess the physical appearance of hands joined in prayer.

Secular architecture soon followed suit. Actually Gothic was far less suitable to the environment than the classical styles: the Greeks and Romans had designed for sunny climates too, but the medieval architects of northern Europe had built for winds, fogs and glowering skies, and when Gothic was translated to the East there was something close and restless to the very look of it. Still, Ruskin had demonstrated from the Venetian example that it did very well as an imperial idiom, and the Anglo-Indian architects applied it to all purposes. So ubiquitously indeed did Royal Engineers' Gothic, Public Works Department Gothic, spread across the face of India, in secretariat and public hall, market and museum, that by a natural association of ideas the whole of Anglo-India began to have a distinctly diocesan look, and the white pillared buildings left over from earlier generations seemed more elegantly pagan than ever.

The grand hybrids

Another change of mode was signalled, after the Mutiny, by the end of the East India Company. The Crown now established its own administration for India, embodied in the Indian Civil Service. The Company's Governor-General became the Queen's Viceroy, Queen Victoria was proclaimed Empress of India, and for the first time a few Indians were admitted to the higher echelons of their own Government. Flamboyant new elements entered the imperial ethos, not easily to be embodied either in the austerity of the orders or the piety of conventional Gothic. The fact that Indians were now fellow-subjects of the Queen seemed to

demand some architectural concession to the indigenous, some manner less unbending than the classical, less utterly alien than the Gothic. Without *in any way* conceding that Indian culture was the equal of British, or abandoning *one jot* of the conviction that they had been called by divine providence to the redemption of India, the British began to introduce Indian features and motifs into their imperial architecture.

This was something startling. In 1772, when the military architect Patrick Ross had tried to adopt Indian patterns for an arsenal he was building at Madras, he had been severely rebuked by the Company, and as late as 1861, when St. Stephen's College went up in Delhi in a vaguely Mogul style, it was violently attacked as being unsuitable for Christian purposes. Times and tastes were changing, though. Nobody now suggested pulling down the Taj Mahal: it had become, for the British as for the Indians, a supreme symbol of romance – had become, indeed, part of their own inheritance. While at home William Morris and his friends were seizing upon the English heritage of craftsmanship, in India a British-fostered arts and crafts movement encouraged the employment of native skills in imperial projects, providing Maratha motifs for railway station waiting-rooms, or ancient Rajasthani patterns for the embellishment of vegetable markets. When in 1903 Lord Curzon presided over the durbar held at Delhi to celebrate the coronation of Edward VII, he saw to it that the great tented encampment was decorated entirely in Indian styles and Indian materials.

The British were trying to imply that they were, though still an imperial people, organically a part of the Indian scene, and weird hybrid styles were evolved to express the synthesis. William Emerson thought that particular buildings erected 'for any purpose connected with the natives' should show 'a distinctive British character, at the same time adopting the details and feeling of the native architecture'. Eclecticism was rampant enough, Heaven knows, at home in England – one design for a new Liverpool Cathedral, presented in 1886, incorporated a Byzantine dome, a Baroque cupola, Gothic spires and classical porticoes. It was nothing, though, beside its Anglo-Indian kind, which Lutyens once likened to 'the mad riot of the tom tom'.

Fortunately for the architects the Gothic style, with its natural profusion of ornament, its pointed arches and vaulted roofs, lent itself fairly easily to orientalization; all manner of Eastern fancies invaded the orthodox architectural vocabulary, and the forms of the Northern masons found themselves transmogrified with domes, kiosks, and harem windows. 'Indo-Saracenic' was inexplicably the favourite generic name for these combinations, but the Hindu-Gothic, the Renaissance-Mogul, the Saracenic-Gothic, even the Swiss-Saracenic, were all identified at some time or another as architectural types. Sometimes the British erected buildings in a purely Indian way, and in late-Victorian times there arose a lively 'back-to-India' movement among more imaginative Anglo-Indians. Hybrid

The railway Gothic style of roof fretwork, at the Deccan College in Poona *(top left)*. Roof detail from Gujerat Government College, Ahmedabad *(bottom)*. Carvings above a window of St. Stephen's Church, Ootacamund, South India *(top right)*.

buildings remained predominant, however, into the twentieth century, and though purists and connoisseurs scoffed at them, and though they were indeed sometimes preposterous, perhaps we may see them now as proper to their time, and in their blend of the conciliatory, the dedicated and the exhibitionist, not without nobility.

The instinct fades

In Anglo-India as in England, there was a return to simpler modes in the early twentieth century, the flush of imperial certainty, as of Victorian complacency, fading away in wars and disillusionments. British architecture in India was anything but avant-garde, and never really had time to absorb art nouveau, let alone Bauhaus and the new international functionalism. The genre, like the empire that gave it birth, went out gently, even apologetically in the end.

Eclectism was given a last fillip by the establishment of New Delhi, the new capital of India, between 1911 and 1932, but it was eclectism of a more muted kind. Styles and symbol, Muslim, Buddhist, Christian and pagan, were somewhat tentatively blended in this last and greatest creative enterprise, together with emanations of Isfahan and English country life, and tacit suggestions of Versailles. Gardens in the Mogul sort flourished beside Gertrude Jekyll rose-gardens. There was a circular Parliament building on Roman lines, a shopping centre evidently inspired by Bath or Regent Street, and a presiding dome evolved from a Buddhist *stupa*.

Mild reflections of this vision drifted across the subcontinent, to be solidified here and there in Lutyens's favourite upturned domes, or Baker's Persian-like pavilions. In general, though, British India bowed itself out in an unmemorable blandness of the neo-classical. The sort of architecture made popular by the Wembley Exhibition of 1923 well suited the needs and preferences of officials and businessmen alike, and could easily be touched up with ornamental elephants, or even corner kiosks, to show willing to the indigenes. It was hardly architecture at all really. It might almost have been devised as an allegorical backdrop to the end of Empire – so soon to disappear not in any fires of Valhalla, but almost sheepishly into history.

'Shut-upness'

Of all the constructions of the British in India, few are more telling than a pretty white building which stands to this day upon the waterfront at Madras, a little tumbledown and patched about nowadays, but still full of character. Built in two storeys, it has a gracefully rounded front on the seaside, rather like an apse, an

The manhole-cover industry remains one of India's world monopolies: most of those found in America today were made by firms like Nortons of Calcutta, Delhi and Simla. The leonine fire-hydrant on a Simla street is of almost wholly decorative use – water pressure in the overcrowded town is nearly nil.

Indian wedding-cakes: the Ice House, Madras (*top*), built in 1842 to store ice brought by clipper from Boston, USA; and the old 'chummery', or bachelor-officers' quarters, in Jubbulpore (*bottom*).

elegant verandah, classical details, and a small shady garden all around. It looks like some tasteful little palace of ease, like an orangery perhaps, or a private theatre, or even a seraglio, but it is really an ice-house, built by the British in the eighteenth century solely for the storage of ice-blocks shipped in to cool them from Massachusetts.

Nothing could be more conclusively *separate*, among the palm trees of that humid shore, and it was separateness, far more than overbearingness, that characterized the stance of the British in India. They ruled in enclave, and their buildings almost always, even when ostentatiously Indianified, spoke of an alien and exclusive presence. Kipling called it 'shut-upness'. Even the smallest bunga-lows tried, with grand gates, wide compounds and ramparts of potted plants, to shut themselves up against the kaleidoscopic life of India all around: and at the other end of the scale, whole cities were arranged so that British communities could shut themselves away from the Indians. If this tendency began *faute de mieux*, the early European traders being obliged by the Indians themselves to live in waterfront ghettos, it grew to represent a maxim of the imperial system – Stay Apart and Rule.

It was not mere racialism, though bigotry was doubtless satisfied by the practice. It was a technique of dominance, and it worked. The more carefully the British stayed their distance, insulated within their clubs, barracks, offices, bungalows and ice-houses, the easier it was to impose their will upon the Indians at large. A touch of mystery, or at least of unapproachability, potently fortified their authority. Most of them were ordinary enough people really, and decidedly thin on the ground, so perhaps the less they revealed of themselves the better. Those Corinthian columns beside the Hooghly River, those Gothic parish chur-ches of the plains, those towered and vaulted railway stations – all were instru-ments of the system. They were the buildings of another, different, separate people, and however old they were, even when the tropic creepers covered them, bright bougainvillaea softened their outlines and apes trampled nonchalant across their roofs, still they always showed it.

They were seldom simply grand for grandeur's sake. The British were gener-ally convinced, it is true, that Indians were particularly susceptible to pomp and display, and they put great store on pageantry. But even the imperial palaces of British India, the ultimate structures of the Raj, were not generally overwhelming in their manner, let alone bullying. These were not the palaces of tyrants. They were the residences of English gentlefolk, a strange and special breed, come from afar to bestow their gifts upon India. They did not bristle with guns, like the forts of Rajahs. They were seldom stupendously extravagant, like Mogul palaces. A calm domestic air informed them. LINDY LOO, 1938–1943, mourned a gravestone in the garden of Government House, Bombay: HER TAIL STILL WAGS IN OUR HEARTS.

Sleeping worker, St. Thomas's Cathedral, Bombay. The repointing goes on, if in a somewhat leisurely way.

Yet their corporate personality was formidable, for they represented a ruling caste altogether sure of itself, secure within its own peculiar enclave of convention, tradition, prejudice and duty. To most Indians, I do not doubt, one viceroy or governor was very much like the next, every pukka memsahib was treated with the same deferential courtesy, each little Alice with her dolls, George on his pony, blurred into one fairly sentimental image of English childhood. It was the buildings themselves, their white serenity so startlingly emphasized by the surrounding flummery of flags and sentries, that were the real images of the Raj.

On assurance

And it was the assurance that counted. It did not matter that the elevation was awkward, if the house sat serene behind its trellises. The fiddly detail hardly showed, if the Secretariat was bold and grand enough. Lutyens and Baker, the most distinguished architects ever to work in British India, faltered in New Delhi because the real meaning of the project was uncertain; but Sam Russell, who was only a sapper subaltern, never put a foot wrong when he designed the Hyderabad Residency, all self-righteous decision, and the mostly unknown architects of the Indian railway depots endued them with the unanswerable fervour of cultists.

Assurance! When a district commissioner made a house for himself out of mud-brick and country tiling, when a captain of engineers blithely took on a cathedral, whatever their professional failings their buildings had the merits of gusto, courage, and sometimes brashness. The Empire itself, in its dynamic years, possessed just those qualities, bolstered too by delusions of divine favour. It had a stern beauty to it in its prime, when bearded patriarchs direct from the Old Testament commanded its armies with missionary fury, when preconsuls of terrific conceit directed its affairs with such authority that more than one of them was locally deified. It was like a huge work of architecture itself then, resting upon massive arcades of Christian faith, mercantile principle and self-esteem — castellated against all comers, turreted for effect, audaciously buttressed, and crowned at the top, as other edifices might be completed with saint or angel, by the portly figure of Victoria the Queen-Empress, holding an orb and a sceptre, and already bathed in the refulgent light of legend.

When it lost its assurance, it lost its virtue: and so did its constructions.

3 · Domestic

Chez Tapworth

On a ridge – beside a river – in a flowered suburb – on the desert's edge – there stands the home of the empire-builder! One building above all others stood for the intimate side of imperial life: the bungalow, which was to remain for ever a symbol of the British in India. Before we explore Anglo-Indian domestic architecture any further, let us in an idle way, during our afternoon hack, perhaps, or from the dicky of our Packard during a Saturday spin with Frank, briefly inspect this archetypal construction.

It stands, almost certainly, surrounded by a walled compound, and whatever its size, it is likely to be built well away from its neighbours. Behind it, there beyond the banyan tree, its kitchen quarters are cluttered beneath a thin haze of wood-smoke; a gravel drive lined with flowerpots runs down to its front gate, which is guarded by fairly pompous gateposts and marked with its owner's name, G. D. L. TAPWORTH. It is a low oblong building, with a *porte-cochère* of some sort in front of it, probably entwined in creepers, and verandahs under deep eaves all around. Wicker chairs and tables, hammocks, sporting trophies and perhaps a ping-pong table are distributed around these stoeps, and beyond them in the shadows we may just catch a glimpse of chintz and flower-vases, or a glint of cutlery through an open french window. It is not a grand house, not architecturally anything special, but even from our distance on the road outside its character is unmistakable. It represents a culture of distinctive strength, however limited, a people of great resolution, however dull. As long as the British in India are remembered at all, they will be remembered against the background of the bungalow, taking sundowners on its verandahs, playing badminton on its lawns, or –

Gosh darling, there's Muriel Tapworth now, just coming out of the drawing-room. Step on it, for Heaven's sake, before she drags us in for tea . . .

Keeping comfortable

Condemned to spend the best years of his life in the heat of Bengal, the great eighteenth-century Orientalist Sir William Jones (a Welshman, as he was once introduced to George III, who spoke every language but his own) devised a dramatic domestic expedient. Within easy reach of his offices in Calcutta, at the village of Safirabad on the Dacca road, he immured himself in a bunker immune to climate. Its roof was several feet thick, and its rooms were ventilated only by narrow heavily shuttered windows. So he survived the awful summers, resolving that so far as possible 'he would never see the sun, and the sun would never see him' (but dying nevertheless before he was fifty).

The first requirement of a British house in India was shelter against excessive heat, torrentuous rain, or more rarely fearful cold – all conditions which the British, brought up in a clime of equable drizzle, found dangerously debilitating. Two monsoons, said an old Anglo-Indian saying, was the life of a man: and though the mortality rate was certainly hastened by unsuitable diet and intemperate drinking, not to speak of battles, still the climate really was a terrible killer. Jones was not alone in his resolution: in the earlier years of the Empire in India, Britons often went to idiosyncratic lengths to keep the climate out of sight.

Often they turned old tombs into houses. Sir Thomas Metcalfe, British Resident in Delhi in the 1840s, bought a Muslim tomb almost next door to the Qutb Minar, the ancient victory tower which still stands on the hills south of the city. He used the coffin-space below its dome as a dining-room, and around it built an octagonal series of rooms, with entrance halls on two sides, which gave the whole a consequential symmetry. Another Muslim tomb became the home of the British Governor in Lahore, the mausoleum itself again providing a cool core to which miscellaneous rooms and verandahs were added in successive generations. Nobody appeared to resent these irreligious measures, and the British themselves very soon forgot, it seems, that they were sharing quarters with the spirits of the dead.

Another popular device was the *tykhana*, a windowless, underground room copied from Indian models. *Tykhanas* were used in the hottest weather of all, and sound very uncomfortable. Sometimes attempts were made to ventilate them with air shafts, but generally they seem to have been horribly stuffy. Nevertheless they were often furnished as grandly as the rooms upstairs. British official houses in Lucknow had whole suites of them, expensively decorated, and eighteenth-century drawings of the *tykhanas* in a house at Delhi show them nicely fitted out with Corinthian pillars, ornamental fireplaces, beamed ceilings, picture-hung alcoves and a billiard table.

They tried all sorts of mechanical methods to keep their homes cool. The *punkah* was universal in the early years, and the *punkah-wallah*, the man who kept those heavy flapping fans in motion, was the first familiar of every Anglo-Indian household. In very early days he often sat, as in the courts of medieval potentates, directly behind the chair of his employer, moving a fan by hand. Later he sat invisibly outside the sahib's chamber, pulling a hinged fan by a string slotted through the wall. Sometimes *punkahs* were small and numerous, sometimes they were few and immensely long, like undulating strips of carpet, and complex arrangements of pulleys were needed to keep them on the swing.

Later more elaborate systems came in. Water was kept constantly dripping, for example, through aromatic screens, erected all around the verandahs of houses like enormous cocoons. There was a device like a gigantic pair of bellows, with its snout inserted into the wall of the house: outside relays of servants sat pressing its huge handles together, inside the air was filtered through ice-blocks and blown in fitful gusts around the living-rooms. Or there was the more sophisticated Thermantidote, whose rotatory fan, puffing draughts of air through dampened screens, was often worked by bullocks in the yard.

Electric *punkahs* came and went, and in the 1880s the electric fan arrived. The slow creaking and whirring of this instrument above one's bed, the sometimes irregular rhythm of it, the always present fear that its huge blade might fly off in the middle of the night and decapitate you, became an essential element of the imperial experience. Air-conditioning never reached far below the upper echelons of British India, and the electric fan was, to the end, as much a part of the ambience as the bungalow itself: spectacular numbers of them were sold in India, and if there was no central electricity supply to power them, why, then steam generators chugged away day and night, in a miasma of coal, heat and Indian sweat, to keep the sahibs cool.

The cold weather too, which could be very bitter even on the plains, tried the British harshly. There was 'hardly such a thing', wrote Honoria Lawrence in 1845, 'as a comfortable cold-weather house in India', and forty years later the Vicereine Lady Dufferin described herself as sitting in 'not one, but twenty draughts at a time'. Snugness was a quality the British pined for, but their houses were generally sadly short of it: huge tall rooms, wide open verandahs, folding doors which seldom fitted properly, and were generally left ajar anyway – it was hard to feel cosy in such a setting, and many a poor memsahib, having dreamed of fresh English autumn days throughout the blistering months of summer, when winter came longed for some warm little cottage in Hants or Somerset, wrapped around with old English oak, with a comfortable country tabby on the hearth.

But there, they were not in India for snugness. They were there for duty, for advancement, for adventure. By and large the British never did live comfortably in this empire – luxuriously often, if only because of their multitudinous servants, but seldom *easily*. They learnt to live rough and ready. They thought nothing of sleeping in tents on the lawn, if the house was full, or on the roof if the heat was unbearable. They abandoned attempts at privacy, in a society were servants were ubiquitous but seldom slavish. When they went to their baths, in a zinc tub in a bare white-washed bathroom, they generally sluiced themselves out of tin mugs, sponges offering such convenient nesting-places for scorpions. The Vicar of Holy Trinity Church, Karachi, incumbent of one of the hottest livings in the world, was not provided with a refrigerator until 1946; when in the 1930s Lady Brabourne, wife of the Governor of Bengal, encountered an Indian urchin wandering about the Marble Hall of her palace, she was told that he was one of a family of squatters which had, for several generations, been living behind a screen of coconut matting on the south verandah.

'Bungle-ohs'

The Anglo-Indian bungalow, then, was evolved to make the best of things. It was called a bungalow probably because it was adopted from Bengali patterns, and it was variously spelt bungalla, bangla, bungelow, banggolo, bangala and bungalo – 'For Sale', said the *Bombay Courier* invitingly in 1793, 'a Bungalo situated between the two Tombstones on the island of Coulaba'. In the early years a bungalow generally meant a humble *cutcha* house, built of mud-brick or rushes, but later governors and even viceroys were not ashamed to sleep in one, and it was only when the term came to England, at the end of the nineteenth century, that it acquired a faintly pejorative social meaning, as in 'bungalow-land' or 'bungaloid developments'.

The first Anglo-Indian bungalows were pretty awful. In 1801 somebody defined them pithily as 'stationary tents run aground', and the explorer Richard Burton, in the 1840s, described the bungalow style simply as 'a modification of the cow-house'. Here and there even now you may still see an example still in use. It is likely to be an oblong structure on one floor, its roof rising unsteadily to a pyramidical centre, its stepped verandah pillared with square mud columns and shaded by low eaves. Its roof was doubtless thatched once, but is now of irregular rough tiles. It is a very primitive house, hardly more than a big hut, and really does look, as a matter of fact, a bit like a cow-house. With lesser regional differences (flat roofs in upper India, for instance, stilted floors in Assam) it was built in its thousands all over British India, generally containing a single square living-room and a bedroom opening off it, with the kitchen quarters in separate shacks.

Most such bungalows were built as bachelor quarters (and they sometimes had a *bibikhana* tucked away behind, for the accommodation of native mistresses). When, especially after the advent of the steamship, more British women and children came to India, the form of the bungalow became rather more complex, and sundry changes were rung upon the theme. It remained nevertheless

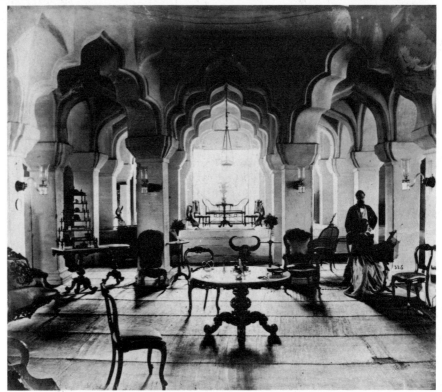

The cool of indoor life. A verandah in a Poona bungalow (*facing*); and a sleepy afternoon on the marble floor of a large private house in Secunderabad (*above*), once home to a senior soldier. Now it is owned by one of Hyderabad's most prominent Parsee traders. The Moorish drawing-room in Madras is shown in an 1860s print (*right*).

a simple structure to represent a great empire, and often struck visitors as quaint or even faintly comic, when they contrasted its modest arrangements with the flurry of servants that surrounded it, the impressive space of its compound (fifteen times the area of the house was thought a proper proportion for officers' bungalows in 1925), and the almost limitless authority that it frequently housed. Until the end of the Empire it often had no running water, and even in elegant city suburbs its toilet arrangements were generally limited to the noxious thunder-box.

It did evolve, though, into more pretentious versions of itself. Sometimes it just grew bigger. The bungalow of the Commissioner at Chittagong in the 1870s, for instance, was a hilltop structure that looked like four or five of the old-style structures put together – still thatched, even then, but surrounded by elaborate successions of verandahs and surmounted by a long balustrade ('I have never seen so lovely a place to look at', wrote its inhabitant in 1878, John Beame, 'nor one so loathsome to live in . . .'). Such a house now was likely to have three or four bedrooms, with dressing-rooms attached, a study, a playroom for the children, and a dining-room opening through an arch into the drawing-room, while a covered passage connected the serving pantry with the kitchen quarters at the bottom of the compound.

The bungalow became more stylish, too. The portico was the first sign of higher things: it could serve as a *porte-cochère*, or it could be a mere extension of the verandah, and it did wonders for the dignity of the establishment. We see it in many kinds – flatroofed, ostentatiously pedimented, curiously gabled, trellissed all over to make a sort of gazebo. Innumerable pots of chrysanthemums or geraniums often gave it charm. Castellation along the top sometimes gave it grandeur.

Behind it the simple shape of the building could be further disguised with parapets, ornamental urns, turrets, wooden spikes, barge-boarding. Though bungalows generally remained single-storeyed, clerestories made their rooms still higher and cooler, attics were sometimes added, and there could be terraces above their verandahs – 'too high for one storey, too low for two', the journalist George Steevens thought they looked when he arrived in India in 1899. Elaborate fenestrations appeared. Regency fanlights blossomed above heavy wooden doors, mullion windows framed stained glass representations of *Ivanhoe* or *The Idylls of the King*. A wonderful variety of accessories came to clothe the Anglo-Indian bungalow down the generations, and many architectural traditions were drawn upon – only the international style of the twentieth century was altogether ignored, the bungalow being, if essentially rather formal, distinctly not formalist.

By the time it came to the building of New Delhi, in the 1920s, the bungalow had reached the climax of its development. Lutyens, who was responsible for the residential layout of the new capital, was not an admirer of British domestic arrangements in India, which he thought 'extraordinarily unintelligent'; he liked to scoff about 'bungle-ohs', and his own designs for the capital's bungalows, which he wanted faced in marble, were rejected as too expensive. Nevertheless as you drive around the streets of New Delhi today the bungalows of the more senior officials, mostly designed in the end by Government architects, look most agreeable houses. Their gardens are lush and mature by now. Creeper drifts into their wide verandahs. They are of all sizes, being graded according to the importance of their occupants, and in several styles too, but they nearly all give an impression of spacious and airy charm. It is a long way from the stationary tent to these handsome structures, some of them palatial in manner if not in scale, but still the line of descent is direct: it is a curious truth that the British, having chosen the form of their housing in India in the seventeenth century, never devised a better one during the 300 subsequent years of their residence.

On the verandah

A diversion just for a moment, to consider the verandah. It was in some ways the most important part of the bungalow, fulfilling all sorts of socio-economic functions. Just occasionally it was rather a nuisance – Richard Burton, experiencing one during wet weather in the hills, said that it was 'only calculated to render the interior of the domiciles as dim and gloomy as can be conceived'. But in two particular ways it was essential to the purpose and significance of the house.

First, it was the one place the imperialists had just for messing around on. Everything was easygoing about the verandah. Its furniture was meant for lounging. Its floor was covered, if covered at all, with the memsahib's least valuable carpets, or with Chinese matting. Its pictures and trophies were beloved rather than precious. Funny old chairs lay round about, bamboo couches, rocking-chairs sometimes, or sofas with wide arms for the accommodation of glasses. Potted plants were everywhere, and here the little dogs of the household were indulged, lying around on sofas or begging titbits at breakfast time.

And secondly, the verandah was the place where the British woman, in particular, could feel some tentative personal contact with the alien world of India outside. Here hawkers and tradesmen might bring their wares, without actually entering the house proper. The watchman sometimes slept upon the verandah; the tailor was often to be seen cross-legged there in the afternoon. When Mr Tapworth felt obliged to bring one of his native colleagues home for a drink, it was upon the verandah that Muriel generally arranged things: and after dinner, as often as not, when the moon was high, the distant jackals were howling and there was a distant beat of drums from the bazaar, it was upon the verandah that the memsahib, already sketching out her entry for the day's journal, felt herself to be most truly amidst the romance of Old India.

In short, the verandah was a sort of bridge: it linked the rigid and conventional life of the imperialist with the lost liberties of home; it linked the rose-petals of the drawing-room with the dust and dung fires of the land outside; and perhaps, too, it tenuously joined the dreams of the Anglo-Indians with the reality of their existences – for on the verandah sometimes, with a drink in one's hand, or an embroidery frame, friends to laugh with and faithful servants just out of sight, empire-building really could seem, just for the moment, all it was cracked up to be.

Nabobian

Of course the bungalow would not do for everyone. Rich indigo-planters, who lived like lords, built themselves sprawling country houses; senior officials often indulged themselves with villas – Metcalfe, besides his tomb, had a splendid house in Delhi; and in the Presidency towns the nabobs, uninhibited alike by conscience, red tape, or restraint, commissioned impressive residences. When William Hickey went out to Calcutta in the 1780s he put up what he frankly called a mansion, without regard to expense, 'the bricklayers' carpenters' materials all being of the best'. He was very proud of it – it gained him, he reported, the reputation of having great taste. It looked much like a London terrace-house of the period, built on three floors, symmetrically windowed, with balconies on the *piano nobile*, and tall shuttered doors from which Mr H. might emerge, as a nabob should, to survey the colourful native scenes below.

The principal apartments, he tells us, were furnished with immense mirrors and many beautiful prints ('the expense was enormous'), and indeed the town houses of Calcutta could be very splendid. Gleaming in their lime or plaster facings, aristocratically free in their classical allusions, there was certainly no false modesty to them, and they were much grander than equivalent London houses of the time. The drawing-room of No. 5, Russell Street, by no means unique in its grandeur, was a double cube eighty feet long and forty feet high, and James Fergusson observed once that the Grimani Palace in Venice, one of the greatest of the great houses of the Grand Canal, 'both in dimensions and arrangement would range perfectly with the ordinary run of Calcutta houses'.

They were generally square, solid buildings, with flat balustraded roofs, generally with porticoes and nearly always with verandahs, half-closed with venetian blinds, on the first floor. Their ground floors were often rustically arcaded, while upstairs they were dignified with tall pillars or pilasters, usually in the masculine Tuscan order, and crowned with pediments. They were commonly built at right angles to the highway, great gateways leading between high walls into their compounds, and so they stood there one after the other along the city's main residential street, Chowringhee, like so many embassies or scholarly institutions. Today they are mostly buried in the urban mass of Calcutta, but still

Mansions. Metcalfe House, Delhi (*top*), was the home of the city's celebrated Commissioner from 1835 to 1853. It was badly damaged during the 1857 rising, but has recently been lovingly restored by the Indian Ministry of Defence, for whom it now houses a science library. Guindy Lodge, Madras (*bottom*), the former country residence of Governors of Madras Presidency, now provides the home for the Governor of the state of Tamil Nadu. It was acquired by the British Government during the governorship of Thomas Munro, and still houses a herd of deer in its huge gardens. The building is faced with *chunam*, a mortar made with crushed sea shells.

you may find their hapless relics if you look, overwhelmed by the sad congestion of it all, glimpsed up foetid alleys, embodied in sprawling tenements, or detectable only in a few crumbled pillars and a disregarded pediment.

One of the best of them, however, has survived in perfect condition, and gives an enviable impression of life among the Calcutta bigwigs of Company times. It is now the Calcutta Turf Club, but it has been little altered since its days as the home of the Apcars, a prosperous shipping family. It was erected in the early years of the nineteenth century in a distinctly patrician kind. Palladian in style, it is brilliant white of course, built on two floors, with a verandah on the south front and a portico on the north. A fine vestibule, extended through both floors, greets the visitor to this palace, and a beautifully detailed wooden staircase leads upstairs. Downstairs two large public rooms overlooked the gardens: above were family sitting-rooms and bedrooms. It is a meticulous house. Everything fits. The fine teak doors, the marble flooring, the sculpture-niches, the richly carved fireplaces – all are expensively and stylishly executed, and give an unexpected impression of cultivated restraint (for all too many of the nabobs were, as it happens, hardly more than avaricious sots).

In the south, in the outskirts of Madras, merchants and Company officials built no less elegant retreats. Down there the favoured orders were the Corinthian and Ionic, and the houses were more light-hearted and rambling in effect, with curved verandahs often, and bowed fronts, and they sported wide wings with connecting arcades, and shallow domes sometimes, and frivolous towers. The local artists John and Jonathan Gantz, in the 1830s, painted a number of these Madras suburban homes, and delightful they seem to have been, set in their wide green compounds, with their shady porticoes and the wispy Coromandel trees that soon grew up around them.

There is a handsome survivor of these houses, too, in the Adyar (now called the Madras) Club, originally the home of a merchant called George Moubray, and for years familiarly called Moubray's Cupola after its most distinctive feature. The Adyar River flows gently past this mansion, just as the Ouse or Trent might pass a gentleman's seat in England, and the house is full of urbane surprises – a hall thickly clumped with white plastered pillars, intimate alcoves here and there, a whole esplanade of terraces above the lawn: if you wish to catch the evening breezes – 'eating the air', as the Anglo-Indians used to say – you can climb by a succession of ladders into the eponymous cupola itself, high and fresh above the river, where you will find a garden bench waiting to accommodate you, and where a servant will presently follow, no doubt, with your sundowner and your letters from home.

Moubray's Cupola was more like a squire's place than a commuter's villa: here as at home, the British pined for landed consequence. The Anglo-Indian householders of Madras went in for ornamental lakes, landscaped gardens, even

The elegant mansion, rarely attainable in England, was far less costly in India. Scores remain, few of them in the pristine nineteenth-century condition shown here.

A fine private house in the inner suburbs of Madras, now owned by the British Government and – hence the flag – the official residence of the Deputy High Commissioner.

deer-parks, and around Calcutta, too, country properties called garden houses spread far out of the city centre. In the 1770s the Governor-General Warren Hastings built himself a country residence at Alipur, south of the city, which still stands. It was a simple enough building to start with, a square classical block with a bit of land: but in the way of country proprietors Hastings soon added to it, and by the time he left India in 1786 he was offering for sale two separate houses on the estate, a bath-house, a bungalow, and a range of outbuildings that included four coach-houses and stabling for fourteen horses.

In the hills

The nearest thing most Anglo-Indians got to a place in the country, though, was a rented house in one of the hill-stations. To these high retreats the central and provincial Governments habitually withdrew during the worst of the summer heat, and they were followed by many of the richer businessmen, all the grass

Senior soldiers, vital to the governance of the Indian Empire, were given quarters as grand – almost – as those of the civilian rulers. Flagstaff House, Secunderabad (*top*), would have housed the commanding general; the great garden house in Madras (*bottom*), its lawns running down to the River Adyar, was designed for one of the great lieutenants of 'John Company'. Today it is used as a naval pay office.

widows, all the officers on local leave, all the wandering globe-trotters and investigative Members of Parliament from London, giving rise to a unique pattern of resort.

The hill-stations were mostly, like Bath or Cheltenham at home, developed by speculative builders. Few Anglo-Indians actually built homes up there (Mr John Sullivan, who did, was repeatedly reprimanded in the 1820s for neglecting his duties as Collector in the awful lowland town of Coimbatore in favour of his garden high in the hills above). Some got houses ex officio, like the Commander-in-Chief of the Indian Army, say, or the Chief Secretary to the Government of Bengal, while others rented them for the season, generally from Indian landlords. Nevertheless it was in the hill-stations that the British in India achieved the most distinctive of their vernacular styles, and places like Simla, Darjeeling, Naini Tal or Ootacamund remain the most evocative concentrations of Anglo-Indian domestic architecture.

The hill-stations first came into their own in the middle of the nineteenth century, and the influences behind their architectural manners were distinctly varied. First there was the Gothic pleasure-villa, derived from the exuberances of Strawberry Hill Gothic, and given a more general lease of life by John Loudon's textbook. Horace Walpole, Pope, Beckford and Nash were all present in spirit at the building of the hill-stations, and so perhaps was Marie-Antoinette, for the cottage orné was everywhere. Then there were the festive terraces of the Georgian spas and resorts: Bath with its happy blend of the rural and the urban, the simple and the fashionable, or Brighton crowned by the supreme Anglo-Indian folly of them all, Nash's Brighton Pavilion. And finally there was the influence of the Grand Tour, which had accustomed Englishmen to the chalet styles of the Swiss and German Alps, and made them think that wherever there were mountains, there ought to be half-timbering. Add to this a contemporary taste for ornamental woodwork, elaborate it with the porches and verandahs engrained by then in Anglo-Indian design, festoon everything with guttering and down-pipes, cap it with a marvellous variety of convoluted chimney-pots, essential to the tone of the thing as to the brisk mountain climate, wrap it all up in the familiar imperial bungalow, and you have the fundamentals of the hill-station style.

Most of the hill-stations were remote – generally only primitive tribal people lived in those high places before the arrival of the British – and their first houses were nothing if not defiant. The first house at Simla, built by Captain Charles Kennedy in 1822, looks in old pictures rather like some sort of forest temple, Incan perhaps, with very high-pitched roofs and a central chimney apparently built upon a kind of pyramid – the wood for it was felled on the spot, and the house was put up by local hill-men: yet in it, so a French traveller reported in 1830, Kennedy gave his infrequent guests splendid dinners, with hock, champagne, and excellent coffee (being as the Frenchman admirably put it 'the first of all artillery

Houses in the hills: 'Knockdrin', a typical large Simla bungalow (*top*), is now used as residence of the Commanding Officer of one of the many units based in this vital military region; Kennedy's Cottage (*bottom*) was built in 1822 as the Simla hot-weather residence of the Commander-in-Chief, India.

captains in the world'). The first house at Ootacamund, Mr Sullivan's, was built entirely of stone, hitherto unknown as a building material in those parts, and nearby another stone house soon arose that might have been brought to that high tropic moorland, roamed by tigers, wild elephants and aboriginals, direct from some granite coast of Ayr or Cornwall. A few early houses were built in the classical mode, too, to demonstrate the sang-froid of the imperialists in all circumstances: but by the later decades of the nineteenth century, when the hill-stations had become tamer and more accessible, from the Himalaya in the north to the Nilgiris in the south villas sprouted everywhere in what might best be called Himalayan Swiss-Gothic.

When in 1888 Lady Lytton moved into the Simla house called Peterhof, then the summer residence of the Viceroy, she said it was the smallest house she had ever lived in, while her husband called it a pig-sty; but what seemed poky to the Lyttons then would seem to most people wonderfully spacious nowadays, and some of the hill-station houses were far more than mere pleasure-cottages. Take for example Barnes Court at Simla. This was remarkably like a curiously reconstructed kind of English manor-house. Its gardens were landscaped in the English style, its trees were cunningly disposed, and the whole house was built in nostalgic half-timbering. Patterned dark woodwork beneath its projecting eaves gave it, it is true, something of the air of a Swiss hotel; a gabled verandah acknowledged that this in fact was India; but by a cunning sleight of hand or *trompe l'oeil*, from some angles the octagonal steeple which stood at one corner of the house looked tantalizingly like an English church steeple, and made one think that the squire might easily emerge from Barnes Court on Sunday morning, to a chime of bells across the meadows, to walk through his private wicket-gate to morning service.

Other Simla houses were grander still – Snowdon, for instance, for many years the summer residence of the Commander-in-Chief, which had a façade of six half-timbered gables, and looked like a rather expensive spa. More characteristic of the genre, though, were the middle-sized villas, surrounded by modest lawns and shrubberies and often called My Abode, or Fair Lawns, which speckled every hillock of the hill-stations, and were to give many Anglo-Indian families the happiest weeks of their careers. 'It is impossible to describe the delicious feeling of awakening at Simla for the first time', wrote a visitor in 1846. 'The intensity of such a moment can neither be described or forgotten'.

There were thousands of such houses, and like the bungalow of the plains, they adapted readily to circumstance. At one extreme they suffered a lake change, and became Kashmiri houseboats – first built in about 1875, because the Maharajah of Kashmir allowed no European buildings on his land, and evidently derived too, with their shingle roofs, dormer windows and flag-poles, from Oxford college barges, or the boats of the City livery companies. At the other extreme the hill villas became even more English than English holiday houses, and remain to this day virtually untouched by time and history, preserved in architectural amber.

The best selection of all is at Ootacamund (which they used to call Ooty) in the Nilgiri Hills of the south (which they used to call the Neilgherries). Most of the Ooty houses are built of mud-brick, timber being short in the district, but they are nicely dressed up in scalloping and merry chimney-pots, and set in genteel gardens rather like so many small vicarages, this way and that on the slopes of the gentle wooded hills. They are mostly roofed in rustic tiles of a mild red colour, and with their drawing-rooms opening on to wide verandahs, their little bedroom balconies, their neat paths and trim wooden gates, they seem just made for the gentle English flowers which bower them still.

They hardly seem like India at all. So heartfelt was the emotion that built them there, so potent was the culture behind it, that even now one is surprised to find Indian families living in them, the music of the sitar sounds strangely from their mullioned drawing-rooms, and one listens in vain for the knock of croquet balls beyond the herbaceous border, or *Come Into the Garden, Maud* from the upright pianoforte.

The Club

Most Anglo-Indians had another home, separate from the bungalow or the hill-station villa: the Club. This resilient Anglo-Indian institution came in all kinds – social clubs, sporting clubs, yacht clubs, elegant institutions of the Presidency towns or ramshackle affairs of corrugated iron and beer-ringed bars, droned about by flies in up-country stations.

Calcutta, for instance, in 1913, had the Bengal Club for Government civilians (which carried associate membership of the Hong Kong and Shanghai Clubs), the United Service Club for military officers, the Turf Club, the India Club, the Calcutta Club, the Tollygunge Club, the New Club and the Saturday Club, a sort of beginners' club, open to men and to women, which specialized, says a handbook of the day, in 'games and amusements'. Bombay and Madras were just as well-supplied, there were fine clubs in the larger inland stations like Lahore or Allahabad, and they went on building new ones well into the twentieth century: Willingdon Sports Club in Bombay was founded in the 1920s, and long after the end of the Empire, I am told, if a gentleman stood impassive for long enough beside its changing-room showers, sooner or later a servant would appear and remove his trousers for him.

The Willingdon was a rarity in that it admitted both Britons and Indians from the start. Generally speaking all but the least pretentious of the clubs excluded Indians until the Second World War – in the case of a few of the most ludicrously

Calcutta's Clubs were the most exalted. The Tollygunge (*top*), to the south of the city, offered hundreds of acres of lush parkland: today, the new underground railway has consumed much of it, and the Members' tennis-courts have had to be sited elsewhere. The Royal Calcutta Turf Club (*bottom*), from its headquarters at 11 Russell Street, organized all the major racing events on the banks of the Hooghly River, besides offering its members the finest of European cuisine.

exclusive, actually until the end of the Empire. The Indians sometimes responded by building clubs of their own on the British model – at Bombay the British Gymkhana Club was followed by Hindu, Parsee and Muslim Gymkhanas, side by side along the waterfront. The Club, though, with a capital C, remained pre-eminently an Anglo-Indian symbol, and when you spoke of it everyone knew what you meant, whether you were a Chief Secretary discussing the Bengal Club burgundy, or an Assistant Traffic Superintendent on your way to tiffin at the Railway Institute. The clubs were islands of Britishness in the great Indian sea, to which the imperialists might withdraw whenever they felt a personal, social or ritual need: for a drink at the bar, that is, for a stag dinner, for a dance, a horse show, a wedding reception or a game of bridge.

Though they were seldom distinguished buildings, the architectural symbolism of the grander clubs was at least frank – Come In! it cried to suitable sorts of Briton, Keep Out! it hissed to everyone else. Visually their tone was generally dictated by their setting, which was above all prohibitive – daunting gateways, stern name-plates, sentry-boxes for deterrent watchmen, long drives to make the intruder feel uncomfortable, terraces from which he might feel he was being stared at by superior officers. It took nerve to gatecrash a really upstage Anglo-Indian club, and this sense of impeccable exclusivity impressed itself upon everyone. It helped to give many of the imperialists a spurious sense of aristocracy, so that when they went home to England in retirement they sometimes felt vulnerable and betrayed: but it also gave rise to much of the best writing about British imperial manners – Kipling, Forster, Orwell were all fascinated by the deliberate insularity of the club.

In its most ostentatious kinds the club could be very splendid. The Old Madras Club for instance, which now houses the local offices of the *Indian Express* newspaper, was described by Ivey's Club Directory at the end of the nineteenth century as 'one of the most magnificent clubs in the world', and was built to a princely scale. It was a heavy assemblage of several classical blocks, all columned and pedimented, with a monumental staircase leading up to its formal entrance in the middle. The central block housed the longest bar in India, with a dining-room and reading-room above it: the flanking buildings contained rooms for single men and married couples, with an excellent library, a billiard-room, a bridge-room, and sundry verandahs everywhere for drinks and gossip in the evening cool. In old photographs it all looks less like a place of pleasure than some great institution of authority: its servants are posed stiffly here and there, one or two gentlemen are grouped commandingly about the lawn, and in the background the great white buildings stand severe and imposing in the sunshine.

The Bengal Club in Calcutta was hardly less impressive. Founded in 1827, in 1845 it took over two of the big houses on Chowringhee, one of them the former home of Lord Macaulay. Several lesser houses round about were also acquired

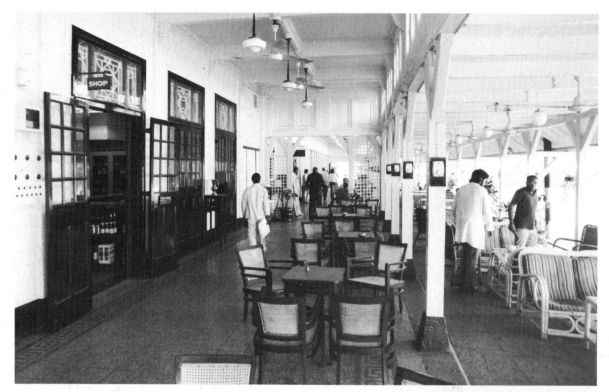

Clubland. After tiffin in the Gymkhana Club, Bombay (*top*); and the Madras Club (*bottom*), once the private home of one George Moubray, who built it in the 1770s. The gardens running down to the River Adyar are still very fine, with scores of magnificent casuarina trees.

The Old Madras Club, said to be 'the finest Club in all India – the Ace of Clubs'. The ballroom, now unused and decaying, was reckoned by dancers to be the best in Asia.

The Royal Bombay Yacht Club, a curious mixture of Swiss and Hindu styles. It is now off limits to yachtsmen, who make do with a rather less handsome structure tucked in behind the Taj Mahal Hotel.

over the years, until in the end the club formed almost a little village of its own, its gleaming white buildings separated by yards and gardens, guarded by spectacular doormen, and criss-crossed perpetually by hurrying domestics. With its balustrades and window-shades, its ornamental gaslamps, its beautifully tended gravel paths and this inescapable profusion of minions, the Bengal Club in its prime really did feel rather like some royal compound, the sort of place that revolutionaries eventually storm, and turn into museums.

Or there was the astonishing Yacht Club at Bombay, built in 1880. This was one of the very first buildings the newcomer saw upon his arrival in India, and with its long lines of al fresco tables beside the water, at which parasol'd ladies and topi'd gentlemen sat taking their tea in the afternoon sun, it must have made an encouraging if misleading first impression. A peculiar impression, too, for it was a building that defied architectural analysis. It looked partly like a railway station, and partly like a Chinese castle, and partly like an Alpine hostelry, and party like something in Port Said, and a bit like a prison, with tall watch-towers, and a bit like a covered market; and outside it, beside the sea, above the tea-tables, an immense white flag-pole capped the whole baffling gallimaufry with a small but distinctly bossy club flag. Suitable new arrivals soon found themselves at home there: 'tone it all down', wrote J. A. Spender bravely in 1912, looking out across the harbour from the Yacht Club terrace – 'tone it all down and in the dim light the view might be that from Plymouth Hoe'.

Light relief

For lighter relief the Anglo-Indians resorted to the gymkhana clubs, which were ubiquitous, and were devoted to the outdoor sports that lay so close to the heart of the imperial ethos. So important was the gymkhana club to the imperial way of life that its very name was to pass into the English language, to be used in very different contexts far away for ever after. Your gymkhana was an easier-going sort of place, where women and families were welcome, and it had tennis, badminton and racquets courts, skating-rinks sometimes, cricket-pitches, golf-links in later years, and a generally cheerful ambience.

We perhaps see its prototype in the eighteenth-century Assembly Rooms at Madras. This charming building, conveniently close to the racecourse, was clearly made for pleasure. Built on two floors, arcaded on the ground floor, balustraded around its flat roof, it had two three-sided protruding fronts with a steep staircase between, leading to a first-floor terrace. An enormous Union Jack flies from its roof, in an eighteenth-century picture of it, and people seem to be enjoying themselves all over it, on the roof, on the terraces, under the arcades, and all around the entrance, which is a lively jumble of palanquins, carriages, horses and sightseers.

The gymkhana clubs generally perpetuated this festive tradition. A good example was the Bombay Gymkhana Club, which thrives still. The British built Bombay, by and large, in heavy styles and ponderous materials, and the down-town city gave most visitors an impression of solemn zeal and opulence. Contrast was supplied by the Gymkhana Club, for this was built in a rural mock Tudor, all black and white, surrounded by acres of green. Its buildings seemed to consist mostly of verandahs, with views over various kinds of playing-fields. Everything was space, shade, and canvas, and one entered the club through a scalloped canopy which conveyed a permanent suggestion of the celebratory, or even the matrimonial.

There were little cousins of it wherever the British settled, and it is note-worthy that their constructors, encouraged no doubt by club committees, gener-ally chose some sort of Tudor adaptation for their various pavilions: for in the exiled British mind the Elizabethan style seemed to represent gentle, pastoral, particularly English values – like the cricket pavilions of school, maybe, country pubs or sentimental cottages, where butterflies of softer colour fluttered among

homelier blossoms, and tennis was played more or less perpetually through
summer evenings under elms.

Up-country pleasures

The nicest clubs of all were the bigger up-country kinds, and of these we may
choose as representative the Ootacamund Club. It had started life in 1831 as the
residence of Sir William Rumbold, Bt., a well-known usurer of Hyderabad, but
was adapted in mid-century to provide a social centre for Ooty itself, and for the
tea-plantations and military stations nearby. A long, low, classical building, it
stood at the top of a steeply descending lawn, more like a meadow than a garden,
and was approached by a sweeping drive past a gulley full of reeds and water-
flowers. There was no *porte-cochère*, showery though Ootacamund could be:
instead your carriage, crunching on to a gravel esplanade, debouched you directly
on to the wide steps of the verandah, and you were enveloped at once within the
authentic ambience of The Club.

Sofas, magazine tables, pictures of monarchs, Viceroys, club presidents, lists
of Masters of the Ootacamund Hunt (founded 1847), sporting prints, old photographs of Ooty As It Was, slightly mangy heads of hunted jackals, pale water-
colours, a notice-board full of pinned notes, cane chairs, polished parquet floors,
The Times, *The Field*, the *Army List*, the *India Office List*, vases of fairly stolidly
arranged flowers – shuffle of servants' sandals, laughter from the bar, sibilance
from a corner of the lounge, pervasive smells of cigars, vegetables and furniture
polish – somebody's little dog yapping, somebody's anecdote rising and falling
out of sight but never out of hearing – these were the signs and sensations of The
Club, nowhere embodied more pleasantly than in the fine public rooms of Ooty,
where the planters whooped it up at their annual dinners, the Hunt met in high
spirits to elect its Master, and a subaltern named Neville Chamberlain, in 1875,
invented the game of snooker.

Palatialism

The ultimate domestic buildings of Anglo-India were the palaces of the procon-
suls – the Viceroy himself, the Governors of the several provinces, the Residents
in the theoretically independent Native States. They form a category of their
own, more social or anthropological perhaps than architectural, for while they
were political statements in their size and grandeur, they were family homes as
well, domestic in manner if not in scale, with a character very different from the
palaces of most conquering élites.

Clubs in the out-stations, up-country, were essential rather than merely celebrated. The Ootacamund Club (*top*) was
built as the private home of Sir William Rumbold in 1831: the game of snooker was invented there, in a billiard-room
unchanged to this day. The rather more forlorn verandah of the old Central Provinces Club, Nagpur (*bottom*), suggests a
less fashionable part of India. Near here is the grave of a young soldier 'whose heart burst after he was chased by a tiger'.

(*Above and facing.*) Government House, Calcutta, home of the Governor of Bengal; later, until the capital was shifted to New Delhi, the home of the Viceroy. The house, modelled on Kedleston Hall in Derbyshire, was built in 1799 and formally opened in 1803 with a ball to commemorate the Treaty of Amiens.

Palaces they were, nevertheless, and they were very numerous, for often the principal residences were supplemented by lesser houses in the hill-stations, or seaside villas, or hot-weather retreats up the road. The Governor of Madras had three to choose from, his country residence being just five miles from his town house, his hill-station house 250 miles away. The Governor of Bombay had one palace in town, another a mile or two away, a third in the hills at Poona and a seaside villa along the coast. (When, though, in the last years of the Raj the British built a new home for the Viceroy bigger than Versailles, it was officially called, by decision of the King-Emperor George V, simply the Viceroy's House.)

The ideas of a prince

The original great palace of British India was the Company Governor-General's residence in Calcutta, completed in 1803. It stood in a dominating position in the burgeoning city, overlooking the great open space called the *maidan*, and it was a deliberate declaration of power and success. Until then Governors-General had lived in undistinguished rented quarters: when Richard Wellesley, brother of the future Duke of Wellington, arrived to take office in 1798, it took him only a month to decide that he needed something more fitting to his status. As his admirer the young Lord Valentia wrote, during a visit to Calcutta, India should be ruled from a palace, not a counting-house – 'with the ideas of a Prince, not those of a retail-trader in muslins and indigo'.

There was no dispute about the style to be employed. British Calcutta was a classical city through and through, and the prototype of Kedleston Hall, generally considered one of the noblest English country houses, was chosen by the young architect, Lieutenant Wyatt of the Bengal Engineers, as being perfectly suited to site as to purpose. Built like most Calcutta mansions of brick covered with white plaster, Government House consisted essentially of a large, central block on three floors, connected spider-like by long curving corridors with four symmetrical wings, each virtually a separate house. An Ionic portico, approached by a huge processional staircase, faced the official centre of the city, to the north: on the other side, looking over gardens, was a softer, domed and apsidal front, topped by a large figure of Britannia. The palace was approached through splendid arched gateways, based on those built by Robert Adam at Sion House in Middlesex and surmounted by lions and sphinxes: since the grounds around it were, at first, absolutely treeless, it stood in tremendous dominance over everything in sight.

Quite right too, Valentia said. India was a country of splendour, and 'the Head of a mighty Empire ought to conform himself to the prejudices of the country he rules over'. Lordly the palace certainly was: its kitchens were not in the house at all, but outside the grounds altogether in one of the city side-streets – 'somewhere

The Throne Room and the Grand Marble Hall in Government House, Calcutta. Tipu Sultan's throne was one of the best-known treasures kept in the house; guests were also keen to see the ornate, steam-operated lift – supposedly the first installed in the country.

in Calcutta', the Vicereine Lady Dufferin vaguely thought. Six great State apartments filled the central block: a throne room; an Ionically columned ballroom; a Dorically columned Marble Hall; a drawing-room, a breakfast-room and a supper-room, each more than 100 feet long. The shape of the building caught whatever breeze there was, and the house was full of spacious vistas, huge floors of marble, high ceilings of polished oak. It had great dignity from the start, and as age mellowed its details and matured its gardens, over the generations it acquired an unexpected charm as well (though the East India Company was not overjoyed to be presented with a bill for its costs, £167,359, while Edward Lear, staying in the house in 1873 and unsympathetic to its protocol, called it Hustle-fussabad).

Wellesley had still greater ideas for gubernatorial Calcutta. He is said to have planned to connect this palace by an avenue fourteen miles long, straight as a die, with a country house at Barrackpore, a military station up the Hooghly River, making of the two a magnificent complex: 'in the approved manner', Lord Curzon dryly remarked a century later, 'of the railway line from St. Petersburg to Moscow'. The avenue was never made, Wellesley being recalled home for his extravagance, but the Barrackpore house was built after his departure to the designs of Captain Thomas Anbury, Bengal Engineers, and for later incumbents the place did much, so the first Lord Minto said, 'to take the sting out of India'.

Really a very large bungalow, with an eight-columned portico and arcades all around, it stood easily in the centre of its own official hamlet – lesser thatched bungalows for staff and guests, guard-room for the military, kitchen quarters, and later all sorts of pleasant conceits, a Temple of Fame, a dainty bridge leading nowhere in particular, an artificial ruin, a monument to a well-known racehorse, a menagerie housed in airy Gothick cages. From the front of the house a wide straight walk ran down to the river; all around it there were gardens, walks and terraces, ponds with lotuses on them, tunnels of bamboo, palms and poinsettias: across the river at Serampore a church steeple rose above the trees in a startling and comforting illusion of Home.

Between them these two palaces made for magnificent living, and the Governors-General and their wives travelled frequently and comfortably between them, for among their official fleet of 200 vessels was the gubernatorial yacht. In later years this was an elegant steam-craft, but in earlier times it was the marvellous houseboat *Sonamukhi*, 'Golden Face', which was furnished in white, gold, and green morocco, which had marble baths on board, and which was rowed magnificently from one house to the other, up and down the muddy river, accompanied by a flotilla of barges carrying 400 servants: as Emily Eden, sister of the Governor-General Lord Auckland, observed in 1837, 'such a simple way of going to pass two nights in the country'.

Gentlemen's residences

Though their settings were exotic and their arrangements somewhat fantastic, the Calcutta palaces were unmistakably English. Even the line of scarlet lancers welcoming the guests to dinner, even the dream-like progress of the Golden Face, did not disguise the fact that these were the domestic arrangements of English gentlefolk, temporarily transferred. Other early Government Houses were sometimes no more than enlargements of existing buildings, but even so the tradition of upper-class Englishness infused all the palaces of Anglo-India, whatever their styles or origins.

In Madras, for instance, in 1802, the second Lord Clive established a new palace outside the walls of the original British fortress by the sea – a token of growing confidence, no doubt, but also a return to more English ways of life. Actually the first thing one saw on entering its grounds was a free-standing banqueting-hall of tremendous pomp, replete with helmets, shields, and piled trophies, but a few yards away across the drive the house itself was of very different style. It was a wide, low house beside a lake, developed from an earlier building by a local mathematician, John Goldingham, and its broad two-storeyed verandahs and balustraded terraces made it seem above all comfortable and leisurely, just the sort of house a rich English gentleman might have built for his own retirement. It was later Victorianized, and began to look, with its verandahs piled one on top of the other, and its heavy nineteenth-century *porte-cochère*, rather like a grounded steamship; but it always remained a genial kind of place, and in later years even the banqueting-hall was slightly domesticated by the addition of an arcaded verandah, which made it look less like a Temple of the Martial Arts and more like a particularly well-endowed village hall.

Away in the city of Hyderabad, seat of the Nizam's power in central India, the British built the most monumental of their Residences in the territories of the native princes, but though this was pointedly the home of an overlord it too had its homely connotations. It was begun in 1803, and its begetter was J. A. Kirkpatrick, the Resident of the day, a soldier of eccentric habits who was known to the Indians as Hushmat Jung, 'Glorious in Battle', and who had married a Muslim girl named Khair-un-Nissa, 'Excellent among Women'. Kirkpatrick commissioned an officer of the Madras Engineers, Lieutenant Samuel Russell, to design the house, and he produced a building more terrific, if anything, than the palace in Calcutta – and paid for, as it happens, by the compliant Nizam.

Its main block, of two storeys above a basement, was flanked by latticed galleries leading to twin wings one the kitchens, the other staff quarters. It was entered through a great Corinthian portico, forty feet high, guarded by two lions, approached by a flight of twenty-one steps, and capped by an entablature with the royal crest. This led into a galleried hall, rising the full height of the house, with a

Classical magnificence. The young women – students of English – stand on the staircase of the British Residency in Hyderabad, which is now a college. The building (*top*), designed by Russell in Corinthian style, was clearly intended to impress the Nizam. A scale model, built to gauge reaction, stands in the vegetable gardens: it was severely damaged recently when a tree fell on it. The Doric front of the Residency, Bangalore (*bottom*), is still well preserved: the house is now the seat of the Governor of the State of Karnataka.

floor of inlaid wood: tall mirrors, each surmounted by a lion, surrounded this great chamber, and around it lay a series of oval drawing-rooms, while in an apse at the back rose a fine double staircase in the Adam style.

A stately garden lay in front of the house; behind, a formal drive ran through an avenue of outbuildings towards the Nizam's city, and the compound was closed by three arched gates, named in later years after Lord Roberts the Commander-in-Chief, Lord Lansdowne the Viceroy and Queen Victoria herself. The Residency was successfully defended in the Indian Mutiny, but in 1892, as a local guidebook tells us, 'after the Manipuris had murdered Mr Quinton, Chief Commissioner of Assam, the Residents became thoughtful', and the whole complex was fortified with outer walls, gunposts, and a look-out on the roof.

Yet tremendous though it was, the Hyderabad Residency was always more a house than an institution. The Residency billiard-room was so popular with local Britons that according to Sir Charles Metcalfe, Resident in the 1820s, the house was used as a kind of tavern. And in a little secluded garden behind the building, on the city side, there stood a handsome white model of the Residency itself, like a magnificent doll's house, except that it was frequented by snakes and scorpions. This Kirkpatrick had built for his Indian wife. She remained strictly in purdah to the end of her days, living in her own *zenana* beside the stables; and because she could not even walk around the side of her husband's great creation to admire its portico, where the lions stood, and the bees swarmed, and the sentries stamped up and down, Kirkpatrick had built for her this touching plaster substitute.

A variety of houses

Later Government Houses and Residencies were nothing if not varied in style. Government House, Ootacamund, built in 1877 when the Duke of Buckingham was Governor of Madras, had a pillared portico copied from His Grace's seat at Stowe, in Buckinghamshire, but managed to look all the same much like a plush hotel in the Lake District. The Residency at Cochin, which had begun life as a Dutch colonial house, had a high-pitched roof with wide curved eaves, heavy teak doors and shutters in the Arab or perhaps Indonesian manner, and a lamp-lit walk, shaded by magnolia trees, through the gardens to the Residential jetty, where the canoes of the Cochin fishermen drifted by with tattered sails and flashing smiles.

Government House at Lahore was built around the tomb of Mohammed Kasim Khan, who died in 1635. Its centre was the domed dining-room, which was the upper part of the tomb itself: below it was the kitchen, in which the sarcophagus of the late Khan, a cousin of Akbar the Great and a celebrated patron of wrestlers, served as a chopping-board. An octagonal tower hid the dome of the tomb from sight, allowing for a series of triangular rooms around it, and veran-

The remnants of the old banqueting hall of the Residency, Lucknow (*below*), after its eighty-seven-day siege during the height of the Mutiny. The tower was the only place in the British Empire from which a flag flew, day and night, in commemoration from 1857 until Independence nearly a century later. 'Nunc fortunatus sum' – 'I am in Luck Now' – was how General Sir Henry Havelock cabled his Commander-in-Chief, when, after four attempts, he managed to lift the siege. The undistinguished block of flats (*left*) houses lawyers, on the Esplanade in Calcutta – very convenient for the High Court next door.

dahs around them, and over the years the house was embellished with Gothic arches, Moorish windows, classical columns, and Arabesque frescoes executed by Rudyard Kipling's father Lockwood. In the garden, on top of a hump, was a pleasure-pavilion in the Mogul manner, built in 1908, with an indoor swimming-pool columned in the Doric mode.

Another oddity was Ganesh Khind at Poona, the summer palace of the Governors of Bombay – only 2,000 feet about sea-level but still far more comfort-able than the blistering city eighty miles away (as the vulture flew) on the Ma-harashtra coast. This was built by Sir Bartle Frere, Governor from 1862 to 1876, and was at once flamboyant and peculiar, partly because money ran out half-way through and the building was left unfinished. Confusedly Italianate in style, it was inspired no doubt partly by the Queen's contemporary house at Osborne, begun in 1845. Its terraces were regally wide and hugely canopied, and from its eighty-foot tower, iron-decorated at the top, there habitually flew a truly enormous ensign. Ganesh Khind had Romanesque arches here and there, and classical statuary, and stepped lawns like Tuscany, and a winter garden like Scarborough, but it would really have been a splendid ambivalence anywhere on earth.

The first truly modern Government House, the first to have electric light and European kitchens, was the Lodge built at Simla in the 1880s under the auspices of Lord Dufferin the Viceroy, who had long cherished the dream of building a romantic country house somewhere. Where better than Simla, that paradise of aromatic forests and Himalayan vistas, where the Viceregal families were still slumming it at Peterhof? Enthusiastic architects were to hand in the persons of Henry Irwin, Public Works Department, and Captain H. H. Cole, Royal En-gineers, and the style was to be exuberantly Tudor. No expense was begrudged, all the furnishings being supplied by Maples of London, and it was popularly suggested at the time that Indian income-tax was introduced specifically to pay for it all.

It was a showy sort of place – 'a Minneapolis millionaire', sneered the American Lady Curzon when she moved in in 1899, 'would revel in it . . . it looks at you with pomegranate and pineapple eyes from every wall'. The dining-room was hung with Spanish leather, the drawing-room with gold and brown silk. Heraldic beasts supported the chimney-piece of the immense hall, which was as tall as the house itself, and everywhere there were elaborate carved details of teak, deodar, and walnut. There was an indoor tennis-court, a tiled laundry, a Council Chamber, the inevitable ballroom and a half-timbered guardhouse at the gate.

The house was built of grey limestone, quarried five miles away and brought to the site on mules, and from a distance it did look rather faery-like on its high ridge, with its bauble-towers above the deodars, and the glint of the sun on its multitudinous windows. The romance of it was true, too. It was the palace of a satrap, sent from a misty Northern isle to govern the inconceivable millions of

In the hills of Simla, the Scottish baronial style of the Viceregal Summer Palace (*left*) marches with the Tudor of Barnes Court (*below*), since 1879 the Residence of the Governors of the Punjab. Now that Punjab is divided between India and Pakistan, there are four Governors' Mansions, one on each plain, one in each set of hills.

that oriental country: the anomaly of its architecture there, a great mock-Tudor English country house encouched in exotic trees and set against the background of the Tibetan Himalaya, only suited the grand anomaly of its meaning, and gave susceptible Britons, as they rode past its guardhouse to the salute of the turbanned sentries, perceptible frissons of satisfaction.

For modern tastes probably the most desirable Government House of them all was the Governor of Bombay's seaside residence at Malabar Point, on the edge of Bombay City. This was hardly a palace in any conventional sense, but rather a cluster of white bungalows, mostly in traditional Anglo-Indian style, grouped on a rocky promontory above the sea, and surrounded by lawns, gardens and wooded walks along the sea-shore, where cuckoos sang, pet dogs were tearfully buried, and Hindu fishermen habitually came ashore to worship at a waterside temple. The bungalows were at once shady and breezy, being surrounded by wide verandahs and having very tall rooms, and the sense of fastidious retreat was heightened by the careful detailing of the woodwork, neat shutters and complicated fretwork screens, which divided one room from another.

The most interesting building in the group was the big ballroom which formed the heart of it. This was a large wooden structure less like British India than imperial Malaya or Borneo – rather a Conradian thing, except that its paintwork was always impeccable, and its denizens allegedly respectable. In this long clapboard hall, with two drawing-rooms and an al fresco dining gallery, the Governor would receive his guests at fêtes, balls and soirées, while the band stringed away in its trim little stand off the verandah, the crickets hummed in the shrubbery outside, the fireflies hovered here and there, and on the rocks below the waves of the Indian Ocean gently slapped.

Empire was not all hospitable idyll, though, and in later years the life of a Governor of Bombay was frequently at risk. In the last decades of British rule in India, when this city seethed with patriotic unrest, they built an underground bunker beneath the happy bungalows of Malabar, equipped with bedrooms and kitchens for a long stay: a motor-road led into it, big enough to accommodate the Governor's Daimler, and a water-gate in the rock-face gave access to a jetty, in case His Excellency needed to make a hasty get-away when the ball was over.

The last palace

Retreats were not immediately contemplated when in 1912 Edwin Lutyens set about designing a Viceroy's palace for the new capital of the Indian Empire, to be built on Raisina Hill on the southern outskirts of Delhi. Come with me now to visit this palace along the wide avenue called Kingsway, on an elephant if you like, as in some ceremonial parade, in the Packard again, or best of all (if we have the time, for it is a long, long way) directly after breakfast on foot.

We start at the elongated figure of George V, King-Emperor and founder of this new metropolis, crowned and skinny beneath his stone canopy; we pass beneath the tall Arch of India, inscribed all over with the names of the war dead; and so we set off up the exact straight axis of the ceremonial way, flanked by ornamental pools, brownish lawns, and flowering trees. On and on we go, never deviating a foot from the geometric line of the approach, over one intersection, over another, on and on in the gathering heat of the morning as though we are never going to get there. The great clumped buildings at the far end of the avenue, reddish and brownish in the developing heat-haze, never seem to get any closer, but stand there shimmering on their hillock indistinctly, more like a geological outcrop than any work of masonry.

Gradually, though, they do clarify themselves, and emerge from the misty mass, and presently we reach a plaza with fountains spouting, and pass up an unexpected bump in the road between tall red buildings of absolute symmetry, like huge gatehouses on either side. On we go, though, straight as a die, through splendid iron gates into a courtyard, past an honorific column with a lion on top, between sculpted elephants and living sentries, across the gravel yard, up a huge flight of steps, never swerving, never wavering, through a gigantic open door, into a dark domed chamber all of porphyry and marble, where aides bow and ladies curtsey – and there, mysteriously beneath a crimson canopy in the very centre of the room, facing the open door and the long line of Kingsway, there stands a gilded throne.

On the throne there sits an Englishman: and so, bowing and curtseying ourselves a little stiffly perhaps after so demanding an approach, we find ourselves in the presence of the Crown's surrogate, the despot of this vast domain, His Excellency the Viceroy and Governor-General of India. 'Frank, my dear fellow', he says *sotto voce* as he accepts our obeisances (for we were probably at school with him) – 'my dear Madge' (for we are very likely cousins on his mother's side) – 'you look quite done in. Come round the back when all this hoo-ha is over, and have a drink with Mary in the garden . . .'.

The house that Lutyens built for this satrap was the largest of all modern palaces, 600 feet long from end to end, 180 feet to the top of its central dome. Lutyens was known then chiefly as a designer of exceptionally comfortable English country houses, built in a distinctive combination of classical and vernacular styles. He knew nothing about India, and had never been there: it happened though that his wife Emily was not only the daughter of a former Viceroy, Lord Lytton, but was also a devotee of the Theosophist sect, which had its headquarters in Madras, and an irrepressible supporter of Indian independence – India was the last place in the world, she thought, where 'little nobodies can come and play at being kings and queens'. This ironic provenance gave birth, in the Viceroy's House on Raisina Hill, to the most interesting of all the domestic

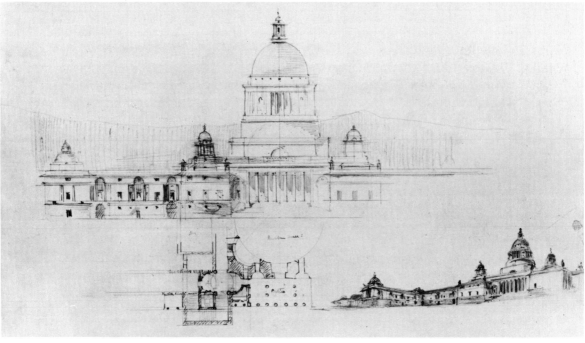

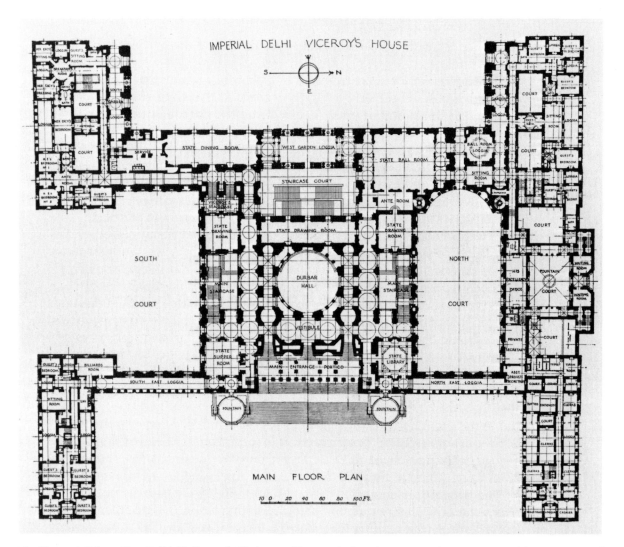

IMPERIAL DELHI VICEROY'S HOUSE

MAIN FLOOR PLAN

10 0   20   40   60   80   100 Ft.

The Viceroy's Palace, New Delhi. Sir Kenneth Clark says of Lutyens's gigantic structure, the centre-piece of the great Imperial capital, that it bore as little relation to India as L'Enfant's Washington did to the southern United States. That it was a work of great genius and beauty, however, is beyond dispute. The architecture is not without its technical flaws: one of the huge fountains ornamenting the approach to the mansion collapsed in 1977 after its iron girdle rusted away. The rest of the buildings, though, are in good condition – particularly the mansion, now used as the official residence of the President of the Indian Republic. Many of the scores of rooms which Viceroys and their huge staffs would have occupied are empty today.

buildings, big or small, that the British erected during the 350 years of their presence in India.

The house was only the centre-piece of a plan for a whole new capital city, New Delhi, which had been decided upon in 1911. At that time, though the new modernism was beginning to make itself felt on the continent of Europe, and neo-classicism too was enjoying a revival, British architecture in India was pre-eminently still in its mongrel phase – Saracenic Gothic, High Victorian Pathan. Also, though there seemed no doubt in most British minds that the empire in India was more or less eternal, Indian nationalism was already stirring, and there were signs of some relaxation in the imperial despotism. The style of the new palace was therefore of double importance, aesthetic and political.

There were of course many advocates of the by now traditional syntheses. Sir Swinton Jacob, 'a walking dictionary of Indo-Saracenic art', was brought in to advise, and the Viceroy of the day, Lord Hardinge, declared himself particularly in favour of pointed arches for doors and windows – 'I should personally like to see buildings of a bold and plain character with oriental adaptation . . . call it bastard or what you like.' Others thought that in this ancient capital of native dynasties the house should be entirely Indian in form – 'for high considerations of State', Lady Hardinge said. Lutyens resisted these suggestions. He loathed the pointed arch, he thought Indian effects tacked on to Western shapes were generally mere 'pictures on a wall', and he dismissed most purely indigenous architecture as 'childish'.

And in the event he built the palace in a style that defied easy classification, either political or aesthetic, being classical in form, country English in manner, and recognizably influenced in the end not only by Muslim forms, but by an Indian cultural heritage hitherto neglected by Anglo-Indian architects, Buddhism. The proportion and stance of the building spoke clearly enough of Lutyens's classical preferences, his boundless admiration in particular for the mathematics of Greek architecture. But the house was sealed, as it were, with indigenous features like sharp Mogul cornices, and sturdy roof pavilions, and in the centre of it all was placed a copper dome which looked at first sight rather Byzantine, but was more probably derived from the great Buddhist *stupa* at Sanchi near Bhopal. All around the house, and even on its roofs, fountains played in the Mogul manner and pools reflected the red and cream sandstone of the construction; behind it there was a great formal garden, direct from Kashmir, deliberately contrasted with a circular rose-garden straight from Sussex.

This house was probably the last of the great royal palaces of history. Its dome rose above the new city, so Robert Byron wrote in 1931, like 'the shout of the imperial suggestion – a slap in the face of the moderate average-man, with his second-hand ideals'. It covered four and a half acres and included within its walls twelve separate courtyards. Three million cubic feet of stone, worked in the world's largest stoneyard, were needed to build it. It was equipped with every kind of domestic office: a printing-room for the Viceroy's private press, a tent-room for his baggage, a bakery, a tailor's shop, linen-rooms like those of a great hotel, sculleries and larders of diverse sorts, places to hang game, and make cakes, and scour pans, and store the vast quantities of coal needed to heat the place in winter.

Besides the circular Durbar Room with the throne in it, the house contained a State dining-room 100 feet long, a huge ballroom, three State drawing-rooms and vast numbers of State suites and guest bedrooms. Everything in them was designed by Lutyens, down to the chairs, and the stamp of his taste was everywhere: in the endless arched corridors, for instance, which seemed to run through the house like sumptuous warrens, in the panelled walls and coffered ceilings, in the whimsical nursery furniture, in the elaborate chimney-pieces and the cool white woodwork, which made the rooms overlooking the garden, with their nice squashy sofas and their country-house selection of books, feel uncannily like cultivated drawing-rooms at home in England.

And in a certain puckish fondness for the unexpected, the pun and the illusion, Lutyens designed his own order for the columns of this house: they were decorated with stone bells, honouring in a back-handed way an old saw which claimed that so long as the bells of Delhi were silent, the reigning dynasty would survive. He ornamented it everywhere with upturned domes, like saucers. And he devised the most delightful of the few architectural surprises that the British bestowed upon India (for by and large, it has to be admitted, the Anglo-Indian architectural imagination was short on fantasy). If you walked out of the ballroom to go to the State drawing-room, during an intermission perhaps in the dancing, you would find yourself in a wide vestibule with staircases on each side. It had a ceiling, you would perceive, of deepest blue, surrounded by mouldings and only dimly to be glimpsed above the bright lights below, against which the dresses of the ladies passing up and down the stairs, the brilliant uniforms of the officers and functionaries, the scarlet turbans of the servants, stood out in theatrical contrast.

A choice of genius, you might think, that deep seductive blue: but as you mounted the stairway, and the ceiling became clearer, you found that it was not a ceiling at all. Lutyens had called the Indian sky itself into his design, and had left his staircase court roofless to the stars.

In exile

Deep Asian skies, cummerbunds, handsome young aides and sunburnt girls, gleam of lance, glitter of lanterns in the Mogul gardens – yet despite the glamour of it all, even at the top of the hierarchy there nagged at the imperialist mind the insidious curse of homesickness. Viceroy or Company clerk, general's lady or corporal's wife, they dreamed of Britain far away. The pull of home remained poignant and powerful, even among people who had spent most of their lives in India, or families who had served this empire for generations – even sometimes, indeed, among Eurasians, half British, half Indian, who had never set foot in Britain at all.

The memsahib suffered most. She was the most exiled of the exiles, and she palliated the old longing in the only way she could, by making her house, be it never so palatial, as much like home as possible. In the earlier years of imperial rule, when there were few British women about, the interiors of Anglo-Indian houses often looked as much Indian as Anglo. They were generally sparsely equipped. In 1823 Bishop Heber the hymn-writer, found most of the great houses of Chowringhee only half-furnished; another visitor reported of his lodgings in Madras that there were no pictures on the walls, no curtains on the windows and no cushions on the chairs; William Hickey, in the same city, was put up in 'a large hall, without a single article in it except a crazy old couch'. And this is how Honoria Lawrence described her bedroom at Lahore in 1851: 'A naked, comfortless look in the room . . . ceiling bare beams and rafters; walls bare lime, coloured grey; floor covered with chintz; bed without curtains or posts'.

Later, as Gothic changed the outsides of Anglo-Indian buildings, Victorian taste changed the insides. By the 1860s the Vicereine Lady Canning was defining Anglo-Indian decor as consisting of 'round tables in the middle, chairs all around, and an ottoman on each side', and a photograph of a Madras drawing-room then shows it rather attractively hybridized. The floor is covered only with rattan matting, somewhat frayed at that, much of the furniture is local cane and straw, the long room is brilliantly light and airy: but the trimmings are already conventionally Victorian – whatnots, cowrie shells, jingle-jangle glass vases, one or two lugubrious sporting trophies, a spinet in one corner and lotus-shaped oil-lamps affixed to all the walls.

Later still the memsahib often succeeded in making her rooms almost entirely British. She did not generally have much furniture, and what she had was still locally made, but she made up for it with ornaments and incidentals. At one end was Lady Canning, in her Government Houses, using chintzes and pictures of the royal family to make her sitting-room 'pretty cool and English'. At the other end was your run of the mill Anglo-Indian housewife, whose aim it was to reproduce the more bourgeois consolations of Guildford, Stowe or Aberdeen in these exotic climes: with pictures jammed together on every wall, water-colours of the Highlands or portraits of Mother and Father in Oxford frames – with flowered wallpapers and looped curtains – with innumerable pots of posies, and ashtrays mounted in chair-arm saddles with dangling spurs, and big brass trays on mahogany legs one day to be reborn in distant retirement cottages – with arrangements of bamboos and grasses in polished brass shell-cases in the corner – with Calcutta-made pianos brightly polished, Mendelssohn or Sullivan on the music-stands – the whole ensemble only faintly stirring in the breeze of the *punkahs*, or the creaking electric fans in the ceiling.

It was the décor of exile: and outside in the garden, potted or bedded lovingly in the shade, phlox, rose, geranium and antirrhinum loyally ignored geography, history and architecture alike ('My violets are in bloom', wrote one poor home-sick memsahib in 1906, 'dear little English flowers . . . carefully, one by one, have I gathered enough to make me a buttonhole').

4 · Public

Diagrams of supremacy

Like all their predecessors, the British were autocrats in India. They maintained their authority by force – force of arms, force of character, force of suggestion. Liberty of the subject might be their watchword at home, but there was no equivalent to Magna Carta in India. The barons of this kingdom were kept severely in their place, beneath the sovereignty of the British Crown; though in the last years of the Empire Indians did join the higher echelons of authority, to the very end the power to make the greatest decisions was reserved for the British themselves. When in 1939 India went to war against Germany, the declaration was made personally by the Viceroy, a Scottish nobleman, and none of the 350 million Indians were consulted on the matter at all.

It is hardly surprising then that the public buildings of Anglo-India were seldom, so to speak, consultative in style. Indians were not often invited to approve their plans. They had by and large the unmistakable stamp of take it or leave it, and were drawn as diagrams of supremacy. In the very last years of the Empire it occurred to some designers that Indians one day might themselves occupy these halls of power, but even then they seldom progressed beyond the condescending: as was written upon Herbert Baker's Secretariat buildings at New Delhi, opened in 1926, 'Liberty Does Not Descend To A People. A People Must Raise Themselves To Liberty. It Is A Blessing That Must Be Earned Before It Can Be Enjoyed'.

The old forts

The first British public buildings in India were warehouses – godowns, as the Anglo-Indians called them – but the next ones were forts. This was always, Company or Crown, a militaristic regime, cap-à-pie against foreign enemies as against native subversives, and uniforms, battle honours, and regimental loyalties were essential to its style: when novelists or film-makers wanted to express images of the Raj, as often as not they were military images, from Kipling's barrack-room ballads to the North West Frontier derring-dos of Hollywood in the 1930s.

Forts, then, were everywhere in British India: story-book forts on the Khyber, island-batteries in the harbour of Bombay, ancient strongholds of Mogul or Maratha appropriated by the British for their own use. Each of the three Presidency towns was centred upon a fort, and for years their original settlements were enclosed within fortified walls.

Fort St. George at Madras, the oldest of them, was re-designed in 1750 by an eminent military mathematician, Benjamin Robins, and enclosed within its high walls not only administrative offices, warehouses, an arsenal, barracks and living-quarters for Governor and staff, but brokers' offices too, an exchange, a church, a theatre, auction rooms, a subscription library and a bank. 'Here you may contrast at every step', wrote a visitor in 1821, 'the man of war with the man of traffic, the muster-roll with the ledger, the bayonet with the pen, the sentry-box with the desk and counter'.

The others began in much the same way, but the original Fort William at Calcutta was largely destroyed when Suraj-ud-Davla, the Nawab of Bengal, briefly took Calcutta from the British in 1756. As a result, the city acquired a new fortress which was to remain the greatest and most famous of the Anglo-Indian military works. It was considered impregnable in its day, and indeed never fell to an enemy (if only because it was never attacked). It looked impregnable, anyway. It was the first thing every traveller saw, when he sailed up the Hooghly River towards the city: a sinister mound of earthworks, surrounded by a wide expanse of bare scorched grassland, rather like a monumental barrow-grave on a down somewhere, except that a large Union Jack flew from the top of it, while over those ramparts one could make out the roofs of grey barracks, the steeple of a church, and the squat black forms of cannons.

It was among the most advanced fortresses of its time, when it was completed in 1773: a Captain Brohier was its architect, and bricklayers and carpenters were brought especially from England to build it. It formed an irregular octagon at the Hooghly's edge, surrounded by a wide moat which was fed by channels from the river, commanding the approaches from the sea one way, the city itself the other. There were five heavily fortified entrances, including a water-gate with a jetty, and successive redoubts surrounded the outer walls. All around the fort a huge area of jungle and marsh was cleared and drained to make a clear field of fire, and this later became Calcutta's *maidan*, the grand park which lies at the heart of the modern city.

Fort William was a third of a mile in diameter, and the plan was that in any future attack on Calcutta the entire European population would be withdrawn within it, instead of being shut up in Black Holes. It was like a municipality of its

Fort William, Calcutta. In both the old and modern views the ships passing by along the Hooghly River can be seen. The great wall appears to have undergone some modification, however, as well as the addition of two centuries' worth of Bengal foliage.

(*Facing.*) Inside the Forts of Madras and Delhi. The latter Fort, however, is a Mogul rather than a British defence. The Victorian structures built beside its delicate marble confections are ugly indeed – a dour and forbidding counterpoint to the ornate splendour of Mogul architecture. The bullock, taking its ease from a lawn-mowing session, plainly cares for neither. Clive's House, deep inside Fort St. George, Madras, was once the residence of the great man. Today it is a pay and accounts office for the Indian Navy.

Dalhousie Barracks, Fort William, Calcutta – the largest single barrack building in the world.

own. The very centre of the fortress was occupied by the garrison church of St. Peter's, and between its grid of alley-ways was a regular warren of barracks, bomb-proof chambers, interconnecting galleries and stables. The garrison commander was provided with a handsome house in the prevailing mode, there was a military prison and a formidable arsenal (containing in Victorian times 600 guns, 60,000 muskets, 20,000 swords and 5,000 barrels of gunpowder).

Nineteenth-century prints show the soldiers of the garrison looking out across the *maidan* almost as from the deck of a ship off shore. Fort William was entirely separate from Calcutta proper, isolated in its flatland beside the river, and its life too was always, to the last days of British rule, suggestively remote from the affairs of the city. In Victorian times, when a visiting feudatory paid a ceremonial call on the Viceroy in his palace, he was usually asked to pause upon the great staircase before entering the presence, and as he waited there in the hot silence, the Viceregal guardsmen with their lances impassive all around, *boom*, *boom*, from the distant fortress sounded the explosions of his princely salute. In later and more troubled times Fort William sometimes replaced Government House itself as the real centre of authority in Calcutta: and it remained until the end of Empire the very model of an imperial fortress, with its sunken gates and lordly ensign, its banyan trees and wandering goats, its hovering kites in daytime, its flitting bats at dusk, and the bugle calls which, in the dry still of the Calcutta dawn, woke not only the soldiers in their barracks, but the Indian poor who slept in their tatters upon the benches of the field of fire.

The cantonments

As British power moved inland in India, so military stations were established all over the subcontinent, but instead of building fortresses within the cities they captured, the conquering generals established separate enclaves on their outskirts. They were called cantonments (pronounced 'cantoonments'), and they were generally set up five or six miles from the subjected city. The gap was deliberately maintained: a road was often built through it, later a railway too, and parade-grounds and shooting-ranges acted as no man's land. By the 1860s there were 175 of these places, and they offered almost allegorical contrasts to the ancient, jumbled, unhygienic, complex, and often beautiful cities they were meant to keep an eye upon.

The cantonment was often elaborately equipped, but remained inescapably a petrified camp. Just as a tented camp was laid out in strictest lines of symmetry, so a ground-plan of the average cantonment shows it severely devoid of grace. All was logic and functionalism, the grid streets of the cantonment being aligned carefully away from the neighbouring city, so that germs would not float directly down them out of the bazaars, while all the principal buildings faced, if possible, into the prevailing wind. Segregation was everything. Officers were separated from other ranks, of course, married quarters from barrack-blocks, British troops from natives, artillery from cavalry, elephants and camels from oxen and horses: the general had a fine big house in the middle of the camp, and at the end of each barrack-block there was a house for the sergeant-major.

Most of the buildings were variations on the standard bungalow. For officers they took the form of agreeable mess buildings surrounded by verandahs, gardens and tennis-courts, not unlike gymkhana clubs; for other ranks they were interpreted in long bleak dormitory buildings, not unlike prisons. The cantonments tried hard to be self-sufficient, and they had their own bazaars, leased out by tender to Indian merchants, their own slaughterhouses, their own water supplies, their own churches, cemeteries, jails and hospitals. They seldom, however, seemed anything but transitory, even the oldest of them: and their rectilinear traces on the map were always to look ironically like the marching-camps of the Roman army long before.

The biggest of the cantonments was at Secunderabad, in the Native State of Hyderabad, sprawled hugely over the boulder-strewn semi-desert country north of the Nizam's capital. Nearly every British soldier in India served at Secunderabad at one time or another: Winston Churchill was there in the 1880s, and reported that at least 12,000 men were based at the station then, keeping guard on a city which contained 'all the scoundrels of Asia'. A military road led directly from the camp to the city, allowing for instant interventions in riots or rebellions, and the cantonment was severely self-supporting – Hyderabad City was out of bounds to British troops.

Secunderabad had a large bazaar quarter, almost another town. It had a fine Club, and a famous hotel, the Deccan (later Percy's), which every British officer knew, and which had experienced every kind of soldierly high jink in its time. The headquarters buildings in the centre of the complex were large and dignified bungalows, the little garrison church was designed to allow one regiment at a time access to its Redeemer, and on the edge of the cantonment was a wide green *maidan*, a mile long, which contained a racecourse, a polo field, a cemetery, pleasant copses for picnicking in, and a vast parade-ground of sand and gravel big enough for the exercising of a complete brigade.

But the ironic crown of Secunderabad was a building which looked remarkably like Windsor Castle, and was indeed universally nicknamed after it: complete with round tower, fortified medieval gateway, cruciform arrow-slits and Tudor turrets, the whole built in a gleaming white stone and standing in splendid isolation above the rocky outcrops. It was the military prison, and beside it was the innermost redoubt of Secunderabad, an entrenched camp designed as the last bunker if ever those scoundrels of Hyderabad rose in arms against the suzerain

Castellated buildings were often designed for the forces of law and order to remind the Indian subjects of the tempered ferocity of Imperial discipline. The police station at Poona (*below*) is made less attractive than it might be by the use of dark trap-stone from the quarries of the Western Ghats. The tall tower of the Secunderabad military prison (*left*) led to its nickname, 'Windsor Castle'.

power. It was surrounded by a ditch seven feet deep, with a seven-foot rampart too, a stone revetment, a bomb-proof shelter, several artillery bastions, and rising above it all, surely an unassailable token of security, the Queen's castle itself with the flag on top.

The cantonments were to keep India in order: away on the frontiers the British stood guard against attack from outside, and in particular for more than a century they manned the forts and watchposts of the Afghan border. Though the dread enemy, Russia, never did cross the 500 miles of Afghan territory that separated the Czar's empire from the Queen's, nevertheless the Great Game preoccupied the British Indian armies until the end of the Empire, enlivened as it was by constant running squabbles with the warlike tribes of the region.

Everything was fortified up there, but the most celebrated and theatrical of the strong points was the mud fortress of Jamrud, which commanded the entrance to the Khyber Pass. It was a fort such as schoolboys dream of. Beyond it the harsh hills climbed away to the Afghan plateau beyond, and crouching there beside the caravan track Jamrud, the flag flying from its central tower, was the very last outpost of imperial command. It generally looked lifeless but menacing, all its power hidden behind its squat brown walls, and seemed ready to explode with rockets, or burst into artillery fire, or erupt into cavalry forays, at the word of command. It was ugly, and full of threat. Curzon, in 1890, likened it to 'a big turret-ship of the most improved and hideous modern kind, plastered over with clay and moored on the plain'. But it was anchored irremovably, and lies there still.

'A delightful station'

The early Anglo-Indian barrack-blocks, in the forts as in the cantonments, were often a disgrace – over-crowded, unhygienic and dispiriting. As late as 1852, the only effective scavengers at Fort William in Calcutta were the adjutant cranes, which lived on cats, rats and (it was said) the occasional baby: the average death-rate for British other ranks in India was fifty-eight per thousand, as against seventeen per thousand among troops stationed at home. In the middle of the nineteenth century General C. J. Napier ('a beak like an eagle', Thackeray thought, 'a beard like a Cashmere goat'), who had recently conquered Sind for the British Empire, led an outcry against the squalid conditions his soldiers were obliged to suffer, and it was consequently decreed that a third of the British troops in India should always be stationed in the healthy hills. A new series of barracks was designed to house them.

Some of these were admirable – even Lutyens thought the British ought to be proud of them – and among the best was the new military station built at Jakatalla in the Nilgiris of Madras Presidency. This was laid out on the flanks and ridges of a low cluster of hills, some 6,000 feet above sea-level, and since there was no big city nearby, only the little hill village of Coonoor on the Ooty road, the usual cantonment form was forgotten. Barrack buildings, messes, parade-grounds, hospital, gymnasium, mansion for the commanding officer, all over the years were disposed gently around the slopes, with green shrubberies interspersing them everywhere, and the steeple of the garrison church of St. George (architect Colonel Morant, Royal Engineers) histrionically above. In the clear mountain light, from a distance it all looked more like a health resort than a military camp.

The centre of the station was the chief barrack-block, and this was very handsome. It was not like a British barracks at all really – more like some show-piece of Napoleonic or Prussian military technique. One entered it through a short dark tunnel, rather as gladiators entered an amphitheatre, and passing out of its shade found oneself in a brilliant parade-ground, 800 feet square, dazzling in the sun, surrounded by two-storey buildings with verandahs upstairs and arcades below. On three sides of the square were first-floor entrances, approached by double flights of steps and surmounted by pediments, and the whole structure, capped with elegant white lanterns and flag-poles, gave an agreeable sense of space and freshness. The soldiers, housed upstairs, were given more room and air than ever before, and had their own verandahs on which, if properly dressed one assumes, they could eat the Nilgiri air in the evenings.

Lady Canning, the Viceroy's wife, inspected these works under construction when she was holidaying at Coonoor in 1858, and reported favourably to Queen Victoria about them. 'It will be a delightful station for the troops', said she. So it was, and it became one of the most popular cantonments in all India, and as Wellington Barracks remained the spanking headquarters of the Madras Regiment long after the Empire itself was disbanded.

Company style

Behind the military, the administration – and sometimes they overlapped, for as we have seen, during the first generations of British rule the only architects available were military engineers. The administrative buildings of the Raj had *gravitas* usually, but seldom inspiration, and since the form of British Government frequently adjusted itself, if not so readily the spirit, new Government offices were constantly in demand.

The first substantial administrative buildings were erected by the Company in Madras and Calcutta, and the best-known of them was the block known as Writers' Buildings in Calcutta, built in 1780 as a hostel and training-centre for young European clerks (or 'writers'). It was replaced in the nineteenth century,

but we know it well from prints, since it occupied one side of the main city square, Tank Square, so called because of the reservoir in the middle of it. The architecture of Writers' Buildings was earnest. Its designer, thought to be a former carpenter called Thomas Lyon, perhaps intended it to have some disciplinary effect upon the young gentlemen, who were notorious for rowdy champagne parties, and it was severely barrack-like in form. Its nineteen sets of apartments, all identical, were contained in a very long, very solid three-storey block, classical in style, with fifty-seven sets of identical windows, a flat roof and a central projection with Ionic columns.

'A shabby hospital', Mrs Martha Graham called this structure when she visited India in 1812, and it was indeed a lumpish thing, unmistakably a Company building, and doubtless helped to put into Lord Valentia's mind his quip about princes and counting-houses. In the more florid atmosphere of Madras, though, 800 miles to the south, the East India Company erected a very different building for its young officials, one which emphasized the romantic rather than the humdrum side of the enterprise. Though a little overwhelmed now by the expansion of Madras, and fretted rather by age, climate and bureaucracy, the Old College still stands, and is wonderfully evocative of John Company's eighteenth-century heyday. You reach it by crossing a graceful contemporary bridge over the River Cooum, and passing through a white ceremonial gateway, and there on your right is a long castellated building which looks remarkably like some Gothick folly in the grounds of an English nobleman, or possibly a magnificent stable-block in Ireland.

You are looking at the back of it actually, for it faces the river, and in its prime there were doubtless lawns running down to the water's edge. All is brown and dusty neglect down there now, but the building itself remains relatively spruce, and retains an inspiriting air of merriment. It forms a single symmetrical block, except for a detached pavilion at one end, and is bisected by a triumphal arch doubtless intended to commemorate the victories which gave the Company its supremacy in these parts. This has the usual clumps of sculpted trophies, the usual guns, cannon-balls and ensigns, but it has some more unusual features too: chiselled crosses, like those on Crusader castles, two blazing suns with wavy rays, and high on the pediment above, one facing the river, one the land, two curious human faces staring enigmatically across the conquered Carnatic.

The Old College is an endearing building all in all, one of the earliest Gothic structures in India, and perhaps designed, like Government House down the road, by John Goldingham the mathematician and astronomer. With its turreted wings, the pretty wooden hoods that mask its windows, all those jolly ornaments and its lovely setting above the river, it reminds us that if there was much avaricious solemnity to the early days of the British in India, there was a good deal of fun too.

New Writers' Buildings, Calcutta – the redbrick home of the Kafkaesque nightmare known as the West Bengal Civil Service. The huge Gothic structure for the then Bengal Secretariat was completed in 1880.

Zeal of State

It is a jolt to move back to Calcutta, move forward into Victorian times, and see
what the British did with those Writers' Buildings when, in 1880, they felt it
necessary to replace them with a new Secretariat for the Bengal Government. By
then the imperial purpose in India had greatly changed, and the imperialists were
not merely making money and campaigning, but Improving the Natives too. The
new buildings perfectly illustrated the change.

They occupied the same side of the same square, but it was now known as
Dalhousie Square, having a large statue of that Viceroy in it: and if the old
buildings spoke of Company earnestness, the new ones proclaimed the zeal of
State. Built allegedly in the French Renaissance style, they are replete with
architectural symbolisms of one sort and another, and ornamented with sculpted
figures of didactic meaning. In the middle stands Minerva, goddess of the
presiding wisdom, and extending from her are pairs of figures, Indian and British,
representing worthy abstractions: Justice for instance (a judge in his judicial
robes), Commerce (a merchant consults his abacus), Agriculture (a farmer in a
slouch hat), the whole supported by a plethora of urns of plenty and lions of
security. The whole effect was depressing: 'chastened gloom', somebody christ-
ened it.

It is a dreadful structure, but perhaps not quite so intimidating as the
Secretariat put up by the Victorians in Bombay, one of a tremendous series of
official buildings looking out over a green *maidan* to Back Bay and the Arabian
Sea. G. W. Forrest, himself an Indian Civil Servant, described this in 1903 as 'the
complete expression in stone of the spirit of an official architect – a massive pile
whose main features have been brought from Venice, but all the beauty has
vanished in transhipment'. Colonel H. St. Clair Wilkins, Royal Engineers, later
aide-de-camp to Queen Victoria, was the designer of this huge structure, and he
took seven years to complete it even with the unlimited cheap labour of the day,
its interior being an impractical labyrinth of poky offices. It was built, as Mr
Forrest said, in Ruskinian Gothic, and to less jaundiced eyes had a certain august
magnificence to it, with its massive and somewhat spiky hulk, its wrought iron
verandahs, and the wide balconies, shaded by gigantic screens of palm matting, on
which its administrators could stroll in the heat of the day, discussing financial
directives or even snatching a moment to watch the cricket on the green below.

Zeal of another class was suggested by a series of three Government buildings
at Simla. These were sited rather picturesquely, skew-whiff and lop-sided down
the slopes of a steep hill, between the Gothic tower of Christ Church at the top of
the ridge, and the jumbled bazaar quarter, flickering fires and smoke-smudge,
falling away below. But structurally they were very forbidding. Each was a solid
square block, brutal of silhouette, surrounded by the usual open verandahs but

The Simla Public Library, a mock-Tudor construction next to Christ Church, at the end of the Mall.

held together visibly by iron stanchions. They had iron roofs, and complicated external staircases, and this made them look like parts of unfinished bridges, or segments of ships, or as suggested by various observers at one time or another, discarded tramcars, toast-racks, salvaged junk, or armadillos. 'Beyond the beyond', Lutyens thought them: but he did admit that it was very English, to build a capital all of tin roofs at the summit of the mightiest of empires.

Last displays

For at least those nineteenth-century designers expressed, in one way or another, the exotic power and improbability of the British presence in India. By the twentieth century the pattern of Government buildings, now more often entrusted to professional architects, was generally much less forceful. A mild classical style was the norm, and the expression was less instructive than persuasive, even slightly diffident.

A characteristic exercise was the new Government quarter of Patna, a city which became the capital of a new province, Bihar and Orissa, in 1912, when the Empire itself was beginning to lose its flair. The presiding architect was J. F. Munnings, of the Public Works Department, and he laid it out spaciously but unassertively, with an engaging rather than extravagant white house for the Governor – flush toilets were excluded as too expensive – and a suitably inoffensive Secretariat. Extreme symmetry was generally a symptom of this school of design, and the Patna Secretariat was no exception. It was built in a neo-classical kind, only faintly impregnated with the Orient, and it had a tall eaved tower in the middle, and exactly symmetrical wings connected to the main block by shallow bridges, and the statutory ornamental ironwork, and carefully balanced gardens, and regularly variegated windows, and was, all in all, a rather forgettable kind of building. Even the local Patna guidebooks ignore it altogether.

On the other hand the most famous administrative buildings erected by the British in twentieth-century India have been endlessly photographed, have been the subject of unceasing controversy, and have entered the permanent imagery of the land. They were the two great sandstone blocks erected by Sir Herbert Baker in New Delhi, the ones between which we passed, as between a pair of huge guardhouses, on our walk up Kingsway to the Viceroy's House. With the palace itself, and the circular Parliament House not far away, they formed the heart of the new capital: they were the Propylea, Baker himself said, of this Acropolis.

These were buildings more conventionally Anglo-Indian than Lutyens's unique palace up the road, but then Baker was by background and by instinct a more conventionally imperial architect – Rhodes's favourite, who was later himself to build a putative Viceroy's House in Nairobi, and had just completed the huge Union Buildings at Pretoria. He loved vistas, arches, courts, galleries, arcades, and all these tastes he was able to indulge in the Secretariat blocks, which were in an orientalized classical style. From a distance they looked, except for their domes and towers, not unlike the pleasure-pavilions of Persian emperors, and their chief merit was indeed a certain airiness, even gaiety of manner. Light played upon light in their galleried recesses, arch peered through to arch, huge winding staircases seemed to be leading nowhere in particular, and once inside the great vaulted offices of the bureaucracy, the visitor could feel strangely disoriented.

They had the unusual gift of seeming smaller than they actually were. You did not realize the size of the Viceroy's House until you were actually in the shadow of its façade: but Baker's buildings did not fulfil themselves until you were far away from them, far down at the other end of Kingsway, or even on the ramparts of Purana Qila, the dead fortress on the banks of the Jumna. Then their red and white jutting shapes, set against the crouching form of the palace behind, had an almost geological look to them: they looked like old sandstone crags, quarried in

(*Top.*) The Banqueting Hall for the Governors of the Madras Presidency, built by the East India Company's astronomer and engineer, Mr Goldingham, in 1802. (*Bottom.*) The circular Parliament Building in New Delhi, designed by Baker as something of an afterthought, which accounts for its rather odd siting, and its distance from the two main ceremonial routes of the city.

Baker's Secretariat Building in New Delhi, with the slope of Raisina Hill on the left and the Viceregal Palace on the right. This building, one of a matched pair, is South Block, where the Indian Prime Minister's office is sited.

places perhaps, cut by age into sharp edges and terraces, eroded by wind and rain. They seemed irrelevant to history then, and more suggestive perhaps, more ironic certainly, than their creator could have imagined: for *his* conception of New Delhi was that 'the spirit of British sovereignty . . . must be imprisoned in its stone and bronze'.

School and college

Of all the schools the British ever made, board school or high school, village kindergarten or fashionable finishing school, none could be *schoolier* than the John Lawrence Memorial Asylum erected by the Anglo-Indians in the 1860s in memory of one of their favourite heroes, John Lawrence of the Punjab, in the Nilgiri Hills near Ootacamund. Its setting is lovely, its intentions were always benevolent, but chill are the vibrations of team spirit, morning assembly and homesickness that it summons. Its buildings are in a Romesque monastic style, executed in a gloomy, yellowish brick. You approach the main block through an open-arched brick screen: behind it the mass of the building rises towards a tall and thoroughly disapproving tower, with heavy Italianate details and a clock to remind you that you are late for prep. It is a school to this day, and the voices of the pupils resound through its tall dark rooms and corridors like the ghosts of all dead schoolboys everywhere.

British Government in India, after its swashbuckling beginnings, was chiefly Law and Order government. Its principal functions were to keep the peace and enable British business to get on with its job. An elevating purpose, though, developed. In the mid-nineteenth century three universities were established, and others presently followed. There were also multitudes of lesser educational institutions, some for the children of Anglo-Indians, some for indigenes, some technical, some religious, some called colleges, some called institutes, some just in every way, like the John Lawrence Memorial, archetypally Schools. Mass education was largely left to the missionaries, and the illiterate millions of India remained illiterate to the end: nevertheless the stones of empire did include, here and there, educational stones, stones of Academe, erected for the most part in the full flush of imperial self-esteem.

In the full flush of Oxford, Cambridge and the English public schools, too, so that college spirit and Old School Tie anomalously recurred. In Peshawar, for example, far away in the north-west, in the bitter light of the Afghan frontier country, the Islamia College was a beguiling mutation of the Oxbridge pattern. A Muslim institution opened in the 1920s, it was set in delightful gardens, and consisted of a widely scattered group of separate buildings. In the centre was the main University building, towered in the Mogul manner, with a huge

Education – complex and simple. The magnificent perpendicular centre-piece of Queen's College, Benares, erected in 1847 by Major Kittoe of the Bengal Engineers. It is on the site of the original Sanskrit College of Benares, and still has a reputation throughout India for excellence in the language. Its ornate buildings contrast with the stark simplicity of Bishop Heber School, Trichinopoly, now renamed Tiruchirapalli and still a centre of cheroot manufacturing.

(*Left.*) The gateway of the Deccan College in Poona – like most public buildings in this cool British military city, fashioned from grey trap-stone.

(*Below.*) The gateway to Raj Kumar College in Rajkot, Gujerat – a school founded in 1870 by Colonel Keatinge to provide British-style education for the princes and potentates of western India.

iron-pillared assembly hall as its core. But over the gardens the students lived in
a row of seven hostels which were part Alma Mater and part *madrasah*, with a
quadrangle, a cloister, and a fountain spouting in the middle. The students' rooms
were grouped vertically around staircases, just like Christ Church or King's, the
courtyard gardens were rather like Isfahan, and each hostel was named, as in
England it might be named for saint or patron, or in Iran for Companions of the
Prophet, after some grandee-benefactor of the Raj – Chelmsford, Grant, Hardinge,
each of them by then, and for the moment, half-sanctified himself.

St. John's College, Agra, which was started by the Church Missionary Society,
was startling too. This was a *tour de force* by Swinton Jacob, and was an
astounding mixture of the antiquarian, the scholarly and the symbolic. The
obligatory quadrangle was there, without which no British college was really a
college at all, but towering about it was a mighty edifice in Jacob's favourite
neo-Muslim, domes and pinnacles everywhere, which seemed deliberately to be
recalling, in that ancient headquarters of the Moguls, the fervours of the Cru-
sades: for besides looking partly like a Moorish castle, it flaunted its purpose with
marvellous insouciance by surmounting the whole Islamesque pile of it with a
gigantic Christian cross.

Other educational concerns were militant in a different way, for many of them
were run along army lines, often for the sons and daughters of British soldiers.
Characteristic of them was the Bishop Cotton School at Simla, founded by a
Bishop of Calcutta in 1863 as a token of thanksgiving for the deliverance of the
Anglo-Indians out of the Indian Mutiny. Bishop Cotton was unfortunately
drowned within a fortnight of the laying of its foundation-stone, but the school
kept his name and honoured his declared intention – to provide an education for
Anglo-Indian boys of the middle classes which would be 'by God's blessing no less
useful than Winchester, Rugby and Marlborough'. Though its headmasters were
invariably clergymen, and though the shape of its buildings were properly
Arnoldian, this place looked on the whole distinctly like a barrack-block, its
central quadrangle more fitted for military parades than for scholastic rituals (and
indeed, as we are told in the old brochures, 'boys who come up to military
requirements of age and physique receive a military training in the cadet company of the Simla Volunteer Rifles . . .').

An exotic paradox

The greater universities established by the British in India, notably those in the
Presidency towns, deliberately set out to transfer British ideas and values to the
Indian middle classes, if only to create a useful client caste. Their curricula were
altogether divorced from Indian tradition – no more of those thirty-foot kings –

and their original buildings were all tinged somehow or other with architectural
suggestions of Cam or Isis. Calcutta University has long since disintegrated into a
melange of more or less unidentifiable buildings, grouped around courts scuffed
and tatty from student demonstrations. Madras University remains a fine con-
centration of buildings, mostly in the so-called Indo-Saracenic style, but extending to derivatives of Lutyens's New Delhi manner, ranged along the city's
magnificent waterfront esplanade. And Bombay University incorporates still the
block which Sir Gilbert Scott, the great English Gothicist, designed for it in the
1870s, and which remained to the last days of the British Empire one of its most
admired, abused, and unmistakable structures.

   It stands in the same formidable row of buildings as Colonel Wilkins's
Secretariat, but is recognizably of higher quality. Scott was at the height of his
reputation when he designed this structure, having already built the Albert
Memorial and St. Pancras Station, not to speak of a cathedral in Newfoundland,
and he was the first British architect of such calibre to be represented in India.
Though he was as it happened a Catholic, he set out to create upon this tropic
strand (in those days there was nothing but a railway line between the University
and the Arabian Sea) a true exemplar of the imperial Christian conviction. He
could not, to be sure, actually build a chapel (such as he had already built for
Exeter College, Oxford, and St. John's College, Cambridge), this being a university mostly for Hindus and Muslims, but he managed to imply nevertheless that a
Christian purpose lay behind the institution, and that the Christian God was
hallowing it.

   The building was completed in 1874, four years before Scott's death. It
consisted of an oblong quadrangle, surrounded by two-storey blocks, with an
open entrance flanked on one side by a library, on the other by a high-roofed
Convocation Hall. The style was pure Gothic, untouched by the Hindu or the
Saracenic, with ogee windows, elaborately buttressed balconies, open spiral
staircases, statue niches, pinnacles and ornately decorated arcades. The library
was upstairs, and was Oxbridge absolute, complete with dark wood panelling and
stained glass windows of ecclesiastical suggestion. The Convocation Hall was in
effect a secularized college chapel. It had a rose-window like all the best examples, though with zodiacal rather than liturgical symbols, and a narthex, and an
apse with stained glass in it, and the interior was embellished all over, in the true
Gothic manner, with stone carvings of animals, kings and queens, the kings often
turbanned, the queens orientally gowned, but all managing to look nevertheless
thoroughly and wholesomely British.

   These handsome if ill-advised buildings, paid for partly by gifts from rich
Parsee citizens of Bombay, were later capped with an immense lantern tower,
based upon Giotto's campanile at Florence, but ornamented with figures representing the communities of western India; and the whole ensemble properly

Bombay University, Sir Gilbert Scott's 'fearsome Victorian Gothic revival'. The clock-tower houses twenty-four statues representing the castes of western India.

summed up, perhaps, the spirit of paradox which so often informed the imperial presence – its buildings being in that setting, as the captious Mr Forrest put it, 'as exotic as the system of education they represented'.

A tropical greenhouse

Here is a happy little public building which, since it seems to fall into no particular category, shall have a category of its own.

In the late 1850s Dr George Birdwood, a Bombay physician of an old Anglo-Indian family, prodded Authority into draining one of the Bombay swamps and making gardens of it. They were called the Victoria Gardens. Trees and shrubs from all over the East were planted there, flowers lavishly bloomed, and near the entrance gate they erected the most delightful of tropical greenhouses. This is our building. It is made of cast-iron struts covered all over not with glass, as it might be in Europe, but with wooden lattice strips, and it is shaped like a little cathedral, with a dome, a nave and a long porch. The idea perhaps came from Loudon's *Encyclopedia*, where a rather similar building was illustrated, or perhaps, in a casual or roundabout sort of way, from the Crystal Palace, built a few years before.

Certainly inside the greenhouse there is a distinctly 1851 feeling. The iron struts stand boldly among the palms and banana trees, there are pools and benches between the foliage, the crowds seem to saunter, the light streams through the lattice-work, just as in old prints of the Great Exhibition. The porch, which has an iron roof, is brightly tiled, and in the middle of it, just for fun, there unexpectedly stands an ancient cannon.

Outside the building is no less charming, for some of the more virile trees within have burst their bounds, and squeezing through the woodwork dapple the whole structure with splodges of their vivid green: at the very top of the dome, as in Loudon's model, the iron framework emerges into the sunshine in a curled elaboration of flourishes. While the children play on the gun below, the mynas frisk within this open and ornamental cage.

Aldermanic

Municipal pride blossomed early in British India, and the Presidency towns had their vociferous local patriots almost from the start. Hardly had the settlers burst out of their waterside forts than they set up municipal organizations: city councils were among the earliest institutions upon which Britons and Indians sat ostensibly as equals. No wonder then that the Town Hall, or the Municipal Building, was among the proudest constructions of nearly every Anglo-Indian city.

Colonel John Garstin's unfortunate Town Hall, Calcutta – a Doric structure that suffered from subsidence and flooding from its beginnings in 1809 until well after its formal opening in 1813. Garstin completely overhauled it at his own expense in 1819.

Calcutta's we have already met, because it fell down during its construction, but it is worth looking at again because it was really the archetype of them all, being completed in 1813 when Calcutta was approaching the climax of its commercial confidence. Its designer, John Garstin, was one of the most interesting of the early engineer-architects, unusually knowledgeable about Indian native buildings, but oddly enough in Calcutta Town Hall he made no concessions whatever to local conditions. Strictly Palladian in style, this was a building as British as Yorkshire pudding, *sans* verandah, *sans* arcades, *sans* anything which might help to temper the Bengal climate. It was paid for by public lottery, and it spoke uncompromisingly of British municipal pride, at a time when Calcutta was to all intents a British city. It was not in the least ashamed to stand just along the Esplanade from the newly-finished Governor's Palace, and with its heavy balustrading, the six giant Tuscan pillars of its portico and its rich *porte-cochère* behind, it properly proclaimed the burgeoning consequence of the place.

Directly opposite its entrance, enhancing the monumental effect, they later erected a tall bronze statue of the Governor-General Lord William Bentinck, with an inscription composed by Macaulay himself, and the Town Hall looked southward over the *maidan* portentously towards the bulk of Fort William in the distance. Inside it was very grand, too. A thickly pillared hall, 162 feet long, occupied most of the ground floor; upstairs was the ballroom with the uncertain floor; all over the building stood effigies of eminent Calcuttans, generals, law-makers, philanthropists, a bishop and even an Indian or two.

Soon afterwards Bombay, though still something of a backwater by Calcuttan standards, countered with an even more prideful Town Hall. This was the masterpiece of an otherwise unknown officer of the Bombay Engineers, Colonel Thomas Cowper, and was finished in 1833 in the neo-classical style, purer than the Palladian, which was then fashionable in England. It was built to house the library of the Asiatic Society, as well as fulfil its municipal functions, and it had a less mercantile and aldermanic, more artistic feel to it than Calcutta's. Its site was the best in the city, opposite the cathedral on the green which formed the heart of the old fort area, and it lay broad and low above a very steep, very wide monumental staircase, flanked by iron railings. It had a portico with six fluted Doric pillars beneath a wide pediment, and its façade was given a curious tropical allure by a series of sharply projecting wooden hoods, deeply shading its doors and windows. It looked fine. Everybody liked it, even in later years the novelist Aldous Huxley, who detested everything else in Bombay.

It was the interior, though, which really showed Colonel Cowper's great gifts, for it was designed as an intricate exercise in lights and shades. The central hall of the building was huge and thickly pillared, lit by sunlight coming through the louvred windows, but at the end of it were smaller chambers illuminated by skylights. Spiral staircases complicated the scheme, there were niches, pillars and statues everywhere, and the effect was mysterious and theatrical – the light streaming down in rods and patches, the heavy columns all around, and dimly glimpsed on plinth and platform, or suddenly picked out by sun-shafts from above, the silent marble figures of the imperial worthies.

The British never built another Town Hall like that, but they continued to express their civic pretensions grandly enough until the end. In Bombay in 1893 the architect F. W. Stevens built a marvellously miscegenated Municipal Build-ing in his best Oriental Gothic: it had a bulbous dome 250 feet high, numerous pinnacles, and a central gable crowned with a thirteen-foot statue representing the Spirit of Bombay. In Simla, in 1887, they built a Town Hall which, though said darkly at the time to be 'by no means free of structural defects', nevertheless housed, until in 1911 they lopped off its upper floor for safety's sake, not only the municipal offices proper, but also a supper-room, a Freemasons' Hall, a library and the Gaiety Theatre, *the* place for amateur dramatics in Anglo-India. In Lahore in 1890 Prince Albert Victor, the Queen's grandson, opened a new Town Hall which had twin domed towers, windows in the Moorish shape and the words TOWN HALL written enormously in English and Urdu in the middle.

And in Karachi, a city the British created from scratch on the sea-coast of Sind, the Karachi Municipal Buildings included not only Ionic columns, Hindu

Public architecture of Madras and Bombay. The Ripon Building (*top*), the present headquarters of the Madras Corporation, was designed by a Mr Harris, consulting architect to the Government, and was named after the Viceroy who introduced local government to the huge country. Bombay Town Hall (*bottom*) is a Doric triumph designed by Colonel Thomas Cowper of the Bombay Engineers. It took workmen fifteen years to complete, and was opened in 1833. Columns shipped over from England proved to be too large and were incorporated instead into the Byculla Church, which was under construction at the same time.

decorations, Mogul domes and Gothic stained glass windows, but a large clock erected to commemorate the Silver Jubilee of King George V and Queen Mary in 1935 – alas for their complacency, for to the City Fathers of the day it evidently seemed one of the great occasions in the immemorial progress of India.

The Law

The Law! Nothing caught the spirit of the Victorian Empire better than the idea of legal majesty, embodied in India as in England in the presence of grave judges and still graver buildings. Fair Play was the noblest maxim of the British Empire everywhere, even in the breach of it, and in the most corrupt and venal days of John Company it used to be claimed that the lawcourts of the British offered a fair hearing to every claimant, brown or white (though when in 1885 it was proposed that Europeans might be tried by Indian magistrates, that was *quite* another thing). Later the establishment of one code of law throughout British India was considered one of the Empire's proudest achievements.

It is true that in the up-country districts law courts were hardly more than huts or sheds – tents often enough, indeed, when the District Magistrate was on tour. But the High Courts of India were very conscious of their own importance, and into them the architects tried to build the loftiest meanings of empire. They were of course prominently embellished with blindfold goddesses and scales: they were also habitually the largest buildings in their neighbourhoods, towering above the rest like legal maxims (axioms that is, not machine-guns). This was true from the start: the original court-house at Calcutta so dominated its quarter of town that to this day, though it has long since vanished, one of the main business thoroughfares is called Old Court House Street in its memory.

The High Courts did not often express a quality of mercy, but generally made the malefactor feel as alarmed as the judge was all-confident. The tremendous High Court of Calcutta, built in 1872 to the designs of Walter Granville, a Government architect, was decidedly the most daunting building in town. It was modelled upon the thirteenth-century Cloth Hall at Ypres in Belgium, and Anglo-Indian legend claimed that when the original was destroyed in the First World War, the Mayor of Ypres asked the Mayor of Calcutta for a set of the plans, so that they could start reconstructing it. Actually the adaptation was loose, and the tower was all wrong, but at least the Calcutta building possessed the same sense of mass and rootedness, and stood with a similar grim importance overlooking the *maidan*. The High Court at Bombay, erected in 1879, was designed by Colonel J. A. Fuller, Royal Engineers, who spent £100,000 on it, and built it in a modish mixture of Venetian Gothic and Early English styles. The Lahore High Court, completed in 1889, was claimed by knowing guidebooks to be in 'the late

(*Left.*) The severely practical corridor of the Western Court, New Delhi. (*Right.*) The High Court, Madras, built, like the nearby University, and like other, more distant courts – such as Lahore – in the somewhat eccentric mongrel style known as Hindu-Saracenic. It was completed in 1889.

(*Top.*) Walter Granville's High Court, Calcutta, modelled after the Ypres Town Hall and completed in 1872.
(*Bottom.*) The formidable Municipal Buildings, Simla, with Scottish baronial brick overlaid by Swiss chalet.

fourteenth-century Pathan style'. The Karachi High Court, opened in 1929, was in a classical mode not altogether untinged with the Lutyenesque.

But the prodigy among them, and one of the most romantically exciting of all the British buildings in India, was the High Court on the waterfront at Madras. This huge red sandstone building challenges description, so splendidly jumbled was its presence, so elaborate were its forms, so complex and disturbing its effects. It was designed 'in the Hindu-Saracenic style', by two Public Works Department architects, Henry Irwin (of the Simla Viceregal lodge), and his assistant, J. H. Stephens, and it was opened in 1892. Next door to the courts stood the Law College, and every traveller arriving by sea in Madras saw the buildings before they disembarked, for they stood on the Esplanade a little way from the docks: and with their multitudinous towers, pinnacles and domes, some brightly coloured, some decorated in stucco patterns, they presented a terrifically fanciful welcome to the city, in grandiose partnership with the classical restraint of Fort St. George along the foreshore.

'The arrangement of the interior', reported Murray's Handbook, 1894, 'is good'. In fact it was spectacular. The great building was like a Piranese jail in its contrapuntal and crypt-like surprise – court after court, staircase after staircase, warrens of arcaded and vaulted corridors, half-hidden alcoves where the lawyers gossipped, huge verandahs thronged with litigants, cool galleries in whose cavities mendicants and holy men reposed on public holidays, a palatial *porte-cochère* beneath whose shade the omnipotent justices of the Raj stepped from their carriages, to walk through gloomy cavernous halls, up wide staircases open to the sky, to their robing-chambers and portentous judgement rooms.

Wide dusty gardens surrounded these splendid courts; great iron gateways separated them from the traffic of the street outside; and on top of the building, surrounded by clusters of lesser protrusions, Messrs Irwin and Stephens erected a last symbolic construction, a bulbous and eccentric tower. It had, as a matter of fact, an unsuitably phallic look to it up there: but it was really a lighthouse, a beacon above the benches, which continued to flash its message of security and punctuality when the judges had long gone home up Mount Road to their tea, and the villains were safely locked away below.

Houses of wonder

There was one class of public building in which the British in India truly excelled: the museum. It was the one class of public building, too, which the Indian masses treated with reverence, hushing their irrepressible children as they entered, and moving in awe among the archaeological relics, the ancient guns, the fabrics and gigantic representations of British history which the imperialists thought proper for their instruction. They called a museum a House of Wonder.

Some of the collections were very fine. They were frequently founded, and largely supplied, by amateurs, but in later years they got Government funds, and they were powerfully encouraged by the example of Albert the Prince Consort, with his enthusiasm for public scientific education. The great complex of museums of South Kensington in London went up in the aftermath, and with the profits, of the 1851 International Exhibition at the Crystal Palace, and the Indian museums were essentially mid-Victorian flowerings too, meant to be not only archives for the educated, but schools for the illiterate.

Architecturally they were often interesting. The Indian Museum on Chowringhee in Calcutta, the most important of them all, was an Italianate palace, built in 1875 around a colonnaded courtyard full of shrubs and trees. The Victoria and Albert Museum at Bombay was a French Renaissance building, ornately detailed: behind it was stationed one of the stone elephants which had given their names to the Elephanta Caves, a swart and bloated object, while in front there stood a particularly horrible but fascinating memorial tower, Osbornesque in allusions, which the financier Sir Albert Sassoon had dedicated to the Queen. Down the road the architect George Wittet designed the Prince of Wales Museum, founded in 1905 but still unfinished at the end of Empire, in a resplendent local style, said to be based on fifteenth-century models, with a large concrete dome and outlying domelets on a structure of blue and yellow basalt.

The museum at Karachi was housed in the delightful Frere Hall, a display of Gothic pinnacles, buttresses and stained glass which might stand in any exhibition as an example of that popular genre, the Victorian Monstrosity. At Madras there was a whole cultural complex, rather like South Kensington and begun at exactly the same time, set in handsome gardens and built in varying styles: a museum proper, a technical institute, a library, a theatre, and a startling art gallery, the Empress Victoria Memorial Hall, which was built in 1909 in purest Hindu style by the versatile Henry Irwin.

The most ambitious of them all was the Victoria Memorial in Calcutta, dedicated entirely to the history of British rule in India, and opened in 1921 as a token of gratitude to the memory of the lately-deceased Queen-Empress. Lord Curzon, the Viceroy of the day, was the true begetter of this inescapable pile. He wanted, he said, 'a building stately, spacious, monumental and grand . . . where all classes will learn the lessons of history and see revived before their eyes the marvels of the past'. To this end he enlisted as its designer an English architect with Indian connections, William Emerson, to be assisted locally by the learned and prolific Vincent Esch, then City Architect of Calcutta.

Curzon was in no two minds about the nature of the building. It was to be his Taj Mahal – the grand symbol of love and devotion by which both Queen and Viceroy would always be remembered. If it was not exactly a tomb, like the Taj itself, it was at least a kind of allegorical sepulchre. It was built of the same marble

as the Taj, from Makrana in Jodhpur, and when the poet W. H. Auden visited it in
Calcutta in the 1930s, he was assured that it was by the same architect. There was
a difference, though. Shah Jehan's Taj was essentially sad, commemorating as it
did a woman who died young, and built by a man who ended his days in captivity;
Lord Curzon's Taj was to be altogether happy, at once monumental and festive,
proud and serene, and it was to be packed to its every attic with the annals and
artefacts of imperial success.

And there was no denying the success of the building, either. It stood among
sixty-four acres of garden at the southern end of the *maidan*, a prison having been
demolished to make way for it, and you approached it through high ornamental
iron gates. Long before you reached the entrance Queen Victoria herself greeted
you, in a gigantic white effigy by Sir George Frampton, sitting on a throne and
supported by Art, Literature, Justice, a lion, a tiger, two Indian soldiers and St.
George: behind her the museum awaited you, gleaming white.

Like its great prototype at Agra, it was reflected all about in ornamental pools,
and was described by its architect as being in the Italian Renaissance style, 'with a
suggestion of orientalism in the arrangement of the domes and minor details'. It
consisted of a central block with four wings, each of them domed; the tall central
dome, which was supported by Baroque scrolls like the Salute in Venice, was
surmounted by a revolving figure of Victory, sixteen feet high and three tons in
weight, while supplementary statuary, much of it made in Italy of Carrara
marble, paid tribute to imperial abstractions like Motherhood, Prudence, Learning and Charity.

Inside the museum was sumptuous, and replete with royal mementos, besides
being equipped, as Curzon intended it, with every kind of imperial scroll, print
and trophy, from locks of Lady Canning's hair to the surrendered swords of
defeated vassals. It was a building full of excitements, both for the subjects and for
the imperialists of the day, and of all its lesser frissons, perhaps the best occurred
when one looked out of the window across the east quadrangle: for there, looking
past Sir Thomas Brock's touching statue of Victoria as a young girl, one saw
perfectly aligned with her profile, across the brown *maidan*, the west window of
Calcutta Cathedral, seat of the Anglican Primate in India – the spiritual always
over the shoulder, so to speak, of the imperial.

(But poor Curzon never saw it: he had left India for ever before even the
foundation-stone of his great creation was laid in the ground).

Where Kim took the Lama

The ultimate Anglo-Indian museum, all the same, was the one Kipling made
famous in *Kim* – the Ajaib-Gher in Lahore, where Kim took the Lama in the
opening pages of the novel. It was rebuilt in 1894, when the Kipling family had left

Hindu-Saracenic architecture on a small scale: (*top*) the Punjab Public Library, Lahore. (*Bottom*.) The interior of the
Victoria and Albert Museum, Bombay, built to mark the assumption by the Queen of the title Empress of India, in 1877.

India, but Rudyard's father Lockwood, formerly its Curator, had indelibly stamped upon it his own devotion to craftsmanship and meticulous design. It remains even today much as it was at the end of the Victorian century, only just beginning to look shabby in its corners. From the outside it may not seem much – it stands upon the Mall, the chief thoroughfare of Lahore, and is built in a fairly restrained Anglo-Mogul style: but the moment you set foot inside it, its magic is all around you.

Each of its display-rooms is arranged around groups of iron columns, and affixed to these are the illuminated show-cases, like fungi on tree trunks; this gives it a suggestively foresty look, the ironwork black and heavy above the clustering old mahogany cases. But then everywhere in the building, up the great staircase, in every alcove, a mass of lovely carved woodwork adds intricacy to the whole. Nothing was done patchily or carelessly in this House of Wonders, and nothing was uncontrived. Even doors into lesser offices or cupboards are exquisitely worked, and there is a mass of polished brass, too, and heavy teak beams loom splendidly above one's head, and the whole building is rather dim-lit, almost opaque in fact, as though wood-smoke is perpetually drifting through it.

All around are the strange images and artefacts of the collection, massive recumbent Buddhas, manuscripts in ancient containers, opulent doors from demolished houses of old Lahore, silks and lacquer-ware, prayer-wheels, temple banners, archaic lutes and trumpets, curious weapons, incomprehensible utensils – all to be wandered about silently with your friends, holding each others' hands for reassurance, perhaps, among so many arcane objects, and shuffling your feet rather, as in a temple, over the polished and gently creaking floorboards.

The ante-rooms

We cannot leave the public buildings of British India without mentioning the legislative chambers which, in the late years of the Raj, came into being in all the provinces of India. They were not very interesting buildings, but they were the ante-rooms of liberty. It was not until after the First World War that the British first gave their Indian subjects some real share in the government of the country, elected legislative councils then being established in the several provinces, with a central legislature in New Delhi. 'We march round the fortress of bureaucracy', the patriot leader G. K. Gokhale had said, 'seeking entrance but finding none'. Now, in the flurry of liberal activity that succeeded the Treaty of Versailles, a chink of a door was opened. Legislative Assembly chambers went up all over the country without much sign of architectural enthusiasm. In Calcutta they were unobtrusively neo-classical, tinged with the New Delhi style but altogether overwhelmed by Granville's High Court across the way: in Bombay they were tacked on to the back of the disused Royal Alfred Sailors' Home: and in New Delhi, the home of the central legislature, the future Parliament of India, they were added to the city plan purely as an afterthought, and feel like one to this day.

When the new capital was devised, in 1911, nobody had thought of a Parliament. A semicircular Council Chamber within the Viceroy's House was the most that seemed necessary. The reforms in 1918 changed everything, and a huge new building, altogether an intrusion upon the original plans for the city, was built by Herbert Baker in his Secretariat manner, a few hundred yards to the north-west of the palace. It was entirely circular, colonnaded all the way round, and its scale was generous: within its cirque it contained three assembly chambers (one the Chamber of Princes), offices, gardens, and a library in the centre surmounted by a dome and a lantern – theoretically at least, a perfect modern Parliament building. But the hearts of the Anglo-Indians were not in it. Lord Irwin the Viceroy opened it with hopeful words in 1927, and in later years it was to be the seat of the most populous democracy on earth, but architecturally it was a loser from the start. It cowered beneath the sneer of the palace across the way, and for all its bulk was soon to become, topographically speaking, hardly more than another roundabout or intersection in the imperial diagram of the capital.

5 · Practical

Captain Garstin's masterpiece

From a boat sailing down the holy Ganges at Patna, in Bihar, one may see a queer and wonderful building protruding above the straggly junipers and acacias that line the bank. It looks rather like a huge white old-fashioned beehive, dominating the flat-topped houses of the town, and any ramble through the more down-to-earth structures of the British in India, the structures of trade, technique, profit and pleasure, may very well begin with it: for if its appearance is extraordinary, its purpose was purely utilitarian.

It is the Gola, a granary built by the British in 1786 as a precaution against famine, and known to Patna people as Golghar, the Round House. It was designed by Captain John Garstin, Bengal Engineers, a quarter of a century before his Town Hall in Calcutta (and thirty-four years before his death – he is buried beneath a properly architectural catafalque in the South Street Cemetery in Calcutta). The Gola is the one building that gets him into textbooks and architectural treatises, and is indeed much the most famous of the purely practical structures of the Raj: and this is because, though it turned out to be an abysmal failure, it looks at once functional and excitingly symbolic. It was a pure work of engineering technique, but it was touched, whether by chance or calculation, with the machismo of the imperial presence.

The singular shape of the Gola probably had Indian origins, for the indigenes had been building conical granaries for centuries. The scale of it, though, was unprecedented. Built of stone slabs, it was ninety feet high, and 426 feet round at ground level. The idea was that grain would be poured into the Gola through a hole in the top, allowing it to spread all over the floor, and build up in decreasing diameter to the summit. Spiralling up the outsides of the huge cone, accordingly, Garstin built two brick staircases; the workmen, labouring up one side and emptying their grain-sacks into the summit orifice, stumbled down the other side for more (and once a visiting Nepali prince galloped his pony all the way up, and all the way down, for the sheer panache of it).

The building has always fascinated travellers, and people have often read

The remarkable 'Gola' (or 'Golghar') in Patna built by engineer John Garstin as a storehouse for grain, which was to be carried in sacks up the winding stairs and poured in through a hole in the top of the structure. Garstin's imaginative plan to build a string of such storehouses across the Gangetic plain never materialized.

deeper references into its shape. Was it meant to represent the thrifty garnering of the bees? Was it, as the architectural historian Sten Nilsson has wondered, derived from the *architecture parlante* then popular among the designers of revolutionary France, buildings at once mysterious and allusive, globe-temples, pyramids? Garstin himself evidently saw something heroic to its hefty func- tionalism, and had this inscription carved upon the side of the building:

No 1
In part of a general Plan
Ordered by the GOVERNOR-GENERAL and COUNCIL
20 January 1784
For the perpetual prevention of Famine
In these Provinces
THIS GRANARY
Was erected by CAPTAIN JOHN GARSTIN, Engineer
Compleated on the 20th July 1786
First filled and publickly closed by . . .

But the rest is blank. Though the Gola has been used in time of famine, and indeed is habitually stocked with quantities of grain to this day, it was never filled to the top, and was never used as Garstin intended it – as a perpetual grain store, that is, always kept stocked for emergencies. Nobody really knows why – 'it was found', simply wrote Emily Eden in 1837, 'to be useless' – and it is certainly not true, as frivolous guidebooks suggest, that its only door was made to open inwards, thus preventing entrance anyway when the granary was full. It is true, though, that the usual emptiness of the building gave it its popular fame: for the acoustics of the Gola are prodigious, and tourists loved it from the start. There was never a more startling whispering-gallery. The voices of the officials inside it, counting grain- sacks or totting up accounts, echo around its masonries like the voices of canons in some great cathedral, and the faintest touch upon its floor, the tap of a pen upon the flagstones, is marvellously magnified by the shape of it, and reverberates into the empty roof in hollow praise of Captain Garstin.

Roads of Hindustan

The British were not, at least by Roman standards, great road-builders. Their empire in India, nevertheless, depended upon swift and certain communications, so vast, diverse and widely-separated were its provinces, and in the days before railways they did some build some grand highways. By the 1850s, for instance, they had linked Calcutta and Bombay by a metalled road clean across India; they had thrown a highway, the Great Hindustan and Tibet Road, through the foothills to Simla, and hoped that it would eventually link the British and the Chinese Empires across the Himalayas; and they had recreated the Grand Trunk Road, otherwise known as the Grand Military Road, which was to be the backbone of their dominion in northern India.

It was based upon existing highways, built in bits and pieces by previous rulers of India, and long since fallen into disrepair. In 1839 the East India Company decided to restore and modernize it, and an elaborate works staff was established at Allahabad under the direction of one of the Empire's great innovators, James Thomason, who even went so far as to establish a college for the training of native engineers. It was a terrific task – linking together, and bringing up to modern standards, thousands of miles of derelict intermittent highway, bridging thousands of streams and rivers, establishing ferry services on others, and fitting out the whole great work as a practical military and commercial highway.

As the Empire extended its hold further to the north-west, so the Grand Trunk Road was extended too, and when it was done, it was not only one of the great sights of Asia, but truly one of the great power-factors too. It began in the outskirts of Calcutta, just over the river from the Governor-General's palace, and it went by way of Agra, Delhi and Lahore to Peshawar, the gateway of Afghanistan, almost in the marches of Russia. Mogul precedents were honoured in its design, and it was planned in regular stages, marked everywhere, all the way from Bengal to the frontier country, by monumental milestones. There were regular transit camps, too, for marching troops, and official lodgings for individual travellers, and police stations, and post offices, and even cemeteries for those who died along the way. It was metalled throughout, and though the average speed of bullock-carts along it was some two miles per hour, taking a year to go from one end to the other, it was described by one contemporary traveller as being 'as smooth as a bowling-green'.

Kipling loved it, and immortalized it in *Kim*. It was, he said, 'a stately corridor . . . it runs straight, bearing, without crowding, India's traffic for fifteen hundred miles – such a river of life as nowhere else exists in the world'. Most of it was in three lanes, the centre sixteen-foot carriageway being reserved for fast traffic, and much of it was shaded by double avenues of trees. Its grading was gentle everywhere, and in its last section alone, the 260 miles between Lahore and Peshawar, it crossed 550 bridges and tunnelled through six mountain ridges. 'Aye', cried Kipling's old soldier affectionately, 'this is the Road of Hindustan!': and long though it has been challenged by railways and airlines, it is a noble thoroughfare still – so old, so powerful, so elegant to this day, for all the pot-holes that scar its bowling-green surface now, and the endless scraggly, higgledy-piggledy, hooting, sagging, scrambling traffic of Hindustan that travels slowly, oh so slowly, along its uneven tarmac.

The railways

But the British Empire was the empire of Steam, and the fulfilment of its dominion in India coincided with the climax of the railway age. The prodigious construction of the Indian railways, which very soon replaced the roads as the chief arteries of dominion, together with all their bridges, tunnels, culverts, viaducts, stations and workshops, was the greatest of the imperial achievements in India, and perhaps the supreme British monument of all.

The railways were built, by private capital under Government guarantee, in an amazingly short time. The first twenty miles of track, between Thana and Bombay, was opened for traffic in 1853, but by 1869 some 4,000 miles were working. Immense construction forces were set to work on railway lines in every part of India, and against all kinds of hazard, disease, political unrest, climate, the engineers pushed their lines into the remotest corner of the country, the last main line, through the Khyber Pass, being completed in 1926.

The first purpose of the railways was commercial, but they were also conceived from the start as strategic conveniences, and their lines were laid to military advice. They seldom actually entered Indian cities (doubly suspect to British eyes after the Mutiny of 1857), but generally stopped at stations on the outskirts, under the protection of the cantonments: important junctions, too, were generally sited well away from centres of Indian population. The first major line followed the route of the Grand Trunk Road, from Calcutta to Delhi and the north-west: thereafter trunk-lines were laid to link the three Presidency cities, and a myriad feeder tracks, from rack-railways winding precariously to hill-stations to infinitesimal narrow-gauge lines serving the Native States, eventually meant that the whole of India was criss-crossed with railway lines – more than 30,000 miles of them in the end, from Cape Cormorin at the very southern tip of India to the Khyber Pass itself.

The railway engineers approached their task with a sense of high significance. These were great works, symbols of an Age, tokens of an Empire, even symptoms of a Faith, and their style was deliberately magnificent. The honour, the dignity and the glory of Victorian Britain were concerned, wrote the engineer W. P. Andrews in 1846. 'The complete permeation of these "climes of the sun" by a magnificent system of railway communication, would present a series of public monuments vastly surpassing, in real grandeur, the aqueducts of Rome, the pyramids of Egypt, the great wall of China, the temples, the palaces, and mausoleums of the Great Moguls . . . Were we driven out of India tomorrow, we should leave them behind us as glorious monuments of our rule . . .'. Half measures were not encouraged, on the railways of India, and it was the pride of the railway engineers that nothing they made should be without style. The trains themselves were certainly stylish, speeding over the scorched plains with their plumes of white steam and their flash of burnished brass, and stylish too were the works that serviced and attended them.

The bridges in particular were unforgettable. They often carried roadways too, the double-track bridge becoming a speciality of Anglo-Indian engineering, and in many other ways they were boldly innovative, especially in dealing with problems of river flow and sediment. They did not generally aim at beauty – many of them were built after the disastrous collapse, in 1879, of the great suspension bridge over the Tay in Scotland, and they were accordingly designed to a brutally complex cantilever technique. In their time, though, they were some of the most ambitious and technically interesting in the world.

Aesthetically, too, they could be stunning in their power. The Attock Bridge across the Indus, for example, which took the Punjab Northern State Railway up to Peshawar and the frontier, was a marvellous spectacle. Completed in 1883 to the designs of the engineer Guilford Molesworth, it was built on two decks, the railway crossing above, the Grand Trunk Road below, and it was approached through huge iron gates, sentry-boxes and gunposts. Slowly and carefully the trains eased their way across its exposed upper deck, high above the river; below, the bullock-carts, the camels, the marching soldiers, the pedestrian thousands made their way; and this remarkable iron corridor, always full of movement, the clanking trains above, the jostle below, provided a focus for a dun and treeless prospect of Sind, out of which, from high ridges all around, forts, guns and embrasures looked watchfully down.

Or there was the spectacular Lansdowne Bridge over the Indus at Sukkur, perhaps the ugliest ever built, but among the most memorable too. Sir Alexander Rendel, one of the great bridge-builders of the day, was responsible for the design of this structure, which was opened in 1889 and which was variously described even at the time as bizarre, monstrous, and as a design in which 'the lamp of truth shines with too lurid a flame'. Certainly there was something suggestively timeless to the grotesque mass of ironwork by which this edifice carried the Indus Valley State Railway across the river. Two enormous cantilever structures held the weight of the bridge, like a couple of dozen cranes bolted permanently together in dense meshes of struts and girders. Each was 170 feet high, and the railway entered their towering shadows through fortified stone gateways. The whole thing, then the longest cantilever span ever built, stood there less like a bridge in fact than some nightmarish fish trap, and though the trains cross the river now by a less remarkable structure downstream, it stands there in eccentric splendour to this day.

Some of the Indian railway bridges were built on tall wooden trestles, like those on American railroads. Some, like the ones that carried the trains to Simla, looked like Roman aqueducts, with piled rows of masonry arches. Some were so remote that hardly anybody ever saw them, some so hazardous that trains

The Howrah Bridge, built across the treacherous Hooghly River in 1943 by the Cleveland Bridge and Engineering Company. Despite promises by the West Bengal Government of a second Hooghly bridge, this remains the only crossing. The photograph is taken from a terrace of Howrah railway station, principal terminus for trains to north, south and west India. The city of Calcutta itself is on the far bank of the river.

crawled across them at walking speed, their passengers holding their breaths. Some were so familiar that they became an essential part of the Indian scene, and the landscape would be almost unimaginable without them.

Of these last, the most familiar of all, to the greatest number of Indians, was undoubtedly the Howrah Bridge across the Hooghly at Calcutta. It did not carry a railway proper, only a tram-line, but it was the only connection between the main railway termini of the city, one on the east bank of the river, one on the west. Engineered by Hubert Shirley-Smith, again one of the most distinguished of his generation, this was completed in 1943, replacing a bridge of boats as the only bridge across the river in a city of two million people. It was built in a single cantilever span, more or less 1,500 feet long (it stretched some four feet in the heat of every Calcutta noonday, contracting again each evening), and stood so high that it dwarfed all the buildings around it, hovel and palace alike, becoming at once the popular hallmark of the city, like the Harbour Bridge in Sydney, or Tower Bridge in London.

It was a lumpish thing, but at night especially it made up in drama for what it lacked in grace: for then, as the ox-carts and the bullocks, the taxis and the thousands of bicycles, the rickshaws, the claptrap buses, the diesel-belching lorries, the thousands of commuters, country folk, beggars and hawkers poured over it in an endless multitude beneath the dim street lights, it looked like a great escape route, jammed with refugees swirling this way and that from some uncertain but imminent catastrophe.

An operatic tunnel

The most truly operatic of railway tunnels was surely the Khojak tunnel, at the time of its completion in 1891 the longest in India, which carried the Chaman Extension Railway to the western extremity of the Indian Empire, on the Afghan frontier. The line itself was theatrical enough. It was begun in 1883 as a secret strategic line, intended if necessary to take troops over the frontier to Kandahar, then allegedly threatened by the Russians, and code-named 'The Harnai Road Improvement Scheme'. In the event it never got further than the frontier itself, where until the end of the Raj rails and sleepers were stored in case the project was ever completed, but it did become nevertheless the quickest way out of Afghanistan to the ports and markets of British India. Refrigerated fruit trains ran down it every summer day carrying Afghan grapes, peaches and nectarines to the Indian cities: when in 1927 King Amanullah of Afghanistan went on a State visit to Europe, it was by the Chaman Extension Railway that he began his journey (and alarmed by the length of the great tunnel, we are told, he pulled the communication cord in the middle of it).

The tunnel stood almost at the end of the line, almost on the frontier. Immediately outside it the tracks ended in buffers at the station of Chaman, and travellers into Afghanistan had to transfer to road vehicles. It was fearfully wild and arid country, and to drive the tunnel through the Khwaja Amran mountains the engineers employed thousands of Pathans, Hazarahs, Tibetans, Kashmiris, Punjabis, Arabs, Zanzibaris, Sikhs and Bengalis, together with sixty-five miners especially brought out from Wales, where they had worked on the Severn Tunnel a few years before. Many of these men died – 800 in the winter of 1890 alone, from typhus – but the work was finished in three years, the tunnel being 12,780 feet long and made of 19,764,426 bricks, all fired on the spot.

It was the portals of the thing, though, that gave it such a stagy splendour. In the railway age, of course, tunnels were often castellated, but usually just for effect. The Khojak was fortified in earnest. It stood within sight of one of the world's touchiest frontiers, in the very stadium of the Great Game, and it was built recognizably for heroics. It was defended by no mere bunkers or blockhouses: there at the extremity of Empire, its gateways stood like royal bastions in the hills, beautifully carved and dressed, with two high castellated turrets at each end, battlements all around, and high loops apparently for the pouring of boiling oil.

When one of the great steam trains of the North Western Railway came out of India this way, pulled perhaps by a couple of its big 2-8-0 locomotives – when with a hiss of steam, a hoot of whistles, screeching of brakes and clouds of black smoke a train emerged from that castle-cavern in the mountains, it was *tunnelissimo* indeed.

Stations

Just over Howrah Bridge in Calcutta, almost skulking in its shadow, stands Howrah railway station, one of the largest in Asia. It began, long before they bridged the river, as a huddle of tin sheds beside the ferry-quay, where the thatched country craft lay off shore like flotillas of floating haystacks: in 1906 it was rebuilt to the plans of Halsey Ricardo, a well-known English advocate of the arts and crafts movement, and became a huge redbrick conglomerate of mixed Tibetan monastic and English penal suggestion. Eight towers dominate its jumbled façade, six of them with wide eaves (the monastic part), two with solid square tops (the prison). There are also domes with spikes on top, and the fenestration is partly Moorish in provenance, partly Romanesque. Two *portes-cochères* flank the main carriage entrance, and the whole immense façade is rigidly symmetrical, even to the flag-poles (but excluding the great clock, which is mounted in the north tower where it can be seen from the bridge above).

Inside all is thrust and movement. It is true that huddled here and there across the concourses are silent heaps of humanity, lapped about with bundles, mattresses, baskets and cardboard boxes, apparently permanently inert. But all around these lifeless deposits there is motion. There is a whirring of great fans, an incessant flashing of lights from automatic vending-machines, a drifting and spouting of steam from the platforms beyond, a shuddering of diesels, a rattle of trollies, an unimaginable rush of people here and there, and when one of the great trains slides heavily from its platform in the background, the whole place seems to swing into one mighty rhythm with its departure. The sun streams in through the open entrances of Howrah, and casts its dust-heavy rays through the inner murk: but actually night and day, dark and light, have little meaning in this vast caravanserai, which looks much the same at any time, snorting, seething and flashing indifferently.

Not all the Indian railway stations were like that, Heaven knows. Most of them were simple in the extreme – beyond the beauty of a good design, the Board

Howrah station, Calcutta, built in 1906 as the terminus of the East Indian Railway. The booking office is unchanged, in both style and speed of service, today.

The fantastic exterior, and pleasantly cool interior, of Egmore station, Madras, from where trains can be taken for the Blue Hills, or for Ceylon.

of the Madras Railway declared in 1866, all ornamentation should be avoided, and the building should be as simple as was consistent with its purpose and situation. ('Will a single traveller be willing to pay an increased fare on the South Western', Ruskin had lately asked, 'because the columns of the terminus are covered with patterns from Nineveh? . . .'). When they built a railway station north of Jacobabad in Sind, where there was a convenient water-supply but no habitation whatever, they did not even have a name for it, so they called it Jhatpat, 'Immediately', after a favourite injunction of the construction engineer. And this is how Miss Olive Douglas, in 1913, described the ladies' waiting-room at another less than metropolitan halt: 'A large, dirty, barn-like apartment with some cane seats arranged around the wall, and an attempt at a dressing-table with a spotty looking-glass on it, in one corner. One small lamp, smelling vilely, served to make darkness visible, and an old hag crouching at the door was the attendant spirit'.

But then there was room for all sorts, and many of the Anglo-Indian railway stations were full of charm. Sometimes the engineers responded to the injunctions of that Board by erecting buildings of a delightful innocence, simple wooden shelters sustained by elementary but elegant wrought iron, made out of old railway lines. Often they honoured the environment by building in local styles – a dome here, an arch there – and on the hill-town railways they built halts which were like little resort bungalows themselves, idling there in the sunshine, with a few familiar loafers always in their yards, and once or twice a day an echoing hoot and a chuffing as the train bustled in.

After the Mutiny it was decreed that new stations in the north must be easily defensible in time of trouble, and this instruction was interpreted exuberantly by the Chief Engineer of the Amritsar and Multan Railway, William Brunton, when he designed a new station for Lahore in 1864. He made it actually a station-fortress – 'a passenger station' as he said, 'which shall be perfectly defensible in every aspect'. It seemed at first sight simply a romantic extravaganza in the Balmoral kind, and guidebooks generally treated it so. Its medieval castle towers did look quaint, standing as they did so neatly one at each corner, and its eight bartizans gave it a playful look, like a toy fort of stiffened cardboard. But it was no joke really. That long stone curtain-wall was massively constructed, and its decorated arrow-slits were loopholes for muskets. Those towers were designed to be bomb-proof, last strongholds for the defence of the station, and the picturesque arches through which trains entered or left the station could be closed with heavy iron doors, turning the whole building into a huge bunker.

Lahore railway station never went into action, but from then until the end of the Raj, in times of trouble British soldiers manned its beguiling ramparts: and when they prepared to leave in 1947, and the Muslims and Hindus of the Punjab leapt at each other's throats, ironically upon its platforms the dead were laid out.

'VT'

Indeterminately beyond the traffic in Hornby Road, Bombay, there looms an edifice which seems to be rather blurred than clarified by the burning sunlight – something vast, fretted and ornate, with a tower like Wren's Tom Tower in Oxford on the top of it, and multitudes of galleries, loggias and elaborate windows all around. The structure does not much elucidate itself when we get nearer, tangled as it is in the turmoil of the city, but at least the effect of it, as we enter its railed forecourt between two great lions couchant, is altogether explicit. It is a statement of pride. It bespeaks the incomparable power and beauty of steam, and the uncountable blessings of empire too. It is Victoria Terminus, 'VT' to everyone in Bombay, the southern terminus and headquarters of the Great Indian Peninsula Railway. The Bombay architect F. W. Stevens designed it, it was opened in 1887 in time to celebrate Queen Victoria's Golden Jubilee, and it could make a persuasive claim to be truly the central building of the entire British Empire – the building which expresses most properly the meaning of the imperial climax.

Look up now, at the sandstone mass of the buildings above, rising high over their attendant palms. There are monkey-gargoyles and sculpted dripstones up there, to remind you that this is a sort of secular cathedral. There are portraits of Queen Victoria and her Viceroy in India. There are medallions of the chairman and the chief engineer of the railway line. There are heraldic medallions of elephants and locomotives, and high on the central tower an allegorical figure of Progress raises one prophetic arm into the sunshine. The building has many domes, pinnacles and protruding turrets, and at one end of it a squat little tower, like the gatehouse of an academic precinct, stands watch upon the covered platforms of the station, stretching away in a sheen of glass and iron up the track.

Within, the Victoria Terminus is more diocesan still. It contained the head-offices of the railway company as well as the depot, and no expense or embellishment was spared. Lockwood Kipling, then director of the School of Art a few hundred yards away, supplied the talents of his most gifted students for its ornamentation, and all is done with exuberant richness. Corinthian columns of polished Aberdeen granite line the great staircase to the offices of the chairman beneath the tower; tall stained glass windows illuminate it; meticulous carvings of birds, beasts and foliage, curly tendrils, whirligigs and fanciful devices ornament the banisters; handsome glazed tiles line the floors. The whole effect is sumptuous, and though rebuilt internally in 1921, the station was to be rivalled only by Lutyens's palace in New Delhi, among all the buildings of British India, in its mastery alike of scale and detail.

Its spectacular nature was recognized from the start. Lady Dufferin the Vicereine, whose husband's head is up there with the Queen's, thought it 'perfectly magnificent', but perhaps *too* magnificent for 'a bustling crowd of

Fortresses for the railways. In the far west of India, towards the borders with Afghanistan, railways went in constant and understandable fear of attack. Lahore station (*top*), designed like a medieval castle by William Brunton, Chief Engineer of the Amritsar and Multan Railway, has massive walls, gun-slits and heavy iron sliding doors. The Khojak tunnel (*bottom*), built to take the railway from Quetta to Chaman, on the Afghan frontier (there had been plans to take the line all the way to Kandahar), is well fortified too; a necessary precaution in view of the constant skirmishes between British troops and the Afghans.

railway passengers'. W. S. Caine, visiting it in 1890, thought it the finest building in Bombay, and 'a fitting monument to an unbroken prosperity that has nearly doubled the value of its shareholders' property in twenty-five years'. The difficult G. W. Forrest, in his description of Bombay in 1903, pointedly did not mention it at all, but Murray's Handbook, describing it helpfully as 'Italian Gothic, with certain Oriental modifications in the domes', declared it the finest railway station in any country in the world. J. H. Furneaux, in 1895, called the top of its central tower 'the first masonry dome that has been adapted to a Gothic building', and Mr Gavin Stamp the architectural historian tells us that this is probably true: perhaps its nearest rival is the ogee which Christopher Wren put on the summit of his Tom Tower at Oxford, a building surely familiar to Stevens, and still poignantly brought to the minds of Christ Church alumni strolling up Hornby Road with the sun in their eyes.

In 1983 'VT' handled nearly 900 trains a day, and some two million passengers passed beneath its gargoyles and medallions every twenty-four hours.

Steam city

The railways were the biggest capitalist enterprises in India, and they were run on the most progressive lines. The companies were paternalistic in style, rather in the kind of Japanese capitalism a century later, in particular giving employment to thousands of Eurasians, and all over India stood monuments of their method. It might be one of the palatial residences provided for the Railway Agents or Managers – houses sometimes on an almost princely scale, rivals to all but Government Houses in the scale of Anglo-Indian domesticity. It might be one of the railwaymen's hospitals, or the Railway Institutes, or the housing estates, mostly inhabited by Eurasians and called Railway Colonies, which stood some-where near the railway stations on the outskirts of most Indian cities.

Or it might be one of the boldly self-sufficient workshop towns which the companies built and administered. These were social enterprises beyond the scale of almost anything in England then, and put to shame the mill and mining towns being built at the same time in South Wales and the north of England. Kharagpur, the carriage-works town of the Bengal-Nagpur Railway, included not only the workshops themselves, of course, handsomely detailed brick buildings, but housing for every range of employee, from the substantial brick bungalows of the European railway foremen, with their impressive arched entrances and scalloped window-shades, to the long rows of brick huts, with vaulted cement roofs, classed austerely as Indian Type B. There was a homely apprentices' boarding-house, rather like an English prep. school with its polished teak dining-benches, silver-plate cruets and framed improving texts. And there was a European Institute, a private club for the British employees, with deep pillared

Victoria Terminus, Bombay – possibly the most famous British construction in India. F. W. Stevens built this terminus and headquarters for the Great Indian Peninsula Railway as a blend of Venetian Gothic and Indo-Saracenic styles. The bustling crowds of today's Bombay barely notice their good fortune in using so splendid a construction.

arcades, redbrick pediments and a bandstand on the lawn outside, which some-how managed to express, in its solidity of bulk and stolidity of ornament, the very spirit of railwaydom.

The first and most famous of these towns was Jamalpur, of the East Indian Railway in Bihar. This had its own armed force (service was compulsory for male employees), its own brass band of course, its own Masonic Lodge (St. George-in-the-East) and churches of several denominations. Kipling, who wrote about it in 1888, said that everything in Jamalpur had 'the air of having been cleaned up at ten that very morning and put under a glass case'. Its streets, laid out in a geometric grid, were given English names of high import, Church Street, King's Road, Victoria Road, Prince's Road, but a master-avenue crossed and dominated them all: *Steam Road*.

Tradesmen's work

'A palace fit for a prince, not a counting-house for a linen-merchant'. The opening of Government House in Calcutta in 1803 emblemized the end of the era when commerce was the chief preoccupation of British Government in India. By the middle of the nineteenth century, when the Crown assumed authority from the Company, though profit was still the true *raison d'être* of the Empire in India, its officials were generally indifferent or even contemptuous towards commerce, habitually despising its practitioners as box-wallahs or counter-jumpers – until the very end of the Empire, it was difficult for a commercial gentleman to get into one of the grandest clubs of the Presidency towns. The Government assured the security of what later came to be called the infrastructure of commerce: the rest was tradesmen's work.

In the early days, though, Government *was* commerce, and the first commercial buildings of British India were erected by the Company itself. The original 'factories' or warehouses on the coast were hardly more than fortified trading-posts, but later some ambitious structures were erected, perfectly expressing John Company's romantic and sometimes swashbuckling view of finance (most of its servants earned far more from private trading than they ever did in salaries). We will look at two of them now.

First, a building in Calcutta. There, in 1831, they built a mint, in which the Honourable Company's gains in specie were stored or converted into currency. This was actually designed by the Mint-Master himself, W. N. Forbes, and a bust of him was very properly erected in its Bullion Room. It was a building to gladden any speculative heart, a heavy, rich and portentous structure around a central courtyard which looked as though, like the statue of Pallas Athene in the Parthenon, it might almost be made of money itself – and the Parthenon indeed was obviously the inspiration for its Doric portico.

It was a particularly solid building – its basement rooms were twenty feet deep and there was said to be as much brickwork below ground as above. With the serried columns of its long façade (forty in all), it stood temple-like on a high platform above the river, approached by reverent flights of steps. It was a building full of hints. Around it, on the road called Strand Road which overlooked the wharves and shipping of the Hooghly, a number of smaller classical buildings were erected: and with their domes and columns and Grecian porticoes, clustered around this great sanctuary of hard cash they were like lesser shrines or offertories, in attendance upon an oracle.

Secondly, a structure far away in Patna: the Company's principal opium godown. Patna was the headquarters of the north India opium trade, in which the East India Company, and later the British Government, maintained a fierce monopoly: it made vast profits, and enabled the British also to attain a political stranglehold over the affairs of China, their chief foreign customer for the drug. The Patna godown was therefore one of the most important of all the Company's installations; it was built along decisive, not to say intimidating lines, and every important visitor made a point of inspecting it.

It stood some five miles east of Captain Garstin's Gola, directly on the banks of the Ganges, where the country boats could pick up the opium bales for delivery downstream to Calcutta, and consisted essentially of three long, plain buildings grouped around a yard. There were arcaded porticoes on each side, giving the ensemble a distinctly monumental appearance: facing the river the Governor of the factory was provided with a two-storeyed, colonnaded house, while round about were bungalows for the British foremen and administrators, and for the Government chemist who, we are told, tested every tenth sample of each consignment to make sure it was unadulterated.

The whole group, tight-packed beside the Ganges, gave a powerful impression of single-minded, not to say evangelical, purpose: and so immense was the flow of opiate through the factory, over several generations, that the substantial river embankment in front of it was made entirely of the smashed pots in which the raw materials were supplied (the untreated opium, which was rather like putty, was trampled into the right texture by the feet of workmen, hanging on to ropes above their heads as they stamped and waddled in the vats).

An imperial store

When it came to private enterprise, the British mercantile community did not as a rule put its money into showy buildings. It had no need to, competition being strictly limited. Banks, newspapers, shipping-companies sometimes built themselves imposing offices in the Presidency towns, in whatever architectural style was fashionably respectable, but the shops and office-blocks of British India seldom matched the houses of the great merchants, and for the most part even the grandest emporia of Bombay or Calcutta were hidden away unobtrusively in great city blocks. No Selfridge or Joe Lyons put his money into India, and there was generally a bazaar-like quality, shambled and untidy, to the shops the memsahibs patronized. Even when, in the 1920s, the Government architect R. T. Russell created an elegant commercial centre, Connaught Circus, for the new capital of New Delhi, somehow the shops that acquired premises within its colonnades, however fashionable and expensive, never displayed much panache of décor or self-advertisement.

One famous exception was Spencer's, a concern which began in humble circumstances in Madras in the 1860s. By the end of the nineteenth century its name had become a household word in Anglo-India, the firm having branches everywhere, and dealing in everything from furniture to paraffin, besides manu-facturing its own famous Spencer's Torpedo No 1 Cooking Range, running railway refreshment rooms, and representing in India both A. S. Margarin-centralem of Oslo and Stokely Van Camp Inc. of Indiana. In 1896 this institution built itself, in Madras, a headquarters worthy of its profits. It stands there still, in Mount Road, still bears the same name, and still sends out its teas and saucepans, pattern-books and sewing-machines, to branches from Jullundur to Trivandrum.

The building owes nothing to European or American shop architecture of the time, for it does not look like a shop at all. Its façade is a gentle redbrick crescent, approached from the street under a long *porte-cochère*, boldly signed SPENCER AND CO. LTD, arcaded from one end to the other and fronted by pleasant lawns with palms and shrubberies. There is a touch of the Moorish to its design, and its general feeling is rather scholastic, or even religious, like a theological college. At each end of the building there are pairs of towers with mansard roofs, heavily ornamented, and there is a centre-piece with a pediment and turreted pinnacles which looks as though its use is reserved for the Reverend the Director of Studies. Pairs of windows, between pilasters, run all the way round the upper floor of the building, and in a publicity picture put out by the company early in the twentieth century Spencer's modern fleet of delivery vehicles is seen lined up for display on the forecourt below: two spindly covered motor-vans, two stout lorries with gigantic radiators, and the company traction-engine.

On each of the towers of this singular store there are four weather-vanes: and the sixteen of these devices in all, wavering gently with the breeze off the Bay of Bengal, give the whole structure a final touch of the collegiate, besides emblemiz-ing Spencer's well-known ability to foresee which way the wind would blow – long after the end of the Raj, in 1957, they built the First Air-Conditioned Syrup Room in South India.

Higginbotham's sold books to travellers all over southern India. This branch is in Ootacamund, the 'Queen of the Nilgiri Hills'. The little shops huddled into their Gothic shells are in Simla, far away from where the good coffee is found.

A disastrous fire wrecked Spencer's famous department store in Madras, but an extensive rebuilding programme was ordered, despite the cost. The David Sassoon Library and shops on Rampart Row, Bombay, remain unchanged since their construction during Bombay's golden age at the end of the nineteenth century.

Crawford Market, Bombay, and the Moore Market, Madras. The latter, despite howls of protest from the English community in Madras, was due to be pulled down during the Eighties. R. E. Ellis designed it for Lieutenant-Colonel Sir George Moore, and it was opened by the Madras Governor, Arthur Havelock, in 1900. The floor of Bombay's Crawford Market is kept cool by the liberal use of Caithness granite; the bas-reliefs were executed by Rudyard Kipling's father.

In the market-place

If the city stores were not generally imposing, the city markets were frequently tremendous. The British were very keen on covered markets. They afforded some control over the wildly enterprising commerce of the indigenes, and enabled the imperial inspectors to report on hygiene, check weights and measures, recommend prices, and apprehend rascals. So proud were municipal authorities of their markets that many of them were named after British worthies, whose names were thus incongruously immortalized. Hogg's Market in Calcutta, Moore's in Madras, the Frere and Bolton Markets in Karachi – not one Indian in a million could identify these long-forgotten civic improvers, but their names went irrevocably into the Indian vernacular.

Most of them were mid-Victorian structures, and they were rich in the elaborations and symbolisms popular then, and variously disguised as castles, university buildings, palaces or remote imperial progenitors – Mr Geoffrey Moorhouse, writing in 1970 about Hogg's Market, built in 1874, said it transported him instantly to Huddersfield. Let us choose one of the best of them. Crawford Market in Bombay, to stand for all the rest. This was completed in 1869, designed by William Emerson, decorated under the supervision of Lockwood Kipling, and named for Arthur Crawford, the Municipal Commissioner of the day.

Fruits, fish, meats, poultry and various craftwork were all sold in it, and it looks today, in its functions as in its substance, almost exactly as it did when it was built. Inside it is unexpectedly fine. A central hall with two wings, Moorishly arched, it is lined with wooden stalls, often set on several tiers, so that market-people are to be seen high above their produce, bawling offers or reaching down for cash. The floor is clad in flagstones from Caithness, there are ecclesiastical windows at each end, and the whole structure is fitted out, wherever you look, with whimsical iron lamp-brackets in the shape of winged dragons – perched upon by pigeons, and fouled by their immemorial droppings, but still graceful and surprising.

Outside the building is hardly less fetching. You have to stand well away to get the hang of it, but if you walk boldly backwards into the flow of the traffic you will discover it to be finished in modes variously Swiss, Flemish, and Moorish, with half-timbering, eaves, and a clock tower. It occupies a commanding position at a junction of streets, conveniently opposite the police station: and over its entrances there are granite friezes designed by Lockwood Kipling himself, depicting ideal market-people and their clients, women with plump babies, well-built porters with luscious loads, and presenting a paradigm of what a market ought to look like, in the dreams alike of the imperial British and the arts and crafts movement (and though they have officially renamed the building now, after the Hindu social reformer Mahatma Phule, Mr Arthur Crawford ICS need not be distressed, for everybody calls it Crawford Market still).

But before we leave the imperial marts, here is a glimpse of a very different kind of market-place, the great open *souk* called the Shahi Bazaar in Hyderabad, Sind. One of the longest bazaar streets in Asia, one and a half miles of unbroken stalls, shacks, and traders' carts, this famous bazaar begins beneath the towered grey walls of the Fort, whose subjugation in 1843 gave the British mastery of the city. In Victorian times it must have seemed, to anybody starting a stroll or a haggle down its tumultuous length, a very epitome of Asia – all the spiced smells and colours, all the vivacity, the brays of donkeys, the yelps of kicked dogs, the shouts of insistent butchers, snatches of flute or drum, sometimes the tall humped shape of a camel passing through, sometimes the clatter and squeak of carts. At the northern end of the bazaar, though, the visitor would find a sharp if comical reminder of historical reality: for there, high above the scrambled stalls and seething shoppers, the British had straddled the Shahi Bazaar with a brave Market Tower in truest Anglo-Gothic, with flying buttresses, and church-like windows, and a protruding turret over the central arch, and a huge clock high above, beneath the pointed and pinnacled skyline, so that one passed out of that ancient market-place of the East beneath a petrification of Victorianism itself.

On the waterfront

The British were always proud of their imperial ports, the show-pieces of their maritime supremacy, and the ports of British India were among the most important of them all. Nobody sailing into one of the Presidency cities could fail to be impressed by the scale, the momentum and the prosperity of this empire, and the buildings of the Port Trusts set up to administer their docks and harbours were among the most imposing in town.

Their engineering works, too, were often on the grandest scale, for most of the Indian ports had to be artificially enlarged, deepened or developed. Even the port of Calcutta, along the banks of the great Hooghly, had to be kept continually clear of silt: for years they postponed building the Hooghly bridge because they were afraid its piers might upset the hydrology – and in the end they decided that it must have no piers at all, and so built it in one gigantic span. At Bombay, where until 1875 ships had to unload their cargoes and passengers into lighters off shore, wonderfully elaborate proposals were made for the creation of a modern port – the building of huge arched piers, for instance, carrying railway lines far out to sea, or the making of an artificial harbour by reclaiming hundreds of acres of land, cutting an entrance canal and building seventeen miles of walls ('The most sceptical', claimed the Bombay Dock and Land Reclamation Company Ltd. in

1860, 'cannot stigmatize the scheme as hazardous, the most lukewarm cannot deny the greatness and magnificence of the undertaking', but in the end they built a series of more orthodox docks instead).

In Madras, too, there were no docks until the nineteenth century, and hilarious old prints show the nabobs and their ladies carried ignominiously through the breakers on the backs of coolies, to be deposited sack-like on the foreshore. In Karachi, when as a hangdog fishing-village it fell into British hands in 1838, a port was constructed altogether from scratch. The engineers created a deep-water harbour by building a causeway to an offshore island and dredging its basin: they fortified it and laid a railway there, hoping it would one day be an ocean outlet for most of central Asia, and it came into its own after the opening of the Suez Canal.

The most enterprising development of all happened only in the 1920s, when it was decided to create a major new port in the congeries of waterside towns known as Cochin, set among a web of lagoons on the Malabar coast 600 miles south of Bombay. Cochin was a Native State under a Maharajah, but there was one square mile of British territory among its islands, and the imperialists had long envisaged it as an outlet for a vast hinterland of southern India, there being no natural deep-water harbour between Bombay and Calcutta. To see what they did about it, let us board a ship sailing in from the west, and enter Cochin harbour, between its palmy breakwaters, out of the Arabian Sea.

This is a happy experience. The lie of the coast is low there, thick with foliage and speckled with small islands everywhere, and all along the foreshore stand fishing-towers – tall wooden contraptions which, if the tide is right and the fish are running, dip and bow slowly in the sunshine, in and out of the water, like oil-rigs in Oklahoma. Through a narrow inlet we pass, and inside we find a calm labyrinth of waterways, running this way and that, richly banked in green, and thick with shipping: fishing-boats racing urgently past us out to sea, a dredger clanking in the shallows, tankers and deep-sea freighters – stylish Indian Ocean dhows, too, and solid country schooners, and dug-out canoes with tattered sails, and ponderous barges deep with gravel being poled laboriously inch by inch towards the shore. To the right is Mattancherry, the Muslim township, with its minarets and wide-eaved roofs. To the left, on a green promontory, an agreeable old waterside house stands encouched in gardens. A long, many-arched bridge spans the waterway ahead.

And directly before our bows, imperturbably incongruous in that sticky scented setting, there stands a clean-cut, no-nonsense, well-kept, white and not un-elegant official building, with lawns down to the sea and a flagstaff on top. It is the headquarters of the Port of Cochin, built on an artificial island during the 1920s and 1930s, and one of the most visionary and successful of the later undertakings of the Raj. The island was named Willingdon Island, after the

Viceroy of the time, and despite many political and economic vicissitudes was developed along the very latest lines under the inspiration of a brilliant modernist, the engineer Sir Robert Bristow, founder and first Director of Cochin Port.

New bridges brought roads and railways to the island; an airport was built at its southern end; deep-water berths were dredged all along its eastern and western shores. The island was then criss-crossed with grid streets, austerely named Street No. 1, or First Cross Street, and the whole paraphernalia of a twentieth-century port was concentrated within them. The main administrative buildings were built at the island's tip, symmetrically arranged, rather like Ismailia on the Suez Canal, or the Panama Canal Company settlement at Colon. Set diagonally to a central plaza were two square arcaded buildings, each with a pair of red-tiled octagonal towers; one was the Customs Office, the other the Berthing Office. There was a ceremonial fountain in the middle of the square, and beyond it, fronted by lawns, lay the long low headquarters building of the Port Trust, the one that greeted us from the sea, designed like nearly everything else by Sir Robert himself.

The Dutch had been in Cochin before the British, and so a suggestion of Holland was built into this structure, giving it in fact a distinctly South African look, like a late example of Sir Herbert Baker. It had a central tower of classical form, and its gently curved façade ended in high Dutch gables. At one end of the building a colonnaded passageway ran away to an agreeable villa, built in the same style around a tiled yard, which was the residence of the Port Director. At the other end, separated only by fencing, was the verandah'd front of Spencer's Hotel, where all the businessmen stayed, and where the ships' captains and the port pilots, when their day's duties were done, sat in the garden at sunset beneath the palms, watching the ships go by and sipping London gins and local tonics.

It was a fine place to sit, though it hardly felt like India at all – more like Malaya perhaps, with its fresh breezes, its fragrant sea-smells, and that cool white building at one's back. Cochin Port came to maturity during the Second World War, when its airfield too was strategically important, and it has flourished ever since.

Rooms to let

Only the hotel in Willingdon Island has changed its name – even that dredger is called *Lord Willingdon* still. But then most Anglo-Indian hotels changed their names at one time or another; the hotel business was volatile at best, and depended not only on historical and social events, but on technical developments too. Until the advent of steamships there were few proper hotels at all (Spence's at Calcutta, founded in 1830, magnificently claimed to be The Oldest In Asia).

Young civilians in the Presidency towns lived in boarding-houses or bachelor messes, called 'chummeries'; up-country travellers stayed in the *dak* or post bungalows provided by the Government.

It was only in the mid-nineteenth century that hotels in the European kind made their appearance in British India, often kept by Eurasians or foreigners, and known by the names of their proprietors. Maiden's at Delhi, Flashman's at Rawalpindi, Faletti's at Lahore, Percy's at Secunderabad, Dean's at Peshawar, Laurie's at Agra — these and a dozen more preserved for ever the memories of original proprietors, while others ran through complex pedigrees of hoteliers: the Savoy Hotel at Ootacamund, for example, had previously been Spencer's, Dawson's and Sylk's (and before that was a Church Missionary Society school).

In the Anglo-Indian way, most of the early hotels were anything but luxurious: even as late as the 1890s, many reputable hostelries provided no bedding, while some expected you as a matter of course to provide your own servants. One of the best-known of the Victorian hotels was Reynolds' in Karachi, which changed its name once or twice, but remains in business to this day as the Bristol. The opening of the Suez Canal brought liners from Europe to Karachi, and the design of Reynolds' perhaps owed something to the most celebrated of all British hotels in the East, Shepheard's in Cairo, whose terrace was for generations a social rendezvous on the overland route to India. Reynolds' was a solid pile of three storeys, its central block ornate with miscellaneous knobs and balustrades, its wings deeply verandah'd and latticed in stone. There was a distinctly Shepheardian terrace, where travellers' tales could be exchanged, or shipping prices negotiated, and a nice garden in front with mangoes in it.

Its accommodation was standard for its class. Each bedroom opened on to a wide common verandah, furnished with chairs and sofas, where neighbours could bump into each other in their dressing-gowns in the morning, as they enjoyed their first cigarette, just as though they were still on board their liner at sea. Each bedroom suite occupied the whole depth of the building, allowing servants to enter from their own landings at the back. Each had a somewhat gloomy bed-sitting-room (the only light coming from the front), a windowless dressing-room, and behind, with the servants' entrance, an austere bathroom with a zinc bath but no taps.

Like the form of the bungalow, this hotel pattern was based upon the proliferation of cheap labour, upon the exigencies of the caste system, and upon the 'shut-upness' of the British. If the worst came to the worst the guest need never set eyes upon an Indian in his apartment: the bath-water would be poured discreetly when he was still half-asleep, and even the morning tea would be brought to his bedside silently, by a barefoot servant insubstantial as a shadow. Only the cry of the guest next door, yelling 'Bearer! Bearer!' out of his back door, woke him raucously to his circumstances.

To the end of the Raj many hotels remained much like Reynolds'. In the hills they were more generally spa- or villa-like, occasionally escaping into baronial fantasies. On the plains they were extended bungalows as often as not, with long, long verandahs, *porte-cochères* enclosing the reception office, and wicker chairs upon the lawns. As the years passed, and travel to India became more common, some of them became rather more sophisticated. Percy's at Secunderabad commissioned an artist to paint murals of Westminster Abbey and St. Paul's Cathedral in its public rooms. Spencer's at Ooty installed an American Bar. Running water arrived, and electricity, ping-pong tables appeared upon verandahs, Oriental Curio Shops proliferated, and to the dismay of the older hands the confounded Wireless was all too likely to sound from its walnut cabinet in the smoking room. They did not much change in character, however. The small hotels of Anglo-India remained to the very end marvellously loyal to Victorian mores, from the vaguely military notices (*Guests must NOT repeat NOT leave the Electric Light On*) to the dread table-d'hôte of the dining-room, served in a tenebrous gloom among heads of dead animals and mushy water-colours of Kashmir.

In the great cities things were different. There, in the second half of the nineteenth century, hotels in the latest European or American kind began to appear. The first was probably Watson's in Bombay, still standing though no longer an hotel: built in 1867 in a flourish of metal pillars and galleries, this was the first iron-framed building to be seen in Bombay, though the topographer Gillian Tindall has suggested that its elaborate style really reflects the old Gujerati wooden architecture rather than any European mode of hospitality. A truer archetype was the modernized Great Eastern in Old Court House Street in Calcutta, which occupied a whole block in the most expensive part of the city, and had 300 rooms. To visitors from up-country this was a revelation of new times – Kipling has recorded the excitement of finding hundreds of Europeans beneath the same roof, most of them strangers to each other, after the limited and all too familiar Anglo-Indian society of Lahore. Cavernous and grandiose, with a huge ballroom, a dining-room not unlike an engine shed and a first-floor terrace shaded with awnings, the Great Eastern was surrounded by arcades, and set back as it was from the crowded streets outside, was rather like a fortified citadel of comfort in a city beginning to feel the threat and pressure of the Indian multitudes all around.

Still more womb-like was its younger competitor, the Grand Hotel on Chowringhee, 'The Most Popular, Fashionable and Attractive Hotel in India'. The foyer of this hotel, which was built within a big business block and could scarcely be identified from outside, was connected with the street by a long corridor lined with shops, a device already made popular among the imperialists by the Continental Hotel in Cairo. Cool and shady was this tube – reassuringly

Modest hotels: Percy's, Secunder-abad, still offers cream teas – of a kind; the garden at the small hotel in Agra (*right*) provides a fine place for a final stroll before retiring. Gardens in British-built hotels are invariably well laid out, and con-stantly attended by squads of 'malis'. Indians are very keen – and very good – gardeners.

smiling was the doorman at the far end of it – and only when the tourist reached the outer portal, and stepped into the blinding sun, the heat, the dust, the noise, the whine of the beggars, the blaze of the sky, the clatter of traffic in the street outside – only then, as he tipped the doorman and stepped into the waiting rickshaw, could the globe-trotter of *fin-de-siècle* really be sure that he was in India, the Land of Enchantment.

The other Taj

Prince of them all was the Taj Mahal Hotel in Bombay, which was to remain for many visitors, all their lives, the quintessence of imperial amplitude. This was ironic, for it was not in fact built by Britons, but by Parsees, members of a community which had grown rich and powerful by their amicable relationship with the imperialists (Parsee shipbuilders built ships for the Royal Navy, and Parsee philanthropists contributed to many other kinds of imperial good works). Jamsetji Nusserwanji Tata, one of the most enterprising and influential Parsees of them all, conceived the Taj Mahal Hotel in the last years of the nineteenth century, engaged an English architect named Chambers to design it, and saw it accepted instantly by the British as a very part of the imperial order. It stood enormously on the waterfront at Apollo Bunder, for most travellers their first landfall in the Empire of India, and not since the white palaces of eighteenth-century Calcutta, or the *chunam* offices of early Madras, had the Empire greeted its visitors so grandiloquently.

It was not unworthy of its site, though unexpectedly its entrance faced away from the sea: this was not, as fable had it, an error in the building, but was intended to give more of the bedrooms an ocean view. Like so many buildings of British India, the Taj was built in a style difficult to pin down. Around its central dome of reportedly Gujerati genesis (Tata was born in Gujerat) were grouped a number of small round turrets, upon whose crowning bobbles, very often, pigeons decoratively sat. Its roof-line was thus predominantly globular, but was festively complicated by a profusion of gables in the Swiss manner, supported by elaborate barge-boarding, and jutting windows like the *mashrabiya* casements of Arab houses. Add to this Saracenic arches by the score, wide eaves everywhere, elaborate balconies on all seven floors, a plethora of flagstaffs and decorative chimneys, fancy woodwork of many kinds, ornamental spikes and what Ruskin once called 'the entire race of fringes, finials and crockets', and you have some idea of the impact of the Taj Mahal Hotel upon the wondering traveller.

'The Taj Hotel', wrote G. A. Mathews in 1905, 'is on such a scale of magnificence and luxury that at first it rather took one's breath away'. 'The gigantic Taj', wrote Aldous Huxley in 1926, 'combines the style of the South Kensington Natural History Museum with that of an Indian pavilion at an

The Taj Mahal Hotel, and Gateway of India, Bombay. The Taj, still one of the world's greatest hotels, was built in 1903 by J. N. Tata after he was excluded, by virtue of his race, from the nearby Watson's Hotel. Watson's no longer survives; the Taj has prospered well enough to be able to erect the tall – and memorably ugly – extension behind.

International Exhibition'. 'The Taj Hotel', wrote S. J. Perelman in 1948, 'a huge Mauro-Gothic edifice . . . whose crenelated towers, battlements, and drawbridges more accurately suggested a college dormitory'. Whatever its aesthetic effect, it instantly joined, with Shepheard's in Cairo, Raffle's in Singapore and the Peninsula in Hong Kong, the great chain of caravanserais which sumptuously punctuated the travels of the later British imperialists: what was more, almost alone among the luxury hotels of India, it welcomed Indian guests always, and was so bold in its attitudes that by the 1930s black jazz musicians, direct from the United States, were blowing their horns in its bars.

Imperial entertainments

For entertainment too had a utilitarian part to play in the imperial scheme – even the High Victorians, believing as they did in *mens sana in corpore sano*, recognized the virtues of healthy pleasure. It was not always easy, but they persevered. If there were no foxes to hunt, they chased jackals instead. If there were no hounds, they made do with bobbery packs of terriers, spaniels and pye-dogs. Instead of shooting pheasant or grouse, they stalked tiger or speared pigs.

True to their time and their background, they were outdoor people by choice – young people on the average, and very fit. They loved picnics, gymkhanas, and all manner of vigorous sport, from badminton parties (flowered hats and full skirts) to ferocious blood sports (bucking horses, snarling beasts, last desperate shots between the eyes . . .). Most of all they loved horse-racing. There was hardly a station in India that did not have its track, and the grandstand with its attendant buildings was one of the most characteristic structures of British India – though sometimes to be sure the stand was hardly more than a flimsy tent, for the British took their sports with them even when they travelled or campaigned, and had hardly concluded a punitive expedition, or knocked off that last bridge, before they ran up a judge's box, a row of trestle benches and a starting-post, and staged a race-meeting.

The racecourse was the amphitheatre of this empire, and it came in all conditions. The racecourse at Ootacamund had huge thatched stables, like an African kraal, while the one at Poona was built inside the General Parade Ground. The Lucknow track was straddled by an artillery range, the Simla track, surrounded by pines and deodars, was set so precariously on a ridge that careless jockeys sometimes fell off it. The racecourse at Darjeeling, at 7,000 feet, was said to be the highest in the world, and was perhaps the smallest too: its grandstand, though it catered for all the social niceties of the sport, was like a toy with an iron roof, and its track was so restricted that the racing ponies, when they had finished their break-neck circuit, were obliged to run straight off into the public highway to release their momentum.

At the other end of the scale, the race clubs of the Presidency cities were among the most lavish anywhere, for this was one place where Indian aristocracy and British upper class met on equal terms – each side regarding the other with about the same condescension. The clubhouses attached to these great courses grew ever more opulent as the years passed, until with their magnificent stable-blocks, their spacious official residences, their restaurants and bars, and the great tiered grandstands looming above, sometimes they seemed to be as important as any High Court or Secretariat. The Calcutta course, seen from the bare and dusty *maidan*, looked like some particularly well-heeled village of its own; the Bombay course, seen from the roads which ran from the downtown city to the smoky suburbs of the cotton mills, looked like an enclave of some other country altogether.

The best racecourse buildings were among the most modern structures in India. Rich men of all kinds had a share in their development; race club committees included not only officials and soldiers, but influential British box-wallahs and worldly Indians. There was little penny-pinching in these great

The racecourses in Calcutta (*top*) and Bombay (*bottom*). The Royal Calcutta Turf Club's annual Christmas race week was one of the high points of the social season: the Viceroy and Vicereine would drive, Ascot-style, past the grandstand of the two-mile course.

Once, plays and operatic performances would have been seen at the Globe Theatre, Calcutta, or the Royal Opera House, Bombay. Today, they are but two more outlets for the hugely popular Indian film industry.

institutions, and the latest techniques were imported from abroad. Ferroconcrete, electric indicators, air-conditioning, were seen in Indian racecourse buildings long before Government or business generally adopted such devices, and visitors taken to the races in the 1930s, say (and every important visitor was), were likely to come away with an altogether deceptive notion of the state of the Empire in India.

Stage and screen

Nothing like so much money or energy went into indoor entertainments. This was, by and large, a Philistine society, and did not often pine for symphony concerts, exhibitions of contemporary art, or Ibsen. Still, touring musical and theatrical companies sometimes came to India from Europe, roaming troupes of local actors took Shakespeare to the remoter stations, and for generations amateur dramatics were all the rage in Anglo-India. Theatres sprang up here and there across the wide Empire.

The Presidency towns indeed had them almost from the start – the first theatre at Madras was actually within the walls of Fort St. George: by the end of the nineteenth century Calcutta and Bombay each had three, while Simla had the bright little Gaiety Theatre inside the Town Hall, with gilded boxes, curtained in pink muslin, for the Viceroy and the Commander-in-Chief. Architecturally none of them were remarkable, but one structure at least displayed the proper theatrical flair – the Bombay Opera House. This late-Victorian building was unmistakably the real thing. It had the indispensable first-floor verandah, surmounted by four Corinthian columns, for celebrities to appear at, silhouetted against the lights of the chandeliers within. It had a rusticated arcade below, for flower-sellers of course, and a gaslit forecourt at the side for the arrival of barouches, and a huge Britannia with a shield above the principal entrance, and a pediment chock-a-block full of musical figures, harps, violins, trumpets and cymbals. Far away in the steaming East, where the rickshaw-wallahs padded by, the Bombay Opera House seemed always to await, fresh from the Tuesday P and O perhaps, the arrival of Signor Puccini.

Instead, the movies came. 'Those who judge Bombay by its "talkies" do it an injustice', says Samuel T. Shepherd's *Bombay, 1932*, but the truth was that the cinema almost instantly displaced the theatre as evening entertainment for the Anglo-Indians. Like everything else in India, the cinema was willing to rough it: the first films in Bombay were shown in tents on the *maidan*, outside the Secretariat – they were serials, and the plots being complicated, the instalments numerous, full summaries of the stories so far were published as advertisements in the local papers. But when proper cinemas were built, like the racecourse buildings they were often anomalously contemporary of style. Derived so suddenly from the Odeons, the Roxys and indeed the Empires of America and England, they were the first buildings in India, and almost the last, to venture into art deco; to this day, overtaken though many of them have been by far bigger movie-houses, you may recognize their touch of the 1930s buried away in the streets of the big cities, or hinted at in crude cantonment cinemas among the barrack-blocks.

With their square concrete lines and metal window-frames they also represented, if at one or two removes, the Bauhaus in India – almost its only faint repercussion in these distant parts, to whose ruling society twentieth-century modernism in all its forms was generally anathema. It was proper that the cinema should be the medium of this modest assault upon the imperial sensibilities; for if the theatre stood in an old British tradition, the movies were something altogether new, and mostly alien, which by capturing the imaginations of Britons and Indians alike, and offering visions of another dynamism, presaged the end of the imperial performance itself.

Lions for the museum

Such were a few of the utilitarian monuments the British erected in India. There were hundreds of thousands more. There were post offices from the nobly domed classical palace which Walter Granville gave Calcutta in 1870 to the wobbly wooden contraption at Simla, like a monster tree-house, which for many summers handled the supreme dispatches of the earth's most powerful empire. There were water-towers of varying pose: like a classical shrine in the middle of Madras, like a Hindu tower outside Patna, hugely mounted on a forest of girders beside the Grand Trunk Road outside Calcutta. There were hospitals, though never enough of them ('What sort of architecture ought we to employ in India?' asked the architect T. Roger Smith in 1873, discussing his design for the new European General Hospital in Bombay. 'We ought . . . to take our national style with us . . . raising a distinctive symbol of our presence to be beheld with respect and even with admiration by the natives of the country'). There were airports in later years. There was the mammoth hangar built at Karachi in 1930 to house the doomed airship R101, which was intended to fly a regular mail and passenger service between England and India, but crashed on its maiden journey. There were cotton and jute mills indistinguishable from the Lancashire kind, and tea-drying halls in the hills, and power-stations, and foundries, and many breweries.

And finally, there were the waterworks. Irrigation works were the indices of ancient empires, representing as they did the transition from aridity to fertility, or death to life. When the dams, canals and conduits flourished, so did the despots

The Ganges Canal headworks near Roorkee. The canal is 400 miles long, taking water from the Ganges at Hardwar (the dam having been built in 1839) and reaching both Cawnpore and Delhi (by a branch canal).

and the satraps; when an empire fell, soon enough the works which had brought new wealth to the provinces, and made the name of King or Emperor mighty unto all ages, had rotted into dereliction. The British too saw in the creation of new fecundity the most allegorical of imperial functions, and the irrigation works they completed in India were unrivalled in their generation.

The Ganges Canal, when it was opened in 1854, was then the greatest work of engineering anywhere in the world. It was 810 miles long, with more than 2,000 miles of feeder canals. Two rivers were made to pass over it on aqueducts, and hundreds of road bridges crossed it. It was built in the grand manner, under the supervision of a military engineer, Sir Proby Cautley, and at its climactic moments it possessed a truly classical grandeur. For a taste of its splendour when it was all new, when sightseers went to wonder at the scale of it, artists painted its scenes, and engineering journals around the world reported its statistics with awe, let us look at the grand bridge which crossed it at Roorkee, 150 miles north of Delhi, the headquarters of the whole project and the site of its workshops.

We will see it through the eyes of the artist William Simpson, an old hand at Anglo-Indian scenes, who painted it in 1863. In the foreground of his picture there is a tactful suggestion, no more, of indigenous Indian muddle, a couple of cows and a bullock-cart, a few shrouded figures cooking on a wood fire. On the canal itself, shiny as glass, a thatched country boat slowly passes, barely rippling the surface of the water. In the background are the Himalayas, crowned with snow, rising celestially into an unsullied sky. And dominating the picture, unmistakably, two gigantic British lions, couchant, guard the great waterway, one on each side. They are the foci of a truly monumental ensemble. A long series of steps lines the canals behind them, climbing elegantly to the corners of the bridge, and the animals are mounted on hefty stone plinths above.

They sit there high over the canal like a pair of sphinxes in an earlier empire – just the beasts, you might think, to find and moralize over, centuries hence, when they are dug up from the sand of the silted waterworks, numbered, labelled, and packed away in plastic for their long journey to the museum.

6 · Spiritual

The spire

Brilliantly off the river shines the morning sun: vivid saris swing and settle down there at the water's edge, and the bells of wandering cattle clang in the stillness. We stand on the wide marble terrace above as on the deck of some celestial merchantman. Behind us the mausoleum is colossal in its symmetry, delicate in its mass; downstream sprawls its partner the citadel, a grim man-o-war to the exquisite clipper-ship behind our backs.

But beyond the fortress, rising almost jauntily above the roofs of the city itself, a single slender spire intrudes upon the skyline. It looks altogether out of place, but altogether undismayed, too, by the cluster of the ancient city hemming it in, by the brooding alien castle, by the matchless white presence of the monument upstream. It is the Anglican church of St. George, Agra, built by the British in 1826 against all the environmental odds, and now an integral and familiar element in the view from the Taj Mahal.

This was the empire of a Christian élite, in a vast society of Muslims, Hindus, Buddhists, animists and variegated pagans. Official Anglo-Indian Christianity was not of the proselytizing kind: missionaries were never popular with the British Raj, and in the early days were obliged to build their churches and schools in the enclaves of rival European Powers, French, Dutch or Danish. It was, though, a Christianity always assertive and assured, knowing itself to stand somewhere near the centre of imperial power, and it provided an inescapable reference point among the stones of empire. The warehouse, the fort, the palace, formed three sides of the symbolic imperial square: the fourth, with a Perpendicular tower above the parade-ground, or a Gothic apse over the bazaar behind, was always the Christian church.

A gentlemanly start

The first of the British churches in India were built inside the Presidency forts, as essential to their meaning, it seemed, as barrack-blocks or counting-houses, and serving not only as parish churches for the civilians, but as garrison churches too.

The oldest of them, the first Anglican church in the East and today the senior British building still in use in India, was St. Mary's in Madras. It was consecrated in 1680, and early arrivals in the infant settlement, when they had recovered from the awful shock of their piggy-back disembarkation through the surf, were equally relieved and comforted to be taken through the great gateway of Fort St. George, above the strand, and to find nestling within it this stout little church. Relieved, because it seemed to show that not everything in India was noise, rush and confusion, the roar of those waves, the haggling porters on the foreshore, the peculiar smells and the blazing Coromandel heat. Comforted, because the church of St. Mary appeared to be in all respects thoroughly English and gentlemanly.

Actually to later eyes it may look, there behind its iron railings in the cramped square within the Fort, rather more like New York than London. Though it is a century older than any surviving Manhattan church, in flavour it is a little reminiscent of St. Paul's Chapel, on lower Broadway, a steepled trinket among the skyscrapers of the financial district: for St. Mary's too was hemmed tightly in by bigger buildings of secular consequence, the Company's offices on one side, the barrack-blocks behind, and like St. Paul's it stood demurely in its paved plaza like a good deed in a fairly naughty world. One of its sponsors, as a matter of fact, was the merchant Elihu Yale, after whom Yale University would one day be named; and the men who formed its original parish council, I do not doubt, were very like the original English inhabitants of Manhattan – hard-headed, quick-witted, unscrupulous and devout.

The Master-Gunner of the Fort, it is thought, was the designer of St. Mary's; his name was William Dixon, and as an artillery-man he paid great attention to stress, shock and potential catastrophe. He castellated the parapet, in case of assault. He used no wood in the main construction, in case of fire. Over the nave he built a roof two feet thick, in case of bombardment. He saw to it that there was a well and a cistern within the compound, in case of siege. He built the church in a sheltered site, in case of cyclone.

Nevertheless he made a very charming job of it. It was a simple enough square plan that he drew up, a nave with two aisles, with the altar in an apse and a gallery at the other end. Later a tower was added west of the nave, a steeple upon an octagon upon a square, with round mock windows, pilasters and pediments, topped with a golden cross, while between the tower and the body of the church two curving stone staircases led directly from the yard to the gallery. The church was floored with black and white marble, probably brought in ballast from England, had eight big windows, hooded and unglazed, to catch the breezes off the sea, and was filled with curious carved woodwork. 'Inferior to the churches of London', a visitor thought it in 1703, 'in nothing but bells'.

Others were not so fulsome. Ensign Thomas Salmon, who served in the

St. Mary's Church, Madras – the oldest Anglican church in India. It was built by Streyn-
sham Master in 1680, though entirely rebuilt
in 1759. Robert Clive was married here. One
piece of church plate was given by Elihu Yale,
later founder of Yale University.

Madras garrison in 1699, said that whenever a man went to service at St. Mary's he 'lost some ounces by perspiration', and observed that the congregation seemed to be saluting God and the Governor at the same time, 'for when the Governor comes into church the organ always plays': while in 1709 there were complaints that buffaloes were habitually tethered to the church walls, that coconut toddy was sold among the tombs, and that beggars and vagabonds spent their nights in the churchyard ('and what unclean uses the neighbours thereabouts doe make of that place we forebear to tell').

Eyes of God and Government

St. Mary's Madras was an altogether original design, and so very likely was the original church behind Fort William, at Calcutta. This however was destroyed by the marauding Nawab in 1756, and by the time they came to build its replacement the engineer-architects of the Company had fallen under the spell of textbooks. St. John's the new parish church, consecrated in 1787, was not only obviously in the London tradition, as presented by James Gibbs in his *Book of Architecture*, but was itself the prototype of many later Anglo-Indian churches.

Its architect was Lieutenant James Agg of the Bengal Engineers, that genial young fellow who came out to India in the company of William Hickey, and whose only known extant work this is. It was built in a wide green garden, next door to the old burial-ground of the British colony and only a stone's throw from the site of the new Government House, and while some see St. John's as a direct derivation of Gibbs's St. Martin-in-the-Fields, others profess to recognize in it something of Wren's St. Stephen's, Walbrook, in the City of London. Anyway, it was well-suited to eighteenth-century Calcutta, for it was in effect a classical temple with a Baroque tower at one end, enlivened by variations devised by Agg himself. He did without the portico beneath the tower, so familiar a feature of the Gibbs archetypes, and instead put his entrance at the back of the church, behind the altar and conveniently close to the street; he added to the entrance steps, as wide as the church itself, ramps for the passage of palanquins; and all in all he created a building which was authentically Calcutta – square and burly in the nabob manner, Grecian and yet subtly tropicalized, recognizably London but distinctly Bengal too.

Other developments of the Gibbs pattern went up all over India – a couple more in Calcutta itself, one in Bombay, one in Poona, several in Madras, a particularly fine one (by Captain George Hutchinson, Bengal Engineers), completed in 1822 at Meerut, the cantonment where the Indian Mutiny began – the British troops were actually at evening church parade within the white portico of St. John's when the first bungalows were set on fire in the civil station to the west.

In one case the architect strayed so far from the manuals as to create a truly spontaneous building, in a style of its own. This was St. Andrew's Scottish Church in Madras, completed in 1820, and its architect was Thomas de Havilland of the Madras Engineers.

This splendid kirk was exactly contemporary with the New Town of Edinburgh, and if it had any real progenitor it was perhaps its namesake there, St. Andrew's in George Street, one of whose architects was also a military man, a Captain Fraser. Both churches were curvilinear in plan, the Scottish one oval, the Indian one circular, and each was fronted by a portico of four columns and a pediment, with tower and spire in the Gibbs manner above. There though the resemblance ended, for if the Edinburgh building was elegant and dainty, the Madras one was massive. The portico on its west front was inscribed in huge letters ST. ANDREW AD MDCCCXX; on the east front two malevolent lions, carved in relief, supported with staring eyes and sculpted ensigns the round window of the pediment, while beneath them a second gigantic text read AUSPICIO REGIS ET SENATUS ANGLIAE.

It was done with a majestic opulence, huge Ionic columns, heavy balustrading, and the interior too was very splendid. The floor was of black and white marble, like St. Mary's in the Fort, and the long benches of teak and rattan were curved to form a semicircular congregation, echoing the shape of the walls and the central dome above. Finely carved wooden screens supported fans and lights, and everything was brightly burnished and polished, the woodwork fragrant with polish, the brasswork buffed to a military sheen (for St. Andrew's served, too, as a garrison church for the Scottish soldiers stationed in Madras).

There was no escaping the force of this structure. Standing all alone in its wide compound, it seemed to dominate the area all around: and like the eyes of painted portraits, as demonstrated by tourist guides, the eyes of those two lions, predatory and reproachful at the same time, seemed to follow one away up the dusty streets, eyes of God for the sinner, eyes of Government for the subject.

In the porch

Such noble and expensive structures were beyond the means of most Anglo-Indian communities, when once the imperialists moved out of the Presidency cities into the countryside. The up-country churches were usually simple, but in the early years especially they were often built with a dilettante flair.

Demure within its graveyard among the gum-trees and acacias, for instance, stood the parish church of Ootacamund, St. Stephen's, which is generally thought to have been named not in honour of the holy martyr, but of Mr Stephen Lushington the Governor of Madras at the time of its construction. Settled there so prettily among the tile-roofed villas of the hill-station, just along the lane from

St. Andrew's Scottish Church, Madras, built in 1820 by Thomas de Havilland. The interior of the shallow dome is covered with a mixture of crushed sea shells (*chunam*) and lapiz lazuli, producing a lovely pale-blue paint.

the Club, just up the hill from the Nilgiri Library, this little building looked exactly like a toy church, built of nursery bricks. An iron arch with a lamp on it, erected to celebrate Queen Victoria's Diamond Jubilee in 1897, led into its churchyard, and the building was painted all white, and stood out neat and clean against the green wooded slopes behind.

It was a very nice, homely, family sort of church, designed in 1829 by Captain John Underwood of the Madras Engineers, who used a Gothicky style. Inside it was surprisingly sophisticated, with Tuscan columns and a bowed teak roof, the timbers having come from Tipu Sultan's looted palace at Seringapatam. It had pews originally, later replaced by chairs, and the windows were added over the years in memory of Captain Wapshare, Mrs Watson, Mrs Hughes-Hallett and Mr Higgins. St. Stephen's was the parish church for a wide area of the Nilgiris, where dynasties of tea-planters brought their babies for christening, and generations of hot-weather residents made their Sunday communions; its ambience was, like that of Ootacamund itself, at once intimate and well-endowed.

It is all there still, though painted a rather nasty ochre now, and its porch makes an agreeable shelter, if you are ever caught in the rain on your way back from Spencer's or Higginbotham's the bookshop. Then, if you sit on the step beside the plaque commemorating the laying of the church foundation-stone by The Right Hon. Stephen Rumbold Lushington, Governor Etc, Etc, 1829, you may feel the spirit of the little building pungently all about you: the rain spattering on the roof above your head, the rooks like screeching dogs outside, the smell of the dripping eucalypti from the churchyard, a distant hoot of horns from the bazaar quarter down the hill, the proud but shabby buildings of the local administration framed in that Jubilee gateway – and all around the creak of vanished pews, the gossipy whispers of long-gone parishioners, and the soldierly commands of the late Captain Underwood, shadowily supervising the proportions of the apse.

Eccentricities

A few churches now of more pronounced and individual, not to say eccentric, character.

The first was created by a civilian official, F. S. Growse, who was stationed during the 1870s at Muttra, between Delhi and Agra, the birthplace of Krishna and thus one of the holiest of Indian cities. Growse was a passionate believer in Ruskinian principles – in particular, the importance of spontaneous craftsmanship in the construction of buildings, and the encouragement of talent among ordinary workmen – and these principles he put into practice in sponsoring a new Catholic church for his district.

By then Gothic was almost obligatory among Anglican church architects in

Churches in the hills. St. Stephen's, Ootacamund (*top left and bottom*), with the smaller chapel for 'native servants' outside the west door. The church was built in 1830, and the door contains wood from Tipu Sultan's palace. Christ Church, Simla (*top right*), was built to a Gothic design that offered a sense of security and stability to those who fled to the Himalayas as an escape from the raging heat of the plains. The bells were cast from cannon captured during the Sikh wars.

A doorway in the old St. Peter's Church, Fort William, Calcutta, converted for more secular purposes.

India, but Catholics were not so shackled; Growse created his Church of the Sacred Heart in an astonishing *melange* of architectural types, and entrusted it all to local craftsmen. It looked as though it had been made up as the builders went along, and perhaps it was. It was crowned by a rounded tower in the manner of medieval Bihari temples, but with a cross on top of it. Above the west end of the church was a kiosk in the Hindu kind, but it contained a medallion of the Madonna. The main porch consisted of a classical portico, but had small oriental pavilions on either side, and the whole was completed with an endearing alternation of Eastern and Western decoration, a Gothic kind of surround for the vestry door, oriental steppings on the chancel roof. Growse was responsible for several buildings of similar unorthodoxy: the architects of the Public Works Department greatly resented his work, but that did not worry him, for he considered *their* work to be no more than 'utilitarian barbarism'.

Another striking edifice was Holy Trinity Church, Karachi, now the Anglican cathedral of that city, but originally the garrison church. It replaced, in 1855, a temporary structure known locally as 'The Divine Shed', and was designed by a Captain Hill, Bombay Engineers, in a weird Romanesque. Hill is supposed to have started with the patterns of Italian churches, and the body of the building is

St. James's Church (*top*), and the Anglican Cathedral of the Redemption (*bottom*), in old and New Delhi respectively. 'Skinner's Church', built in 1836, is the oldest Christian church in the city, and was badly damaged in the Mutiny. The Anglican Cathedral was consecrated in 1933; the altar was given by the Dean and Chapter of York Minster, to mark York's thirteenth centenary.

indeed a conventional basilica, but when he came to the tower he disregarded precedent: dissuaded from completing the building fancifully with an English spire, he built instead a grotesque campanile, 150 feet high, each of its five storeys being embellished with an increasing number of windows – one at the bottom, five at the top. This device gave the whole church an astonishingly top-heavy and precarious look, looming freakishly there above its sandy compound, and until two storeys were lopped off it in 1903, Trinity Church, Karachi looked from a distance less like an Anglican shrine than some inexplicable relic of an otherwise disintegrated culture.

The third of our singular churches was built by Colonel James Skinner in 1836. The son of a Scottish father and a Rajput mother, Skinner was the founder and first commander of the irregular regiment called Skinner's Horse, 'the Yellow Boys', and he built the church, he said, 'in fulfilment of a vow made while lying wounded on the field of battle . . . in testimony of his sincere faith in the truth of the Christian Religion'. Cynics might suppose he built it, alternatively, as a step in his inexorable progress towards respectability – from half-caste adventurer, coolie, carpenter and printer's apprentice, to Commander of the Bath and landlord of a large estate granted him by the imperial Government: he had already given up his twelve concubines, and perhaps regretted the mosque he had built for his Muslim wife, and the temple for his Hindu. But whatever his motives, he built the church in fine seigneurial style, looking over the churchyard to his substantial mansion across the way.

He is thought to have designed St. James's himself, and it is certainly an odd, robust and handsome structure – a Yellow Boy among churches, though actually it was painted a muted pink. It was a rotunda, built in the shape of a Greek cross, with a large pillared portico on each side, and a high dome supported by Baroque scrolled buttresses and crowned with a golden cross. It cost the colonel 80,000 rupees to build, and later improvers rather spoilt its outline by pulling down three of its porticoes and adding a squat square bell-tower. Never mind, Skinner was justifiably content with his creation (and was buried within it in 1841): except that, as he is said to have complained to its interior designer, his initials were in fact J. H. S., not, as its altar-front suggested, I. H. S.

High in the north at Mardan, almost on the Afghan frontier, the British built themselves the most touchingly evocative of all their country churches in India. Up there Queen Victoria's Own Corps of Guides had its headquarters. It was a romantic, club-like regiment, very conscious of its distinction, and its cantonment was an aristocratic sort of station – huge swards of brilliant green separating one building from another, great trees like elms in an English park, meticulously gravelled roadways, and this dear little church such as you might well find tucked away, for the use of family and servants, tenants and villagers, in the flank of some vast Palladian mansion of the shires.

It was Victorian actually (like the Corps itself, which was founded in 1846, but had swiftly acquired a manner of venerable pedigree), but Victorian in the gentlest kind. Small and low, it was built of the grey local stone with a tiled roof, and it had a small Gothic porch, and a little eaved belfry at one end whose bell, you might think, was surely rung each Sunday morning by old Tom from the *Red Lion*. Flowered creepers climbed all over this disarming structure, wistaria grew about its gate, and in the hedged garden all around, in whose trees pigeons obligingly murmured, the graves of dead Guides lay peacefully in the sun, as in a family plot.

And the last of our extraordinary churches, churches beyond the call of duty, was built in the last years of the Raj as a garrison church of a very different kind. To the west of the new capital of New Delhi, four miles from the Viceroy's House on Raisina Hill, the British built during the 1920s a cantonment for the new capital – separated from the city, as was usual, by a wide no man's land of unoccupied semi-desert. Of all the visitors who came to wonder at New Delhi, hardly a handful went over there: yet the garrison church of St. Martin's, completed in 1930, was one of the most truly individual buildings erected in the whole history of the Raj.

It was built of red bricks, three and a half million of them, and was perceptibly influenced by Lutyens's Indian manner, doubtless because its architect, Arthur Shoosmith, had gone to India in the first place as Lutyens's employee. Lutyens had advised him, when he started work upon it, to 'get rid of all mimicky Mary-Anne notions of brick work and go for the Roman wall'. Shoosmith complied, but St. Martin's is much more than a mere echo of the master's voice. It is stark, square and almost windowless, like a huge machine-house of some sort, a power-station perhaps, or possibly a fortress – soldiers pronounced it an excellent place to hold in an emergency. Inside it is severely classical, with a brick dome above the chancel, and an almost regimented sense of order. Outside only the curves above its doors and deeply recessed windows soften the massive angularity of the high nave and tower. It has been called 'the most remarkable church in India' (Robert Grant Irving) and 'one of the great buildings of the 20th century' (Gavin Stamp). Certainly it was a genuinely Modern structure of its time, one of the very few the British erected in India: and it is one of only *two* buildings Arthur Shoosmith ever designed.

Episcopalian

There were British cathedrals in India. Where there is a bishop there is a cathedral, and the whole British Empire was episcopalian country, fertile soil for see and diocese. Though in later years Anglican bishoprics came to be occupied mostly by indigenes, in earlier times the Empire offered a fine field for clerical promotion

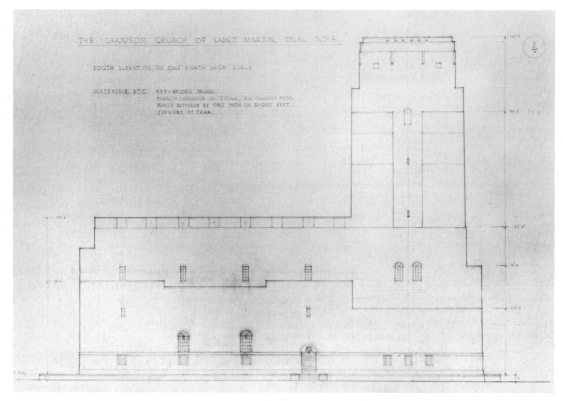

The fortress-like garrison church of St. Martin, outside New Delhi, designed by Lutyens's colleague, A. G. Shoosmith, in 1928.

St. Paul's Cathedral, Calcutta. Construction began in 1839 and the building was consecrated in 1847. The west window, designed by Sir Edward Burne-Jones, was erected in 1880 as a memorial to Lord Mayo.

within the Anglican community, and many a Right Reverend, when he entered into pastoral retirement in England, turned out to have been the bishop of somewhere unpronounceable in the East.

There were Roman Catholic cathedrals in British India too, just as there were non-conformist chapels, but the grandest of the Christian churches of the Raj were inevitably those of the Established Church of England, at whose head was the Crown itself. Most of them were built, as you might expect, during the reign of Queen Victoria. The first of them all, and except for Holy Trinity, Quebec, the first anywhere in the British Empire, was begun almost immediately after her accession to the throne, in 1839.

This was the cathedral of Calcutta, the original metropolitan church of British India. There had been a Bishop of Calcutta since 1814, but at first he ministered from Mr Agg's St. John's Church, and when Major Forbes the Mint-Master submitted plans for a cathedral in 1819, they were considered too extravagant, and conveniently mislaid. Forbes was not discouraged, however: when nearly twenty years later Bishop Daniel Wilson announced his intention to build an Anglo-Indian St. Paul's, he submitted some revised and presumably less spend-thrift plans, and work began.

The site was marvellous. The cathedral arose in *chunam*-covered brick at the south-eastern edge of the *maidan*, at once detached and accessible from the official centre of Calcutta dominated by Government House, the military centre at Fort William across the green, and the commercial centre running down Chowringhee into the southern suburbs. The scale of it was splendid, too. The Honourable Company had promised a substantial grant towards the cost of the building, on the stipulation that it must be able to seat at least 800 worshippers (at a time when the European population of Calcutta was perhaps 2,000). Major Forbes was accordingly able to work to a much grander pattern than Agg or de Havilland.

His formula was plain, but spectacular. The Vicereine, Lady Dalhousie, in the 1840s, thought the interior of St. Paul's very like a railway station. Others might think it more like a vastly distended college chapel, entered through a theatre foyer – carriages at eight, one almost expects the hymn-board to say. Once through the porch and narthex, the theatrical part, you find yourself in a single square chamber, without aisles or transepts, lit by eight tall windows on each side, five at the east end above the altar, and a huge west window above the entrance.

Everything in here seems to be ribbed, lined, or chiselled. It is a restless effect. The high barrel roof is ribbed, the east end is ribbed with stone pilastering, the bishop's throne is spiky, the fine wooden stalls, around the great square of the nave, are complicated with wooden pinnacles. The emphasis is all vertical, and to these long uprights of the building and its fittings, an extraordinary last touch is provided by the myriad iron wands, hanging like tendrils from the roof, which hold the whirring metal blades of the electric fans.

The contents of this unusual building, assembled over the Victorian decades, were remarkable too. The mosaic panels around the altar, telling the life-story of St. Paul, were by Sir Arthur Blomfield. Francis Chantrey made the noble statue of Bishop Heber, second Bishop of Calcutta and author of *From Greenland's Icy Mountains* ('to India's coral strand . . .'). The cathedral plate was given by Queen Victoria, the cathedral organ was built by Willis of London under the direction of John Stainer, organist of St. Paul's in London. The cathedral clock was made by B. L. Vulliamy, the royal clock-maker. The lectern-eagle was designed by Herbert Butterfield. The east windows had first been given by George II to St. George's Chapel, Windsor, and the original west window, blown out by a cyclone in 1864, was replaced in 1880 with stained glass by Edward Burne-Jones. In short St. Paul's was conceived and completed as a true cathedral, the first to be built in the British overseas Empire, imposing in scale, grand in conception, and filled with reverent works of art and craftsmanship. 'It gives', said Bishop Wilson, consecrating it, 'the front and face to Christianity. It claims India as the Lord's.'

Major Forbes has not always been commended for his design (though there is a bust of him here, too, behind the font). It was, though, a brave project for its time and place, and pointed the way for Anglo-Indian institutional architecture in the following half century. The general pattern of the church was orthodoxly classical – the basilica form, rather than the cruciform – but its detail was all Gothic, or at least Gothick. Though Gothic was already the coming thing within the Church of England at home, in Calcutta, where classicism reigned almost unchallenged, this was a radical departure: and to make his point clearer, upon the cathedral Forbes put a tall pinnacled steeple, derived perhaps from Norwich Cathedral and totally different from anything seen in the city before, which stood out inescapably above the green of the *maidan*, and was reflected picturesquely in ponds.

In 1934 this spire was so badly damaged by an earthquake that it had to be demolished. A tall tower was erected in its place, designed by W. I. Kier after the pattern of Bell Harry at Canterbury: this looked uncomfortably professional upon the somewhat amateur old pile below, and made a curious building, now weathered by a century of Bengal heat and rain, curiouser than ever.

Shrine of the Heroic Age

They never built a cathedral, indeed, half so curious again. The cathedral at Bombay is also a mixture of classical and Gothic, but only because it began life early in the eighteenth century as a garrison church, and was incompletely aggrandized after it had become a cathedral in 1833. The cathedral at Madras is a

St. George's Cathedral, Madras. The plans were drawn up by Colonel Caldwell, though, like the nearby St. Andrew's Church, it was built by Thomas de Havilland. It was consecrated in 1816.

massive white classical building, consecrated in 1816, dazzling with *chunam*, designed by Colonel James Caldwell, Madras Engineers, more or less on the Gibbs pattern but done with such self-importance that it feels more regal than diocesan. The Cathedral of the Redemption at New Delhi, designed in Lutyens–Palladian sandstone by Henry Medd, Chief Architect to the Government of India, started life in 1931 looking like a huge Anglo-Saxon church, with a low humped silhouette like Romsey Abbey, but later had a dome added, and came to look more like a rather magnificent mausoleum. (It owed something to Palladio's Church of the Redentore in Venice – hence, we are told, its unlikely dedication.)

The only one to rival Calcutta for interest is a building diametrically opposed to Major Forbes's naïve masterpiece. In the 1840s British power, moving north-westwards towards the Indus valley, came into possession of the Punjab, the fertile and historical country of the Five Rivers. The leaders of this advance were the Lawrence brothers, Henry and John, both Christians of burning zeal, and they were backed by aides and generals of equal evangelical fervour. It was only natural then that the capital of their new province, Lahore, though one of the greatest Muslim cities of India, should become a centre of Christian missionary work and education too. India is the Lord's! Arise a cathedral!

The work was begun in 1883, and the architect was John Oldrid Scott, second son of Sir Gilbert. He provided what most people would now consider the typical Anglo-Indian fane, expressing in itself the mixed aspirations, part so worthy, part so insensitive, part so daring, part so conventional, of the British paramountcy in India. A local missionary, Thomas French, was its first Bishop: and with what pride and gratitude he must have surveyed this brand-new testament of his faith, when he processed for the first time up its tall nave to his episcopal throne beside the altar!

Lahore Cathedral is not large, but it is stately, built of brick with granite columns, and standing in a compound that might, imaginatively, be described as a close. Scott designed it as a pure example, bordering some say upon pastiche, of an Early English cathedral, transferred by the divine will to this exotic location (within sight, that is, of the frowning and ferocious fortress of the Moguls on its hummock above the Ravi River). It is a commissioned cathedral, so to speak. Think of a cathedral, and you get Lahore. Its two towers, side by side, are castellated and rich in drip-spouts. Its chancel is apsed and buttressed. It has a vestigial hint of a cloister, and rose-windows here and there, and a high ornate course of ironwork above its chancel roof-line. Twin mitres surmount its gateway, and there is a cathedral school nearby.

It is the cathedral's high dark interior that is most satisfying now, for this soon became the greatest shrine to the Raj in its heroic age. What feats of bravado, bully and sacrifice are recorded on these brass slabs, tarnished a little now perhaps, but still distinctly engraved with the flowery lettering of the day! How bravely Silas

Swinley must have fallen, leading his soldiers at Safed Sung! How sadly Sir Alexander Lawrence died, 'by the fall of a bridge near Simla'! How tragic that the promising career of John Poyntz Saunders, aged twenty-one, should have been 'abruptly terminated by assassins'! What prodigies General Sam Browne must have performed, to earn his VC, GCB, and KCSI!

And to seal the symbolism of it all, in the dim-lit east aisle one might find a memorial to Bishop French himself: for having raised this great temple among the heathen of northern India, having been rewarded (so his memorial says) with a Doctorate of Oriental Learning, in 1891 he went off to another frontier of the Empire, taking the word of God to Muscat on the Persian Gulf: there he read the Gospel aloud in the streets and coffee shops, and there that May, sixty-five years old, he died without a convert.

The run of them

But most of the churches of Victorian Anglo-India were, to put it gently, unmemorable. Some were dismal, most were just dull, and there was a depressing sameness to the run of them. Many indeed appear to have been built to a more or less standard pattern, based perhaps upon some suggested plan of the Ecclesiological Society, then the accepted arbiter of Anglican church architecture in England, and a prolific source of pamphlets and advice. Whatever their origins, you came across these familiar structures everywhere, in some places more expensively interpreted than in others, sometimes relieved with local materials or devices, or local architects' whims, or the liturgical requirements of the contemporary Bishop, or even occasionally a touch of spontaneous Indian arts and crafts, but in general all too much the same.

Let us visit one, on a Victorian Sunday morning, to stand for all the others. One will be enough, especially if we have been serving in India half a lifetime already. We leave our carriage at the iron gate and walk the last few yards through the compound, which is shaded by big trees and is either very dusty or very muddy, according to the weather, being not exactly turf, nor exactly sand, nor exactly soil, but something very Indian and Anglican in between. At the far end of the green stand the nondescript buildings of the church school, with the potted plants of first-form botany in its windows; at the other are the bungalows of the vicar and the schoolmistress, standard Anglo-Indian style, with standard Anglo-Indian furniture on their verandahs, and standard geraniums potted on their steps.

And here is the church. It is very churchy. No enthusiastic innovator has given life or surprise to it, as eager Captain Underwood vitalized St. Stephen's at Ooty, or excellent Mr Growse gave the gift of true innocence to his Church of the

(*Top.*) St. Andrew's Church, Calcutta, built by Messrs Burn, Currie and Company in 1815. (*Bottom.*) St. Peter's Church, Fort William, Calcutta, is generally reckoned to be the finest garrison church in India. It was built in 1822, but has now been deconsecrated and is used as a military library.

St. Mary's Church, Benares.

Sacred Heart. Christ Church, Muddipore is a textbook imperial church, as rigid and as regular as the Thirty-Nine Articles of its faith. Here we enter the shade of the statutory carriage-porch, here are the steps up to the front door — any experienced Anglo-Indian could negotiate them with his eyes shut — and here inside is the usual oblong pattern of nave and two aisles, separated by pointed arches in the approved Gothic manner. A pale light shines through the plain glass windows of the aisles, and the clerestory windows above; primary colours spill through the east window, erected in memory of gallant Col X., devoted Mrs Y., or the Reverend Mr Z., of St. Mary's College, Oxford, Never To Be Forgotten By His Grateful Flock.

The service follows its appointed course (sermon about Naboth's Vineyard, collection in aid of the diocesan orphanage, *Lo He Comes In Clouds Descending*, banns of marriage of Thomas Henry Lane Tapworth, Forestry Service, and Penelope Victoria younger daughter of Colonel and Mrs Weston, Indian Medical Service). We exchange greetings with the vicar, Major and Mrs Hyde-Robson, Judge Horton and his daughter and old Mrs Weatherby, we congratulate young Tapworth and the simpering Penelope (could they be the grandparents, do you think, of G. D. L. Tapworth?), and excusing ourselves as fast as we can, hasten back to the church gate. As we wait for Abdul to bring up the carriage, though, we take a last look at the church behind us, standing there in inexorable elevation, with the vicar in his white surplice still clustered around by parishioners outside the porch. Nothing different! Nothing changed, not a finial, not a Penelope, since we first set eyes on Muddipore back in '73!

Dear God, how much longer till home leave? *'To the club, Abdul, there's a good fellow...'*

The death cult

Down Chowringhee past the Grand Hotel, turn left past Peliti's restaurant and the Royal Asiatic Society, before the Bengal Club, and before long you came to Calcutta's South Park Street cemetery, a little city of the imperial dead. It had its streets, its crossroads, its little parks. Its displays, too, of architectural kinds, like an exhibition ground: pyramids, colonnaded temples, domes, towers, tombs like beds, or small forts, or frankly coffins; scrolls, and weeping angels, and urns of course, and obelisks, and immense inscription slabs, and long sad epitaphs on marble, and curt obituary facts on granite; and all these shapes and patterns, marshalled into orderly imperial forms, stood there dappled, crumbled, haunted by crows and tinged with lichen, like so many shrouded stone ghosts among the mournful Indian trees.

The cult of death was powerful, in a society that had established itself in war and was beset always by sickness, epidemic or catastrophe. Death came in many

South Park Street Cemetery, Calcutta. Begun in 1767 as a final resting-place for the Europeans of India's then capital city. There are innumerable grandees buried here, but perhaps the best-loved was Rose Aylmer, who died of a surfeit of pineapples when she was twenty.

ways among the Anglo-Indians. There was death by sniper's bullet on the frontier, or by stoning in city riots. There was death by cholera, malaria, dysentery, or by the dread Doo-lally tap, the nervous collapse which the British soldiers mordantly named after the most depressing of their transit camps, Deolali in Maharashtra. There was death in childbirth, in remote stations without surgeons or midwives, there was death often enough from over-drinking, there was death from sheer homesickness, or saddest of all, there was death on the way home, with the coffin sliding melancholy into the tropic sea, and the deceased's topi thrown softly in behind him.

Lapidary constructions were numerous all over British India, and many a designer put his creative all into their mournful conceptions. Many were carved, sculpted or built in India: many more, with a truer symbolism perhaps, were made at home in Britain, and went out to the East as ballast in the deep dark holds of merchantmen.

Kings and captains

Memorial statuary was essential to Anglo-Indianism. 'I doubt', wrote G. W. Forrest in 1903, 'if there is any city in Europe more rich in memorials than Calcutta', and the other Presidency towns were well-supplied too. Half of them were of Queen Victoria, and these were generally anticipatory in nature, for they were erected during her lifetime. She sat elegant beneath a fretted canopy on the waterfront at Madras, she sat voluminous on her high throne outside her Memorial in Calcutta, and most characteristically of all, perhaps, she sat eight feet tall at the junction of Mayo and Esplanade Roads in Bombay, in a marble ensemble described by the traveller W. S. Caine in 1891 as 'one of the finest modern monuments in the world'.

It was certainly a sumptuous affair, presented to the city in 1872 by the Gaekwar of Baroda, carved by the fashionable London sculptor Matthew Noble, and for many years an object of totemic veneration to simple Indians. The Queen, portrayed as a young woman, sat upon a throne of fairy-tale magnificence. The Star of India shone above her head, attended by the Rose of England and the Lotus, and interwoven all around, in four languages, were the chivalric mottoes *God and my Right* and *Heaven's Light Our Guide*, suitably acknowledging the mixture of force and providence behind the British presence in India. Above the royal head a great white Gothic flèche arose, forty-two feet high and richly decorated, and the whole monument was enclosed within wrought iron railings, giving it a mystic feel, like a reliquary.

Four British Emperors of India succeeded Queen Victoria, but none of them were commemorated with the same awe. Edward VII appeared here and there, generally on horseback. George V was just in time to be portrayed in elongated

The only major monuments to Britain's rule in India left officially unmolested are these, at the Victoria Memorial, Calcutta. The structure, which Curzon directed to be built to rival the Taj Mahal in grandeur – something it never quite achieved – was designed by Sir William Emerson, built under the day-to-day supervision of V. J. Esch, and completed in 1921. Victoria herself never visited India. The statue of Lord Curzon, by Pomeroy, shows him wearing the Order of the Star of India.

The All-India War Memorial and
George V Memorial, at the eastern
end of New Delhi's Rajpath, or
Kingsway. Lutyens's plan called
for the eternal flame to burn in the
dome on top of the arch; but today
it burns in a cairn beneath, guarded
night and day by members of
India's armed forces. The statue of
King George was removed, like
many of the movable Imperial
monuments in independent India;
but the offered replacement of the
Mahatma Gandhi looked so peculiar it had to be taken down, and
one of the residual, and unending,
debates in modern Delhi concerns
what to do with the now empty
monument.

form, by C. S. Jagger, beneath a canopy on Kingsway in Delhi, rather more plumply in the street outside Government House in Madras, and actually by an Indian sculptor, Rao Bahadur Khatre, on the Apollo Bunder in Bombay. But Edward VIII was not in office long enough to be commemorated at all, while George VI had only been King-Emperor for eleven years when the Empire came abruptly to an end, and most of the imperial monuments were packed away to unfrequented enclaves, or stored in the back-quarters of museums.

Public reputation

Disused statues of Viceroys clutter those repositories. The *maidan* at Calcutta was once littered with such effigies, and many are now to be seen forlornly clustered together in a compound at Barrackpore. Every Bombay street-corner seemed to have one, and they are now mouldering away in long ranks beneath the palm trees behind the Victoria Museum. Delhi was loaded with them, and they are now grouped in a macabre and leprous crescent on the old durbar ground north of the city.

Governors or mere Civil Servants were less often sculpted, but sometimes they were remembered in masonry instead. In Karachi, for instance, the Merewether Memorial Clock, erected at the junction of Bundar and Macleod Streets, became a focal point for the city's loungers, touts and pickpockets, and to this day immortalizes the name of Sir William Lockyer Merewether, a Victorian functionary otherwise dim in the public memory. And in Bombay Sir Bartle Frere was commemorated by a fountain. He was prone to commemorations actually – a public hall in his memory at Karachi, a statue erected at the instance of Edward VII on the Embankment in London – but unfortunately the purpose of the Bombay memorial, the chief of them all, was soon forgotten. Although it was dutifully called the Frere Fountain during the first few years of its existence, it soon became known to everyone as the Flora Fountain: for it is not His Excellency who surmounts it, dampened by its spray, but a figure of the Roman goddess Flora, attended by less explicit figures of myth, the whole forming to this day one of the city's most familiar and most frequently reviled possessions (and the oddest of all legacies left by R. Norman Shaw, the celebrated and normally fastidious London architect who helped to design it).

Generals too were often commemorated. Lord Cornwallis, whose victory at Seringapatam in 1792 laid the foundations of British rule in southern India, was repeatedly honoured: in a heroic cenotaph at Ghazipur in Bihar, in a toga'd effigy by John Bacon jun. in Calcutta Town Hall, and grandly beneath a cupola, by Thomas Banks, within Fort St. George at Madras (when asked why had portrayed the hero with a squint, Banks replied astutely that, since the squint was outwards rather than inwards, it represented a particular breadth of vision in his subject).

Sir Henry Havelock, one of the most admired of the evangelical generals of the Indian Mutiny, was properly commemorated with a whole church at Agra, built rather less suitably, one might think, in a trim classical style. John Nicholson, another, got a monument on a Punjabi hillock and a garden beside the Kashmir Gate in Delhi, where he had heroically died. A champion of a very different breed, Sir David Ochterlony the American-born conqueror of Nepal, was honoured in 1828 with a tall column on the *maidan* at Calcutta which remains one of the best-known objects in the city: it seemed to combine Greek, Pharaonic and Islamic forms, and was supposed to have been intended by its architect, J. P. Parker, to reflect Ochterlony's well-known social and ethnic pragmatism – in the prime of his life the old rascal was said to have maintained thirteen concubines, each with her own elephant.

And far away at Mardan, near the Guides' headquarters, a curious sort of triumphal arch honoured Sir Louis Cavagnari of the Indian Political Service, who was murdered during a mission to Kabul in 1879, and whose death gave rise to the second Afghan war: built entirely in the Indian manner, with a high curving roof, pavilions at each side, tall pointed windows and a reflecting pool, this strange construction arose in a garden in the very middle of the little town, and though most of the local residents are hazy about its meaning, provides an ironic focus still for the life of the place.

Private worth

A few individuals were thought deserving of commemoration for their private worth, rather than their public reputation. For example, in the old graveyard beside St. John's Church in Calcutta, Job Charnock, the founder of the city, was buried beneath a handsome cupola in the oriental manner, coursed like a Moorish mosque and flanked by tall palms – only suitable for one who allegedly sacrificed a cock each year on the tomb of his Hindu wife, whom he had snatched from her funeral pyre as the widow of a Rajput prince. A few yards away Begum Johnson, Mrs Francis Johnson, lay beneath a fine classical rotunda, with urns and heraldic embellishments: she deserved it too, for, having married for the first time at the age of twelve, she survived four husbands, had six children one of whom married the future Earl of Liverpool and became the mother of a Prime Minister, and was given a State funeral when she died in 1812, eighty-seven years old and the senior British resident of Bengal. Downstream a ghat, a landing stage, on the banks of the Hooghly remembered James Prinsep, who as a young man in the 1830s first translated the rock edicts of Asoka: it was an oblong pavilion of Ionic columns, like a pillared stone thicket above the river. And among these monuments to

Prinsep's Ghat, Calcutta (*below*); and the Ochterlony Monument nearby (*left*). James Prinsep, who came from Essex, was an antiquary, linguist and, most notably, Assay Master of the Calcutta Mint. During his office he introduced a uniform coinage system and a unified weights and measures scheme for the country. The Doric memorial to him on the banks of the Hooghly is now hidden from public view; but King George landed beside it in 1911, when he came to India for the Great Durbar. The Ochterlony Monument – known today as the Martyrs' Memorial, or the Shaheed Minaret – was erected in 1828 after a public subscription, as a memorial to Sir David Ochterlony, President of Malwa and Rajputana. It has an Egyptian base, a Syrian column and a Turkish dome; visitors fortunate enough to win permission can climb the 223 steps and see a fine view of Calcutta. Today it is a rallying point for most of Calcutta's political demonstrations – the Bengal equivalent of Bombay's Flora Fountain.

Britons long forgotten in their homeland, perhaps the most moving is a white marble statue, by Francis Chantrey, inside the Town Hall at Calcutta. It is one of those effigies whose shapes we saw dimly and mysteriously illuminated through the fanlights in Chapter 4, and it represents an eminent Anglo-Indian jurist, Stephen Babington, who died in Bombay in 1822 at the age of thirty-two. He sits in a low chair, one slippered foot before the other, studying a document inscribed *Revision of the Judicial Code,* holding a pen and slightly smiling. He looks to be in his twenties, and with his curly longish hair and slim figure he seems astonishingly, even poignantly contemporary. He is a sociable, bright, rather trendy young Englishman of a kind we all know. Today he might be – a modish photographer? a gossip columnist? an unusually expensive hairdresser?

Then, he had powers of life or death.

'Tell it out'

Much more usual were communal memorials, to armies, to victims, or simply to worthies in a generic sense. The Banqueting Hall beside Government House at Madras was one such: built by John Goldingham in 1802, it was stacked with honorific statues, portraits and symbols, and its picture of General Sir Eyre Coote, who had died twenty years before its construction, was said to have inherited so much of the hero's own natural potency that visiting sepoys habitually saluted it. Another was the Dalhousie Institute in Calcutta, a mid-Victorian Valhalla, a substantial Doric temple intended specifically to 'contain within its walls statues and busts of great men' (such as, for example, the Marquis of Dalhousie himself, the Right Honourable James Wilson, Brigadier-General Neil, CB, and Edward E. Venables, Indigo Planter).

Most of them, though, commemorated the dead of the imperial wars – sometimes, one feels, the wars themselves, for there is no denying that a scrap now and then did relieve the awful monotony of the soldier's life in India. Some of these remembered conflicts of pathetic obscurity. Not far from Prinsep's Ghat there stood a temple-monument to those lost in the Gwalior wars, which had been fought, so it said, in 1843: Colonel W. H. Goodwyn of the Bengal Engineers designed it, inscribing the names of the dead on a catafalque inside, and roofing its little rotunda with metal made from captured enemy guns. The Rohilla Wars, which were fought in the 1790s, were remembered in another sad rotunda, in the grounds of St. John's, Calcutta, while as for the Temple of Fame which stood decoratively beside the Governor-General's country house at Barrackpore, it was built to honour those killed while conquering a country that most people did not associate with the British Empire at all – Java. Lieutenant George Blane of the Bengal Engineers designed this pleasing little shrine in the purest Greek Corinthian style, with thirty white columns surrounding a domed memorial chamber, all thrown into relief by the palms and feathery tamarisks that grew around.

A nineteenth-century invasion of Afghanistan was remembered in a church, the Afghan Church at Colabar in Bombay. For years this was one of the best-known buildings in India, and it remains a landmark to this day. If you stand on Malabar Hill above Back Bay, in the richest, most modern and most dynamic part of the city, you see spread before you, mostly on land reclaimed from the sea, a great panorama of modern concrete blocks – hotels, apartment buildings, offices, white and gleaming above the sea, and giving to the ramshackle old city a spurious sense of progressive modernity. Run your eye along them, to the west, and out on a spit there stands a solitary steeple. It is dwarfed now by the bulk of modern Bombay, but when it was built it dominated the seashore of the city, and like a divine finger beckoned the ships into the haven beyond.

The worst disaster ever suffered by the British in India was the annihilation of an expeditionary army by the Afghans in 1842. Many of those who died had come from the Company's Bombay Army, and in the following decade it was decided to commemorate the dead with a memorial church, dedicated to St. John the Baptist and designed by an architect generally described as 'Henry Conybeare Esqr., son of the Dean of Llandaff'. It was to contain, written on vellum rolls, the names of every officer and man who had fallen in the campaign, while the names of all European commissioned officers were also to be recorded on marble slabs or brasses. By 1865, though the vellum rolls never did materialize, and the proposed steeple was reduced for economy reasons, and though Sir Cowasjee Jahangir's offer of an illuminated clock was inexplicably declined, the church was considered structurally finished: a handsome structure with a tall, tapering spire – the first ecclesiologically 'correct' Gothic church in India, Mr Gavin Stamp tells us.

It was the interior, however, that made the Afghan Church unforgettable. The chancel floor was lined with encaustic tiles from England, to a pattern suggested by Herbert Butterfield; around the font was a magnificent metal screen worked by the craftsmen of Lockwood Kipling's School of Art; but the most marvellous and terrible things of all were the lists of names which were the *raison d'être* of the church. They lined the chancel walls, and they were carved on white, red, yellow and blue marbles, supported by pilasters within Gothic niches. Solemn and sombre they stood there, dominating the tall silent church. The lists were divided force by force – Bombay Army, Bengal Army, Her Majesty's Army – and all around the chancel, in black on blue, ran a great inscription: THIS CHURCH WAS BUILT IN MEMORY OF THE OFFICERS WHOSE NAMES ARE WRITTEN ABOVE, AND OF THE NON-COMMISSIONED OFFICERS AND PRIVATE SOLDIERS, TOO MANY TO BE RECORDED, WHO FELL, MINDFUL OF THEIR DUTY, BY SICKNESS OR BY THE SWORD, IN THE CAMPAIGNS OF SIND AND AFGHANISTAN, 1835–43 AD.

(*Left.*) St. John's Church – the Afghan Church – Bombay, consecrated in 1858. (*Right.*) The Mutiny Memorial, Delhi, standing on the site of Taylor's Battery, on The Ridge. It was erected as a memorial to the victims of the 1857 Mutiny and Siege, and is covered with plaques bearing the names of men and units involved in the action.

So the Anglo-Indians commemorated the most tragic, the most useless, the most incompetent, the most unsuccessful and perhaps the most unjust of all their imperial wars. Eight bells hung in the tower of the Afghan Church. 'Tell it out among the heathen', said the text on number one, 'that the Lord is King'.

Epic of the race

SACRED TO THE MEMORY (said another imperial memorial) OF THOSE CHRISTIANS WHO WERE MURDERED AT DELHI IN MAY MDCCCLVII AND IN GRATITUDE TO GOD FOR HIS MERCY IN HAVING SPARED A REMNANT OF HIS PEOPLE TO ERECT THIS CROSS.

If the first Afghan war was the most hopeless of the imperial conflicts, the most embittering, and the one most entrammelled in Anglo-Indian sanctimony, was certainly the Indian Mutiny of 1857. The responses of the imperialists to this catastrophe were often very pious – gratitude for the sparing of a remnant to erect a cross, thanksgiving for the conclusion or the sacred sacrifice of it ('the Epic of our Race', the Anglo-Indian historian Sir Charles Crosthwaite called the miserable conflict). The memorials erected to commemorate it were equally holy, though they ranged in mood from the stricken to the triumphant, in purpose from the admonitory to the repentant: the doors of the Memorial Hall put up at Madras, hundreds of miles from the scenes of the mutiny, were to be perpetually closed, its statutes said, against 'balls, concerts, theatrical exhibitions, and such like entertainments as have the character of mere worldly amusement'.

Most of them were destined to be disregarded in the end, if only because of their frequency. To the generation of the Mutiny, it seemed an event of cataclysmic historical importance, so that the environs of the several battlefields were profuse with plaques and obelisks. (They were warnings to the defeated as well as reminders to the victors: the Mutiny Memorial on the ridge above Delhi was carefully built to be one and a half feet higher than the nearby Asoka's Pillar, the pride of the Indian patriots.) For a decade or two it was doubtless interesting to relive on the spot the siege of Hindu Rao's House, or follow General Nicholson to his death beside the Kashmir Gate; but by the turn of the nineteenth century only two events of the Mutiny were altogether clear in the general Anglo-Indian consciousness. One was the massacre of Cawnpore, the other the siege of Lucknow, and both were commemorated by striking memorials.

At Cawnpore, after a harsh siege and a treacherous ambush, several score of British women and children had been butchered and thrown down a well, and this event profoundly affected the attitude of Britons to Indians for years to come. Above all other places, Cawnpore (Kanpur now) symbolized in the evangelical mind the gulf of moral discrepancy that separated rulers from ruled in India. No matter that the exact details of the tragedy were never certain, nor that the

British, in repressing the Mutiny, often acted with equal cruelty: the Massacre of Cawnpore, as it became universally known to the British, was remembered as an object-lesson, if not a precedent.

Two memorials commemorated it on the spot, and were visited as shrines, and explained to children as moral examples. The first was a large and sombre church in the Romanesque style, the Cawnpore Memorial Church, from whose steeple visitors were shown, on the landscape spread out below them, the exact locations of the tragedy; the other was the memorial erected above the fatal well, and this was the image that every tourist sketched, and every traveller's book described. The well had been filled in, and upon it a mound was raised, crowned by an octagonal Gothic screen designed by the gifted Sir Henry Yule, part-author of *Hobson-Jobson*, whose brother had died in the Mutiny. On the wall all around was this uncompromising inscription: '*Sacred to the Perpetual Memory of a great company of Christian people, chiefly Women and Children, who near this spot were cruelly murdered by the followers of the rebel Nana Dhundu Pant, of Bithur, and cast, the dying with the dead, into the well below, on the XVth day of July, MDCCCLVII.*'   In the middle stood a marble angel with folded hands, carved by the sculptor Carlo Marochetti, one of the most admired of the time, whose works already stood in St. Paul's and in Westminster Abbey. This was, the visitor was told, the Angel of the Resurrection, but it was not a hopeful figure: there was something baleful and brooding about it, something which spoke, despite its pacific posture, more of reproach than of reconciliation (and it was paid for largely by a fine levied on the Indian citizens of Cawnpore, none of whom were permitted to enter its compound).

The Angel has long been moved to another site, and few visitors go to see it now. The memorial at Lucknow, on the other hand, is still on most guidebook itineraries of India. The siege of Lucknow, as the British called it, was really nothing of the sort, but was, on the contrary, a siege of the British Residency there, into which all the Europeans of the area had withdrawn. It was a heroic affair all the same, the British holding out for three months against powerful odds, losing 2,000 men, women and children, and being reduced almost to starvation when relief came at last. By then the Residency complex, which included an oddly turreted classical house, a Gothic Residency chapel and a small barrack-block, was all in ruin: and it was this ruin itself, preserved just as it was, which the Anglo-Indians turned into their monument of the ordeal.

It was perhaps the very first of the ruin-monuments, the precursor of all the shattered buildings which have in our own times been preserved as mementoes of war's horrors. It was meticulously maintained until the end of the Empire. The rubble was cleared, the gardens were restored, but the old buildings were left as hulks, and upon them there flew, day and night, an imperial standard, remembering Tennyson's famous poem about the siege itself –

Shot thro' the staff or the halyard, but ever we raised thee anew,
And ever upon the topmost roof our banner of England blew.

As the years passed the recrimination left this place, people of both races used the old compound as a place of pleasure, children brown and pink alike played among the reviving shrubberies: and when the British left, and the flag was taken down at last to be presented to King George VI at Windsor Castle, the Indians in their generosity did not abandon the monument, or pervert its purposes, but kept it as it always was, its phlox and sweet peas gentle still among the ravaged structures.

The last memorial

There were no more memorials to the battles that Britons and Indians fought against each other: the war memorials of the twentieth century remembered rather campaigns in which the two peoples fought side by side. After the First World War, when thousands of Indians died in the imperial cause, they built memorials in all the big Indian cities, and most of these were later adapted to remember the dead of the Second World War too. They were usually restrained neo-classical compositions, drawing their inspiration from the cemeteries designed by Edwin Lutyens for the battlefields of France, or his Cenotaph in London. When they came to erect a memorial for New Delhi Lutyens himself was commissioned to build it, and he placed it symbolically athwart the long ceremonial drive, Kingsway, which formed the focal highway of the new capital. It was Anglo-India's last memorial.

It was a tall arch of red and white stone, with a shallow bowl on top for the Perpetual Flame, hefty in construction but deliberately unassertive – nothing like an Arch of Triumph, for all its triumphant situation. Within it were inscribed the names of all those Indian soldiers who had died in the Great War – volunteers every one, regiment by regiment, Hindus, Muslims, Sikhs, Parsees, Christians, names drawn in spirit from the remotest corners of India, and from the far battlefields of the conflict to be remembered for ever here: in a cenotaph built by the best-known designer of English country houses on the road that led, straight as a gunshot, direct to the throne of the Viceroy – the man who had, by the exercise of his limitless imperial power, sent them all to their deaths.

Hail and farewell

Better-known than any of them, better-loved perhaps as well, was a memorial much more festive: the Gateway of India, the grandiloquent triple arch which welcomed new arrivals ashore upon the Apollo Bunder in Bombay, and which became one of the universally recognized emblems of British India. Nothing could be more evocative of the last decades of Empire than the advertisements issued by P and O during the 1930s, when their ships sailed direct from Tilbury to dock in Bombay within sight of this familiar structure: the great ship lies there peacefully at its berth, the vapours still drifting around its funnels, the porters and boatmen scurry here and there, the sahibs and their ladies disembark elegantly, very slim, very svelte, and beyond them, blurred slightly by colour-wash or heat-haze, and attended by fictional palms, the Gateway of India stands like an emblem of pensionable eternity.

Bombay had claimed to be the gate or eye of India ever since the opening of the Suez Canal, and most newcomers to the Indian Empire landed there. The old landing-place, before the development of the docks, was officially Wellington Pier, but it was always called Apollo Bunder, and it was here that the neophyte got his very first taste, smell and hearing of India, in the crowds that milled and swirled around, the beggars and musicians, the conjurors and postcard-sellers – in the extraordinary silhouette of the Yacht Club away to the right, with its members over their teacups on the terrace – in the grand imperial buildings, towered and pinnacled, which stretched away from the quay into the city centre. So this is India, the new arrivals would say to themselves, clutching their topis and sunshades. So this is our Empire!

Some time in the nineteenth century they built an iron pavilion at the top of the steps on Apollo Bunder – a nice little gazebo in a Mongol manner, like a metal tent, but when in 1911 the King-Emperor George V, arrived with his wife on a State visit to India, the first ever by a reigning monarch, this little summer-house was considered unworthy of the occasion, and instead a wedding-cake arch of plaster was erected – white as icing, vaguely reminiscent of the Taj Mahal, having a high dome over its central arch and four minarets at its corners. Through this fancy portal Their Majesties passed, along a wide red carpet, with all possible permutations of salutes and obeisances, to the coach and four and mounted bodyguard which waited to take them up to Government House.

The King and Queen went home again, the plaster arch came down, and instead in 1927 they built a domed arch of yellow basalt to commemorate the visit for ever. Of all the constructions of British India the Gateway is probably the best-known to the world at large. It was designed by George Wittet, Architect to the Government of Bombay, and was originally intended to form part of a much wider ceremonial development; as a result it was set rather oddly in its site, skew-whiff to everything, on a plot of land reclaimed from the sea to allow for a more majestic vista. Wittet based it on sixteenth-century Gujerati models, and it was entirely Indian in style and decoration. It was a reception hall as well as a triumphal arch, so beside its central gateway there were tall domed chambers, each large enough, we are told, to seat 600 bigwigs of Bombay. Four turrets were mounted above the central arch, and the whole building was finished in exquisite detail of carved and chiselled stonework.

This was where the British landed: and this is where, in the end, they left. The Gateway of India did not see many ceremonial arrivals after all, during its three decades under British rule, but it formed the background to one historical departure – the last parade with which, in 1947, the British said goodbye to their Indian Empire. We can relive the occasion in many pictures. The Somerset Light Infantry and a regiment of Gurkhas provided an honour guard, and we see them parading there in the baggy khaki shorts that were a very badge of service in the imperial East. Around the Bunder every window, every rooftop is crammed: guests look down from the rooms in the Taj, members crowd the verandah of the Yacht Club, and every available cranny, attic, eave or platform is jammed with Indian citizens. It seems to be a properly restrained affair – the British upper lip stiff to the end, the Indian courtesies scrupulously maintained. There is a formal exchange of speeches; there is a traditional barking of orders; the band strikes up, and with a solemn slow march between the great arch of the gateway, the last soldiers of the British Raj embark in their launches and sail away to the waiting troop-ships.

Today the Gateway of India has forgotten all its pompous or elegiac meanings, and is a place of pleasure, habitually thronged, inside and out, by companionable crowds out for the sea air. The liners no longer come from London, and the only boats around the pier are pleasure craft touting trips around the harbour, or excursions to the Elephanta Caves. It is a merry place, an ice-cream place, and not one visitor in a million reads the text upon Mr Wittet's parapet above:

ERECTED TO COMMEMORATE THE LANDING IN INDIA OF THEIR IMPERIAL MAJESTIES KING GEORGE V AND QUEEN MARY ON 2 DECEMBER MCMXI.

7 · Civic

<hr>

Urbanism

Among history's imperialists the British were certainly not the greatest builders, but they were the greatest creators of towns. Conquerors since Alexander the Great had seen the strategic and cultural advantages of establishing their own cities across the world, but as the first modern industrial power, Britain was the chief exporter of municipalities, and through the agency of her empire broadcast them everywhere. Half the cities of the American East owe their genesis to the British Empire, most of the cities of Canada, many of the cities of Africa, all the cities of Australasia and the tremendous city-states of Singapore and Hong Kong. Sporting pastimes apart, and the English language, urbanism was the most lasting of the British imperial legacies.

In India this was true almost more than anywhere. Many of the Indian cities, of course, like Delhi, Lahore, Lucknow or Agra, were important civilized centres long before the British set foot in India. The biggest Indian cities of them all, though – Calcutta, Bombay, Madras – were all in effect British creations. Only huddled villages or scattered fishermen's huts were on those strands when the imperialists arrived; the huge ports which presently arose there were born entirely out of British enterprise. So were a host of smaller places across the breadth of the subcontinent, railway towns, cantonments, Government enclaves, or the hill-stations which were the most truly original of British civic developments in India. Some towns, like Calcutta, could trace their beginning to the energy of a single empire-builder; others were actually named for individual Britons – Lyallpur, Jacobabad, Edwardesbad, Campbellpur, Kidderpur, Cox's Bazaar. The British founded brand-new settlements of every size, village to metropolis, even down to a proper seaside resort, Gopalpur-on-Sea, where in the heyday of the Raj twenty-seven authentic seaside boarding-houses regretted that breakfast could not be served in bedrooms except in case of Genuine Sickness.

Village life

Let us start our urban survey upon a village green, *circa* 1930. We have disembarked at Cochin, in Kerala, perhaps to inspect the progress of the new port on
Willingdon Island, but since most of the place is still under the sovereignty of the
Maharajah of Cochin, and Sir Robert's house on the point is not yet ready to
receive guests, we are advised to stay at the Club (to which of course we have a
proper introduction) in the small strip of territory, Fort Cochin, which is actually
British. The approach there, we have to admit, is discouraging. We cross the new
road bridge from the island and plunge into the shambled streets of Mattancherry.
The traffic is terrible. The noise is deafening. The streets are a nightmare of
apparently half-completed concrete blocks, gaudy signs and sporadic derelic-
tions. We are tired after our long journey from Bombay, and Sir Robert's relentless
statistics, and we begin to wish we had not come.

But we emerge, all of a sudden, upon a village green. It really is green, in this
humid and well-watered southern outpost, and it is surrounded by agreeable
half-timbered houses in the English Ideal Home manner – not bungalows at all,
but houses for deputy bank managers in Surrey, say, or stockbrokers working
their way up. There is a village church at one corner of the green, as there should
be, and graceful trees stoop over its perimeter, and they are actually playing –
well, let us *say* they are actually playing, cricket on the pitch in the middle.
Leading off the green towards the sea, whose blue we can see beyond them, stand
rather grander houses, white and Tudorish again, with imposing garden gates and
distinct emanations of Hoovers. Just over there we see the imposing bungalow of
the Collector, which really does look not unlike a tithe barn, with few windows
and huge overhanging eaves: somewhere beyond the square leg umpire there
gratefully appear the unpretentious buildings of the Club, looking genially over
the cricket for all the world like the pub at home.

It is true that when we reach our room, and look down at the beach on the
other side, we see that all along the neighbouring sea-shore stand those eerie
wooden constructions of the fishermen, like giant dipping pumps or insects, that
we saw when we sailed into Cochin harbour in Chapter 5; but never mind, the
bearer will soon bring us a cup of tea, there is a picture of the 1927 Club XI on the
wall, and all around us, we know, the essentials of English village life comfort-
ingly attend us: the inn itself, the green outside, the homes of the amiable
bourgeoisie, the church within its hoary graveyard, the squire's house up the lane.
We can hardly complain. Nice of Tapworth to suggest it.

Hill-stations

That was village life, in one of the smallest of the imperial stations (as the settlements of the Indian Empire were generically called). For small town life among the imperialists we can best go into the hills. There is plenty of choice, some eighty hill-stations having been established by the British as retreats from the heat and hazards of the plains – 'like meat', as one Victorian said, 'we keep better up here'. Less than seventy miles from Bombay, up its own little rack-railway, Matheran stood agreeably above the heat. Only 250 miles from Madras was Ooty, 'the Queen of Hill Stations'. There was Naini Tal in the Kumaon hills, and Mussoorie above Dehra Dun, and Murree above Rawalpindi; most delightful of all, 250 miles north of Calcutta there was Darjeeling, the hill-station *in excelsis*, which stood at 7,000 feet in the Himalayan foothills, looking across to Kanchenjunga, and was the chief sanitarium, as they called hill-stations in Victorian times, for Anglo-Bengal.

Here are the names of some of the houses at Darjeeling, at the end of the nineteenth century: Verbena Villa, Cedar Cottage, Bryngwyn, Meadows Cottage, Nirvana, Willowdale, Meadow Bank, Vale Pleasant, The Dell, Beechwood, Orchard Lea, Emerald Bank. They were the familiar hill-station villas that we visited in Chapter 3, fancy-chimneyed and creeper-clothed, and they nestled, most of them, neatly in the flanks of hills, bright with the lights of evening parties, lively in the daytime with gossip or tea on the lawn. It was a town of pure pleasure. It was, in many ways, the very opposite of Empire.

Its siting, along a hog's back, was characteristic of the northern hill-stations. They were established, sometimes originally for strategic reasons, in precipitous and sparsely inhabited foothill country, heavily wooded and intersected by deep river ravines; and they were built in linear shape along sharp ridges, partly because the British wanted to have views on all sides, and partly because more often than not the ridges offered the only ground flat enough to build on. As far as possible the top of the ridge was occupied by the European quarter of town, the sole reason for its existence after all; the native quarters, bazaars, huts and tenements, were perched on ledges down the hillside on either side, and sometimes looked indeed as though they were liable to slide away altogether into the gulches far below.

Fortunately for the British the ridge at Darjeeling was semicircular in shape, and this enabled them to build the town in an urbane crescent above the valleys. It was placed there with a happy panache, true for once perhaps to the deepest feelings of the British: this was a town they had built altogether for their own indulgence, not for command, not for security, not even for profit, but simply for their own relaxation, where for a few months in the year they need hardly be imperialists at all, but could simply enjoy themselves. Here, for once, women

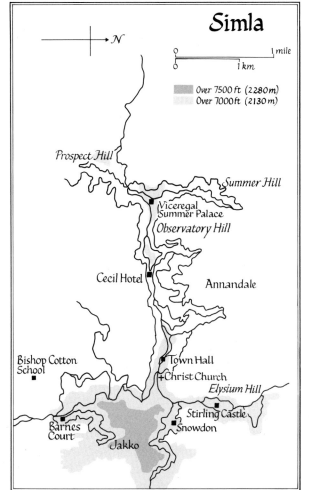

Simla

Over 7500 ft (2280 m)
Over 7000 ft (2130 m)

Prospect Hill

Summer Hill

Viceregal Summer Palace
Observatory Hill

Cecil Hotel

Annandale

Bishop Cotton School

Town Hall
Christ Church
Elysium Hill

Stirling Castle
Snowdon

Barnes Court

Jakko

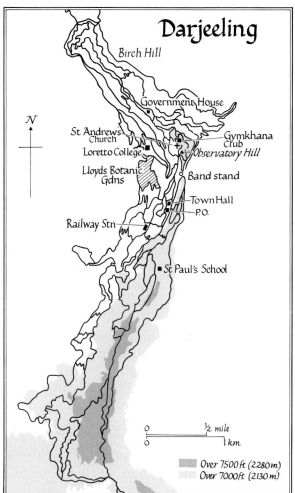

Darjeeling

Birch Hill

Government House

St Andrews Church
Loretto College

Gymkhana Club
Observatory Hill

Lloyds Botanic Gdns

Band stand

Town Hall
P.O.

Railway Stn

St Paul's School

Over 7500 ft (2280 m)
Over 7000 ft (2130 m)

outnumbered men among the Anglo-Indians, and Europeans were almost as numerous as Indians. Darjeeling expressed no elevating message. It made no tactful concessions. It was not even clamped within the usual wary enclave, for there was no very abrupt distinction between the European and the Indian parts. In the summer, it was true, the Bengal Government moved up here from Calcutta, and there were tea estates all around, but it never felt either a political or a commercial town: it was there for pleasure.

The steeple of St. Andrew's Church stood at the apex of the town, and nearby was the Town Hall. Unobtrusively disposed among the deodars here and there were Beechwood, Willowdale and the rest, not to speak of Government House, which was called The Shrubbery, and St. Paul's School, which was very Anglican; and all down the crest of the ridge there ran a wide paved esplanade, with a bandstand in a triangular piazza half-way along, a fountain in a public garden, shops, the Club, the post office, a library, and benches along the way for dalliance or contemplation.

Such was the elongated centre of the town, from which wheeled traffic was excluded. Out of sight was the little racecourse, at one end, and the small cantonment at the other. The rest fell away in layers of decreasing consequence down the slopes – the lesser hotels and pensions, Eurasian sorts of villa, the bazaars, the blur of Indian huts, a market, a square at the bottom where the rickshaws waited, and the buses loaded their passengers for the long haul down the Cart Road to the plains. Somewhere down there was the railway station, too, and ever and again there reverberated through the town, echoing up from distant wooded vales, the hoots and puffs of its little mountain trains (which preferred to travel in company, and came up the serpentine track from Siliguri two at a time).

Seen from a distance Darjeeling, which was very small, but very intense, was a hatched composition. The dominant horizontal was the long line of the ridge itself. The chief verticals were the long thin trees, like cypresses in Italy, which flecked the hillsides everywhere. The diagonals were the slopes of the hills that lay in folds all around the town, gently sliding away to the south, rising in layer after layer, crossing each other, merging, towards the great snowpeaks of the Himalaya to the north.

Yet within this complex pattern it was a neat, functional, well-organized town, sociologically sensible, like a modern shopping centre with its service areas. It was also a very exciting little entity, for its builders had done nothing to disguise its smallness, but rather made the most of it: so that as you walked to your cosy villa on to that infinitesimal mall, pausing in the square perhaps to listen to the band, or stopping off for a cup of tea, you were always conscious of the extraordinary nature of the place, so isolated, so far away. Foreign smells of spice, leather and conifer hung on the air; sly gleams of brass and copper shone from gabled shops; wood-smoke drifted up from the bazaar, tom-toms beat in the evening, slit-eyed tribesmen sauntered past, colourfully booted.

You were so few, you thought to yourselves, deposited up there in that inconceivably foreign corner of the world: and even the pomp of rank or seniority seemed less important, set against the great white mountains, range upon range, pink-blushed or glowering in cloud, which provided the incomparable backdrop to this theatrical but dimunitive belvedere.

'Abode of the Little Tin Gods'

The apotheosis of the hill-station form was Simla, north of Delhi, but it was something different too; if Darjeeling was mostly pure escapism, for several months in every year Simla was one of the great capitals of the world. Here in the hills above the Punjab, from March to October, from 1865 to 1939 the Viceroy ruled with absolute power over several hundred million persons, and surrounded as he was by all his officials, aides and bodyguards, accompanied by experts and ancillaries of every kind, followed by hosts of hangers-on from grass widows to Confectioners By Appointment, portrait photographers to spies – surrounded as he was by this multitude of subordinates, dependants and parasites, his presence gave to the little town a fantasy all its own.

The history of the place ran to pattern, and so did its architecture. 'A middle-sized village', is how it was described by one of its earliest British visitors, 'where a fakir is situated to give water to travellers'. By 1859, when W. H. Russell of *The Times* took time off in Simla after the Mutiny, it had become 'a conical hill, covered with a deluge of white bungalows, dominated by a church behind'. The church (Christ Church) had a tower this time, but Simla's Mall, like Darjeeling's, ran genially along the ridge, lined with Hamilton's the Jewellers, Phelps the Tailor, Peliti's Grand Hotel above its octagonal verandah, Thacker Spink the booksellers and Rubenstein the Hairdresser who boasted a Lady Specialist Direct from Marcel's in London. The chalets, villas, clubs, and hotels were sprinkled as usual among the trees, and beyond the ridge were the pleasure-grounds of Annandale, with a racecourse, a cricket-pitch, polo fields and gardens.

But after 1865 the particularity of Simla was this: that beyond it all, beyond the sociable crowds in the square outside the church, the trysts at Peliti's, the picnics at Annandale or the amateur dramatics at the Gaiety, Power showed. Unlike Darjeeling and its innocent peers of the hills, Simla was a town of great consequence. It was hard to credit, but it was true. On one hillock stood the palace of the Viceroy of India, the most powerful man in Asia; on another stood the residence of the Commander-in-Chief, general of Asia's greatest army; and the scarlet-liveried messengers who hastened between the two of them, down the mock-Tudor Mall, really were the emissaries of one of the world's most terrific despotisms.

Into this little town, then, hardly more than a village, all the departments of a Great Power were crammed: its strategists in those hideous monkey-offices on the slope, its financial planners, its meteorologists and surveyors, its Director-General of Railways, its Foreign Office, its formidable secret service. The telegraph office in its shaky wooden premises above the Mall kept the Indian Government in touch not only with the imperial headquarters in London, but with its own sub-imperial outposts, Rangoon in the east to Aden in the west. Simla might look hardly more than another genteel watering-place of the hills: but it really was, as Kipling had it, The Abode of the Little Tin Gods.

No cars were ever allowed to drive through Simla, except those of the Viceroy, the Commander-in-Chief and the Governor of the Punjab; but the absence of traffic in these streets, the curious hush that seemed so often to hang around the place, only accentuated the significance of the town, and brought its ambiguities into relief. 'Everything is so English and unpicturesque here', wrote the painter Val Prinsep during a visit to Simla in 1876, 'that except the people one meets are those who rule and make history – a fact one can hardly realize – one would fancy oneself at Margate': and to this day, of all the monuments of empire left behind by the world's conquerors, the Imperial Summer Capital at Simla remains perhaps the most surprising.

(But all is relative. When Lord Curzon moved into the Viceregal Lodge in 1899 he was not much impressed by life in Simla. 'It is like dining every day in the housekeeper's room', he said, 'with the butler and the lady's maid . . .')

Binary system

Down to the plains now. Look at any old Murray's *Handbook to India*, with its finely printed maps in several colours, and almost at random you may find the shape of your average Anglo-Indian city of the interior. It looks like a double star, the one revolving around the other, for it consists of two rigidly separated entities, the Native and the European. The Presidency cities of the coast were peacefully settled, but the cities of the interior were mostly taken by force, and the form the British gave them was the form of subjection. What began as a British military presence on the outskirts of the captured city solidified into a permanent British incubus, different in kind, in scale, and in cartographers' colours from the indigenous settlement.

On those old maps the native city looks like a honeycomb within its medieval walls – compact, more or less circular, mazed with a thousand streets and alleys which opened only occasionally into a temple square, the compound of a mosque, a wide bazaar or a prince's palace. By contrast the new British settlement alongside looks tenuously elongated, stretching far out into the desert or country-side round about, and separated from the walled city, as likely as not, by a wide expanse of empty ground and a railway line with two stations – one for the British side, one for the native. The Anglo-Indian planners kept their settlements at a distance, for health and safety's sake, but at the same time close enough to overawe the indigenes, and for the most part they left the old city alone; sometimes they put a garrison into its fort, but it was only in later years that they began to worry their heads about Improvements, like drainage systems, hygienic markets, wider roads and clock towers, or renaming its ancient streets after viceroys and generals.

The British town itself, outside those old walls, was generally divided into two parts, the Civil Lines and the Cantonment: the former spaciously arranged, with lots of green between its bungalows, the latter severely military, as we saw in

Chapter 4, around its magazines and parade-grounds. Often enough each was independent of the other, with its own clubs, churches and attendant bazaars, but this was a relative separation only: Collector often called on Colonel, club met club at badminton, and in Indian eyes the whole British community was an unmistakable unity, demanding in its native visitors special frames of mind, tones of voice, even modes of dress.

As the Raj grew older the divisions between the cultures became more blurred, on the ground if not in the mind. Some of the indigenous muddle infected the Civil Lines and the Cantonment, some of the imperialist hauteur marched through the city gates into the old town, and as Indians began to enter the higher ranks of the administration the clear-cut barriers between the races began to weaken. The best example of a city of this sort in its half-reconciled maturity was Lahore, the capital of the Punjab, whose magical museum, militant railway station, mausolean Government House and lapidary cathedral we have already visited.

Lahore was a fascinating town, standing boldly beside the Grand Trunk Road on the route to Peshawar and Afghanistan, with the great mountains close to the north and the baking flatlands stretching away to the south. The walled city was a palimpsest of styles and regimes, made magnificent by the Moguls, made powerful by the Sikhs, crowned by a great fort and surrounded by its ditch and grand old wall like a city in a Book of Hours. In the heyday of the caravan trade, when Lahore was one of the great entrepôts of Asia, the place had spilled far beyond its walls: but by the time the British arrived, in 1849, it had contracted once more into its ancient shape.

The conquerors distorted that shape, but at least they gave it a new charm. They filled in the city ditch, for tactical reasons, and turned it into a garden: and running away from the southern side of the old city they built a long boulevard called, like so many such main streets of Anglo-India, the Mall. This connected old Lahore with the military cantonment to the east, and along and round its axis the British built their Civil Lines – New Lahore, its centre being the crossroads which, in their homesick way, they called Charing Cross. By the early twentieth century it was in its prime. Lined with trees and green lawns for much of its length, it provided a parade of official buildings that would have been the pride of any English municipality, and managed to achieve a remarkably harmonious balance with the medieval city looming always in the background.

One by one these ambitious structures revealed themselves, as you drove eastward up the Mall: the University, the Town Hall, the Museum with the big gun Zamzama, Kim's Gun, on its plinth across the road, the High Court all fourteenth-century Pathan on one side, the cathedral all Early English on the other. Here was the General Post Office, like an Islamicized bit of Oxford, and the offices of the *Pioneer* newspaper, and the tall-spired Roman Catholic Cathedral,

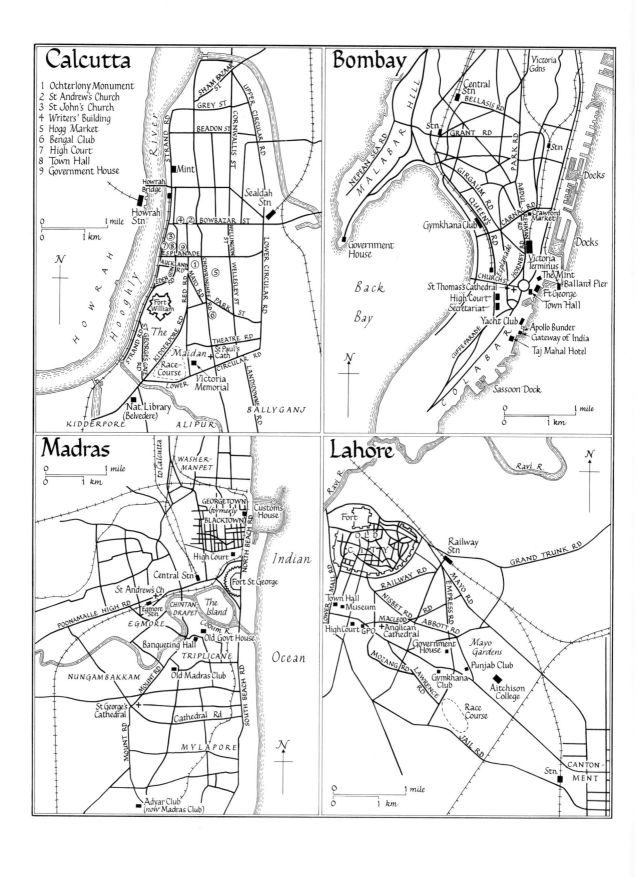

Calcutta

1 Ochterlony Monument
2 St Andrew's Church
3 St John's Church
4 Writers' Building
5 Hogg Market
6 Bengal Club
7 High Court
8 Town Hall
9 Government House

SHAM BAZAR ST
GREY ST
BEADON ST
UPPER CIRCULAR RD
CORNWALLIS ST
STRAND RD
RIVER
Mint
Howrah Bridge
Howrah Stn
Sealdah Stn
BOWBAZAR ST
WELLINGTON ST
CHOWRINGHEE RD
WELLESLEY ST
LOWER CIRCULAR RD
ESPLANADE
AUCKLAND RD
EDEN GDNS
RED RD
MAYO RD
PARK ST
Fort William
THEATRE RD
The Maidan
St Paul's Cath
Race Course
LOWER CIRCULAR RD
Victoria Memorial
LANDSOWNE RD
BALLYGANJ RD
HOOGHLY
HOWRAH
Nat. Library (Belvedere)
KIDDERPORE
KIDDERPORE RD
ST GEORGE'S GATE RD
STRAND RD
ALIPUR
N
0 ___ 1 mile
0 ___ 1 km

Bombay

Victoria Gdns
Central Stn
BELLASIS RD
Stn
GRANT RD
PARK RD
Stn
MALABAR HILL
NEPEAN SEA RD
GIRGAUM RD
QUEEN'S RD
CARNAC RD
ABDUL REHMAN
HORNBY RD
Docks
Crawford Market
Docks
Gymkhana Club
Government House
Back Bay
Victoria Terminus
The Mint
Ballard Pier
St Thomas's Cathedral
CHURCH ST
ESPLANADE
Ft George
Town Hall
High Court
Secretariat
Yacht Club
Apollo Bunder
Gateway of India
Taj Mahal Hotel
CUFFE PARADE
COLABA
Sassoon Dock
N
0 ___ 1 mile
0 ___ 1 km

Madras

0 ___ 1 mile
0 ___ 1 km
to Calcutta
WASHER-MANPET
GEORGETOWN formerly BLACKTOWN
Customs House
NORTH BEACH RD
High Court
Central Stn
Fort St George
St Andrew's Ch
Egmore Stn
CHINTA-DRAPET
The Island
EGMORE
Coum R.
Old Govt House
POONAMALLE HIGH RD
Banqueting Hall
TRIPLICANE
Indian Ocean
NUNGAMBAKKAM
Old Madras Club
MOUNT RD
SOUTH BEACH RD
St George's Cathedral
Cathedral Rd
MYLAPORE
N
Adyar Club (now Madras Club)

Lahore

Ravi R.
Ravi R.
N
Fort
OLD CITY
Railway Stn
GRAND TRUNK RD
RAILWAY RD
LOWER MALL RD
NISBET RD
MAYO RD
EMPRESS RD
ABBOTT RD
Town Hall
Museum
MACLEOD RD
High Court
GPO
Anglican Cathedral
Government House
Mayo Gardens
Punjab Club
MOZANG RD
LAWRENCE RD
Gymkhana Club
Aitchison College
Race Course
JAIL RD
Stn
CANTON-MENT
0 ___ 1 mile
0 ___ 1 km

and then there was Charing Cross, with shops all around it, and the slightly sinister-looking Freemasons' Hall, and the inevitable statue of Queen Victoria in the middle, and Faletti's Hotel, where *everyone* stayed, just a step or two up the road towards the railway station.

Government House now on the left, white and green awnings, with a glimpse of the gazebo on its garden hump, and across the road the Gymkhana Club looking out, from its back windows, handily over the racecourse. The classical Punjab Club looked like a military academy, the Hindu-style Aitchison College looked like a Maharajah's palace, and to mark the end of this happy esplanade there ran beneath the road the still brown water of the Upper Bari Doab Canal, one of the proud creations of Anglo-Indian engineers, lined here with pretty waterside walks and weeping willows.

Scattered off the Mall were the bungalows of the Civil Lines, each within its substantial compound, the Secretariat building long and low, the Mayo Hospital philanthropically towered. Further away, encapsulated within their own enclaves, were the districts of two special societies, distinct alike from the communities of Old and New Lahore: the railway colony for the mostly Eurasian employees of the North-West Railway Company, and a mile or two to the south, at a prudent distance from the fiercely sectarian passions of the walled city, a Model Town laid out by the Anglo-Indians specifically for their Hindu dependants, who built their own houses within its radial pattern, and established their own club upon its central green.

It was a fine city, no doubt about it. Many Anglo-Indians thought it the finest in India, but then the British, on the whole, preferred the Muslim ambience to the Hindu, and the presence of the great Moguls even in memory tempered their insularity rather, and brought out the best in them. They responded more readily to Muslim architecture, too. In Lahore not only did the Governor of the Punjab, as we know, eat his meals inside a former Muslim tomb, but until Mr Scott provided them with their new cathedral the Anglicans of Lahore worshipped in the octagonal mausoleum of Akbar's favourite concubine Anarkali, Pomegranate Blossom, which was inscribed with the Divine Names of Allah, but which they converted to their own uses by removing the lady's sarcophagus to an ante-room, and placing a great gilt cross on the dome.

'A humbug of palaces'

The three Presidency cities came to fruition, found themselves one might say, at different moments, brought to their respective climaxes by historical and economic circumstance that differed from one coast to the other, one generation to the next. The first to get there was Calcutta. Though by the end of the nineteenth century the second largest city in the entire British Empire, still it reached its true apogee relatively early in its history: in the first half of the nineteenth century, when its social complacency was undisturbed, its political supremacy was complete and its prosperity seemed unbounded. The village of palaces, as visitors had called the place in the previous century, had grown into the city of palaces, and Chowringhee was the richest street in the East.

During the centuries of British rule Calcutta was to grow a thousandfold, but to the end the European centre of it, the capital proper, remained essentially as it was then, in shape as in function. Its pattern was deliberately grand. It was laid out as a great capital must be, with authority. It occupied two sides of a square, on the north and the east. The western side was formed by the Hooghly River, the southern was left open to suburban development. Around the whole a defensive ditch was dug, later to delineate the city's inner road, and the centre of the square was occupied by the grand expanse of the *maidan*, with the protective stronghold of Fort William at its south-east corner.

The northern side of the square, at right angles to the river, was formed by the Esplanade, and here most of the great public buildings of the city were grouped. At its centre stood Government House, exactly symmetrical in shape itself, upon which the whole city seemed to be focused. Directly aligned upon its main entrance, north of the house, was Wellesley Place, which was stacked on each side with Government offices of classical pose, and beyond that was Tank Square, later Dalhousie Square, which was lined too with official buildings, dominated in later years by the great dome of the Post Office, and overlooked by the spires of St. Andrew's Church on one side, St. John's on the other. East and west of Government House, in grand array, stood the Town Hall, the High Court, the Mint, and sundry other institutions, and the whole rank of them had as its background the forested masts and riggings of the shipping in the river, at the western end of the street, or in later times the immense latticed silhouette of the Howrah Bridge.

Some of these buildings were in the Gothic mode, creeping in with the nineteenth century, but the shape of it all remained distinctly classical, and old prints of the city are full of clear and elegant vistas: white terraces as John Nash might have built them, arched gates through which palatial casements showed, the steeple of St. Andrew's finely breaking the long horizontal of the Writers' Buildings or framed elegantly at the top of Old Court House Street. Especially in the early years of the century, when Calcutta's trees had not grown up yet, when its plaster was still brilliantly white, its porticoes were not yet cracked or crumbled, there was a Grecian brilliance to it all which painters loved and foreign visitors wondered at.

Such was official Calcutta, a city of protocol and grand pretension, 'a humbug of palaces' as Edward Lear thought, after staying with his friend the Viceroy in 1873. At right angles to it, however, running north to south, was the city's second

T. S. Gregson designed Calcutta's Royal Exchange (*left*) in 1916, and it was opened by Lord Ronaldshay. The General Post Office (*below*) is nearby – a green copper dome above a Greek colonnade. An inlaid brass line on the steps marks the boundary of the original Fort William. The GPO was designed by Walter Granville, Architect to the Government of India.

Views of the *maidan*, Calcutta – showing the Ochterlony Monument, Government House, the High Court and the spires of St. John's and St. Andrew's Churches; and, in the modern photograph, the tower of St. Paul's Cathedral.

façade: Chowringhee, the main commercial street, which ran parallel to the river, down the edge of the *maidan*, to peter out in the pleasant southern suburbs of Ballyganj and Alipur. This, as we know, was originally a residential street, lined with the big, rectangular houses of the nabobs: but as the years passed shops sprang up between the mansions, and hotels, and a theatre, and then they put the Bengal Club there, and the Indian Museum, until by mid-Victorian times it had become a rich metropolitan mixture of a street, which exuded wealth and confidence, and blazed with the brass plates of successful entrepreneurs.

Between these two great arms extended the *maidan*, two square miles of it, with its long riverside boulevard, its numberless walks and gardens, its plethora of statuary, its peculiar Ochterlony column, its pagoda looted from Burma, its cricket pitch where they played the first game of cricket in India, its Red Road built especially for the carriages of Viceroys. Over by the river lay Fort William, half-sunk in the landscape; to the south there arose, in the first years of Queen Victoria's reign, the tall silhouette of Calcutta Cathedral, in the first years of George V's, the Victoria Memorial Museum; and with the towers and domes of officialdom on its northern flank, the opulent blocks of Chowringhee to the east, the masts and sails of the ships in the river and these great monuments of faith and security to the south, the *maidan* at Calcutta commanded one of the finest park prospects anywhere.

It was unmistakably a metropolitan prospect. Indeed, to some sensitive observers it sometimes seemed all too like some heedless European capital doomed to revolution: the royal palace was there for the burning, the mansions swarmed with minions, the generals and the courtiers strutted, the great white official buildings stood side by side like another St. Petersburg beside a warmer river. And beyond it all another Calcutta extended – Indian Calcutta, stretching away almost unimaginably into the flat brown hinterland, over the muddy river, district after district, slum after slum, far beyond the country houses of Alipur and Garden Reach, up the pot-holed track of the Grand Trunk Road and the railway line to the interior, where in an immense confusion of mills, factories, and shanty towns Calcutta petered out at last into the Ganges plain. Indians had flocked to the purlieus of old Fort William from the moment the British had established it there, and they had never stopped coming.

Almost until the end of the Raj British Calcutta managed to insulate itself from this reality, and looked out across its *maidan* as splendidly as ever, but almost from the start, too, there were Englishmen who recognized its horror and its injustice. 'In those quarters of the town occupied principally by the native inhabitants', a committee reported as early as 1803, 'the houses have been built without order or regularity and the streets and lanes have been formed without attention to the health, convenience or safety of the inhabitants'. This was the civic planning of *laissez-faire*, one of the Victorian Empire's nearest approximations to an ideology: if the starving millions of Ireland, during the 1847 famine, were to be left to the mercies of the market economy, the Indians who flocked in search of livelihood to the great emporium of Calcutta must arrange their own social affairs. (And the Irish analogy was noticed early. Lord Valentia, looking behind palatial appearances in 1803, thought the mud-and-thatch houses of the natives 'perfectly resembled the cabins of the poorest classes in Ireland'.)

By the 1820s the British were metalling the streets of European Calcutta, but in 1836 the Chief Magistrate of the city reported that in the native town the lanes were all 'very narrow, very filthy and bounded generally by deep open ditches'. Girish Chandra Ghosh, writing in 1863, described passing through the splendours of the imperial city with 'streets smooth as bowling-greens, wide, dustless and dry, where even the lamp-posts seem to be weekly varnished', into these lanes, where his 'affrighted horse will obstinately back from pits in the thoroughfares wide enough to bury all the rubbish in the adjoining houses'. Kipling, twenty years later, called the whole native city 'a surfeited muck-heap', while the historian H. E. A. Cotton, in 1903, reported that 'not a thousand yards from Government House troops of jackals may be heard after sunset sweeping through the deserted streets . . .'.

Many of the British never faced up to these truths, or really thought of Calcutta as anything more than their own grand part of it. To Curzon, Viceroy in 1903, though the city then contained only 30,000 Europeans and Eurasians to 800,000 Indians, 'yet a glance at the buildings of the town, at the river and the roar and the smoke, is sufficient to show that Calcutta is in reality a European city set down upon Asiatic soil'. They never overcame this illusion, they never caught up with its ravages, and the Calcutta they left behind them when they left, 'the second city of the British Empire', was one of the most tragic of all human settlements, proudly though its towers and domes still stood around the soon to be bedraggled *maidan*.

'Urbs prima'

The port of Bombay reached *its* apogee, without question, in the 1860s. There the British did much better, if not architecturally, at least socially. Florence Nightingale once pointed out that Victorian Bombay had achieved a lower death-rate than London, itself the healthiest city in Europe: 'if we do not take care, Bombay will outstrip us in the sanitary race. People will be ordered for the benefit of their health to Bombay'. 'It had been the greatest good fortune of Bombay', said a local guidebook just a century later, 'that its civil Administration has all along been of the highest order. This has made Bombay the beautiful and has proved the bona fides of the famous proverb "A thing of beauty is a joy for ever"'.

Bombay was different in several essential ways from the other two Presidency towns. It had never seen battles, as they both had; it had come peacefully into British hands, and was never attacked either by foreign rivals or by local potentates. It was not a mainland settlement like the others, but originally a string of islands, separated sometimes by open water, sometimes by mud-flat and marsh, which sheltered the wide inlet of Bom Bahia, 'beautiful bay', from the Arabian Sea. Also Bombay was always more cosmopolitan than either Madras or Calcutta: a great international port, it was also a great manufacturing centre, and the Parsees in particular, who played such a prominent role in its financial and business affairs, were always on easy terms with the British, giving the place a more relaxed, less colonial feeling.

And another difference was that, unlike Madras or Calcutta, Bombay was built against a background of surpassing beauty. Early pictures of the town show it almost Riviera-like. Scattered along the islands are its homes and offices, churches and warehouses, framed preferably in the palm trees dear to every Anglo-Indian water-colourist: behind them the great bay stretches wonderfully blue, with other bumpy islets here and there, and white-sailed dhows winging it to sea, and in the distance the massed blue-green highlands of the Western Ghats, the massif which separated this Maharashtra coast from the interior of the Deccan.

Structurally Bombay began, like its peers, as a fort and warehouse upon the water, and the district around the original castle was always to remain the centre of its business life. Its progress was slow, and for years it remained a backwater, far from the main trading routes, cut off by the Ghats from the rest of India and outclassed by the booming Calcutta. It grew, nevertheless. Over the years the separate islands were linked first by causeways, then by such a mesh of highways that they became indistinguishable as islands at all, and Bombay was no longer an archipelago, but a peninsula. A few buildings of consequence arose in the downtown area, on its eastern shore – Colonel Cowper's splendid Town Hall, the Mint, St. Thomas's Cathedral; and then suddenly, in the middle of the Victorian century, Bombay sprang into life, and became a metropolis.

Four circumstances transformed the place. The opening of the Suez Canal made Bombay the first port of Indian call for ships sailing to the East. The new Indian railways linked it with the rest of the subcontinent. The American Civil War, cutting off supplies of American cotton from European markets, created a vast demand for Bombay cotton instead. And there came into authority in the city a man eager to proclaim all this new pre-eminence in stone, mortar and city plan. All four things happened within a single decade, between 1862 and 1869.

We have already met Sir Bartle Frere, Governor of Bombay from 1862 to 1867, embodied in a museum, a market, a statue, a Flora Fountain and the remarkable Government House he caused to be built up in the hills at Poona. He was the most energetic and imaginative civic reformer of British India. He was immensely proud of his achievements in Bombay – *Urbs Prima in Indis*, as its civic motto said. He it was whose sanitary arrangements so impressed Florence Nightingale, and he presided over a rebuilding of the city so grandiose that by the end of the nineteenth century George Steevens the journalist could say that any Briton would feel himself a greater man for the sight of Bombay, while in the twentieth Aldous Huxley could claim that 'architecturally Bombay is one of the most appalling cities in either hemisphere', and Robert Byron called it an architectural Sodom.

It was a matter of taste. Bombay had no neo-Roman yearnings, like Calcutta. Instead it set out to be the very model of an imperial business town, and in this it succeeded. Its shape, when Sir Bartle and his architectural planner James Trub-shawe had finished with it, was nothing if not functional, and its manner was at once grand and practical. The old castle walls were done away with, and the whole Fort area was transformed from an enclave, tight beside the sea, to an assembly place or entrepôt: the new railway lines ran to its edge, ending in magnificent terminals, while the new docks were so close that the masts of the ships could be seen from the brokers' offices. In the heart of it all, around the green which had been the centre of the original fort, a handsome commercial plaza arose: arcaded like the Rue de Rivoli, with a garden in the middle like a London square, overlooked on one side by the Town Hall, on the other by the Cathedral, Elphinstone Circle was a paradigm of commercial taste and efficiency.

From Elphinstone Circle, and its surrounding streets of shops and offices, a wide central thoroughfare crossed to the other side of the narrow peninsula: and there a line of official buildings arose in a wide variety of Victorian styles. This was a spectacular display, though odious to Mr Huxley. The great structures stood in grandiloquent parade: the Post Office (by Trubshawe himself), the High Court, the University with its high campanile, Colonel Wilkins's formidable Secretariat. Only a succession of green parks lay between them and the sea, and they stood tremendously glaring across Back Bay where every approaching ship could see them.

Another great street ran diagonally back to the Apollo Bunder on the eastern shore; and along this axis there presently arose the Prince of Wales Museum with its glittering dome, the Taj Mahal Hotel flamboyantly gabled, and eventually the Gateway of India on the foreshore. Most of these structures, and many more, went up in less than half a century, and Bombay was to remain one of the most characteristically Victorian cities in the world, displaying all the grand effrontery of Victorian eclectism – Swiss timbering, German gables, Dutch roofs, Tudor casements, French Renaissance turrets, Romanesque arches, Early English vaulting, touches of Olde Englishe, the whole embellished very often with the usual obscurely defined orientalisms. Bombay 'had the misfortune to develop', sneered

Elphinstone Circle, Bombay – today, and eighty years ago, from afar. St. Thomas's Cathedral is seen in the early photograph; today it is surrounded by the high-rise buildings of Bombay's great commercial houses.

Huxley, 'during what was, perhaps, the darkest period of all architectural history'; the Town Hall, he thought, was almost the only gentleman 'among so many architectural cads and pretentious bounders'.

But it worked very well. Frere's vision was bombastic perhaps, but enlightened. He saw to it that Back Bay, on the ocean side of the town, was developed as a pleasure promenade. He sponsored parks and gardens everywhere. A new cantonment was built on the southern island of the old archipelago, Colabar, where the sea breezes would keep the barracks healthy; a racecourse was built to the north; a comfortable suburb grew on the high ground of Malabar Hill, overlooking Back Bay, and Frere himself sensibly moved out of the gloomy old Government House he had inherited, a former Jesuit church, into the delightful complex of white bungalows on Malabar Point. All the municipal virtues dear to the Victorians were skilfully exemplified in his Bombay – profit, responsibility, authority, healthy pleasure – and the city prospered greatly under their influence, and became, so one English visitor boldly claimed in 1891, 'without exception the finest modern city in Asia, and the noblest monument of British enterprise in the world'.

In the early years of the twentieth century the architect George Wittet drew up a plan for the further improvement of the city, on even more monumental lines; later still visionaries proposed bridging the great bay itself, and establishing satellite towns on its other shores; but these proposals came to nothing, and even now it is Sir Bartle's Bombay, clustered all around by upstart skyscrapers, that resists the pressures of time and population on the shores of the great bay, and stands up for the principles of Civic Improvement.

The enclave

Many people thought Madras, on the Coromandel coast, the epitome of British India. Its southern climate gave romance to it, its foliage was picturesque, its natives were lithe, attractive and courtly, the Apostle Thomas was supposed to have been martyred there, and it was the place where, in the old days before the development of Bombay, new arrivals in India generally made their first uncomfortable landfall. It was also the oldest sovereign settlement of British India, its territory having been ceded to the Honourable Company in 1639.

By the late eighteenth century Madras was a fine sight, when your ship approached it at last after so many months at sea. By then Fort St. George, its original nucleus, had developed into a handsome group of classical structures, moated and ramparted, with the tall colonnaded front of the administrative buildings proud above its walls, and the church and barracks all around. Along the waterfront, too, were handsome classical structures, with the urbane silhouette of the Ice House, and a lighthouse in the form of a Doric column, and rows of merchants' offices. Everything was clad in the brilliant white *chunam* plaster of the country, and this too, seen flashing and shining from your foredeck in the sunshine, gave Madras an air of exuberant welcome.

The city had developed in the usual way. There was nothing much on the site until the British settled there, and the Company built a special quarter, Black Town, for the natives who presently came to live around the trading-station. The place was first constituted as 'the town of Fort St. George and City of Madrasspatam' – the town for the Europeans, the city for the Indians – and early maps show the segregation clearly. The Fort itself is built at the water's edge, protected on its south side by the mouth of the Cooum River. Next door to it, separated by a wall and itself fortified, Madrasspatam was laid out in a strict grid system. Inland again, divided from Fort and Black Town alike by a canal, an English residential suburb was established, and well beyond, at the foot of the hills, was the cantonment.

Around this triple core, very gradually, the city of Madras had taken shape. The Fort remained the headquarters of Government until the end of the Empire. Black Town outgrew its enclosing walls and went up in the world, for many of the big British business houses preferred to have offices there, close to the Fort and the waterfront. The European suburb spread slowly, and loosely, inland. In 1800 the Governor, the second Lord Clive, shifted his own residence out of the Fort a mile or two from the waterfront, and by mid-Victorian times the big shops, the churches, the Madras Club, were well away from the sea. Madras assumed on the map a horizontal rather than a vertical look – east to west into the interior, rather than north to south down the coast. Garden houses spread even deeper into the countryside: the Governor acquired *another* palace, five miles from the sea this time, which soon attracted suburbia into its neighbourhood. By 1839 a visitor could report that very few Englishmen lived in Madras proper – 'they live in country houses scattered for miles through the interior, and even the shopkeepers who can afford it have detached bungalows for their families'.

This dispersal gave Madras a spacious but somehow ineffectual feel. The city was soon left behind by its rivals Bombay and Calcutta, and never did come to feel a metropolis. Kipling, who called Bombay 'Royal and Dower-royal', and Calcutta 'Power on silt', could describe poor Madras only as 'a withered beldame'. It was a city without depth: for all its structural changes the waterfront remained its true focus, as it always had been, and the old Fort itself remained the heart of it, with its saluting guns still above the moat outside, with its black granite columns gleaming still on the façade of the Secretariat, and with the Union Jack flying to the last days of Empire from the tallest flagstaff in India outside its great sea gate.

Yet it happened that architecturally Madras came to fruition late in the day, later than either Calcutta or Bombay, and this is because in the 1870s and 1880s there were two remarkable architects working in the city – both dedicated to Indo-Saracenic architecture in its most romantic kind, and both learned in Indian forms and methods. One was Henry Irwin, whose work we have already met, the other was Robert Chisholm, who came to Madras as a young man in 1865. Between them these two men, in the last decades of the Victorian century, gave Madras an altogether new and startling silhouette. If you came to Madras at the start of the nineteenth century you thought you were approaching a foreshore lined with Grecian temples: if you came at the end of the century, it was like sailing into some fantasy of orientalism.

Far down the Marina, the waterfront esplanade of the city, the new structures extended, enclosing within them Fort, Ice House and all. There were the four pepper-pot minarets of the University's Senate House, and the tower of its library, and Presidency College sprawled along the promenade and the huge Chepauk Palace that Chisholm frothily remodelled for the Government when the last of the Nawabs of the Carnatic died: and on the other side of the Fort were the big Gothic Post Office, and the Customs House, and the transcendent High Court with its lighthouse on the top – the whole constituting a marvellously airy and festive waterfront, floating there all pinnacles and bubbles in the southern heat above the surf.

These developments did not much change the underlying character of Madras – they were not, like Frere's constructions in Bombay, true reflections of the city's condition. Madras never did catch up with its rivals again, and remained always an easygoing, overtaken, slightly disappointed place, more charming than decisive. Things changed slowly in Madras, if they changed at all. It was only in 1911, after a visit by the King-Emperor, that Black Town was renamed Georgetown, in his honour.

The last city

So to the last and most calculated of the British civic creations in India. It might seem quixotic, it was certainly extravagant, to build a brand-new capital for an empire which already possessed these magnificent seaport towns, but all mundane considerations apart, the British pined for a plateau more historical from which to rule their great dominion. At a time when Indian nationalism was beginning to stir they wanted somewhere elevated, central and allegorical, somewhere in the line of Indian history, where they could be seen as true successors to earlier dynasts. They wanted to rule as princes! So in the rule of the King-Emperor George V they added another to the seven successive capital cities which had, at one time or another, waxed and waned upon the bitter plain of Delhi, beside the Jumna River in Punjab.

Delhi had held a special meaning for them since they first took it in 1804. The spectacle of those crumbled strongholds of the past powerfully appealed to their imaginations, especially as their own immediate predecessors, the Moguls, had ended up as shadow-monarchs in the Red Fort there. Also the most heroic British exploits of the Indian Mutiny, the last real military campaign in India proper, had been achieved in recapturing the city from the rebels, and its purlieus were thick with the bones of British soldiers and the legends of British arms. Delhi's climate, if terribly hot in the summer, was stimulating in the winter. Its population was a symbolic mixture of the Indian peoples. Hindu, Muslim and Sikh. It was central in a manner of speaking, standing on the Grand Trunk Road midway between Calcutta and the north-west frontier, and connected by rail and road with Bombay, Madras and Karachi.

Also it had already been imperially sanctified by the assemblage in its outskirts of three great royal durbars, in 1877, 1903 and 1911. The tented camps established for these occasions, on flat ground north of the old city of Delhi, were almost cities in themselves. They had their own railways, telephone services, paved roads, water-mains, electric power, and the durbar of 1911, whose tents covered ten square miles and whose railway station had ten platforms, was designed to accommodate 25,000 people – as many as Delhi itself.

It was at the third of these durbars that the King-Emperor himself announced the intention to create a brand-new capital for his empire in India, to bind its provinces into closer unity, and provide a new basis for political advance. It was not the first such project in British imperial history: the Canadians, in the previous century, had cemented their shaky confederation by building a capital at Ottawa, a site allegedly chosen by Queen Victoria by sticking a hat-pin into a map, while the Australian were, in 1911, hard at work on their new federal capital of Canberra. Nor was the idea new in India. They had been talking about it for half a century, and at one time or another Meerut, Ranchi and Agra had all been suggested as possible sites.

Twentieth-century communications made it perfectly feasible (ten months before the King's announcement, the world's first airmail flight had been made in India). Even so, the decision was much criticized. Some people thought it smacked of hubris, others thought it anachronistic, while the citizens of Bengal believed it would be disastrous for Calcutta, for so many generations the centre of British power in India. But the India Office in London, Lord Hardinge the Viceroy and the King himself were all united in wanting it; within three months a commission was set up to establish an exact site for the capital, and presently 'Ned' Lutyens and Herbert Baker were commissioned to design it.

The original intention was to make the new capital an organic partner to the existing walled city of the Moguls, Shahjahanabad – 'one city', said Lord Hardinge', 'not two'. Actually this was already more racially integrated than most

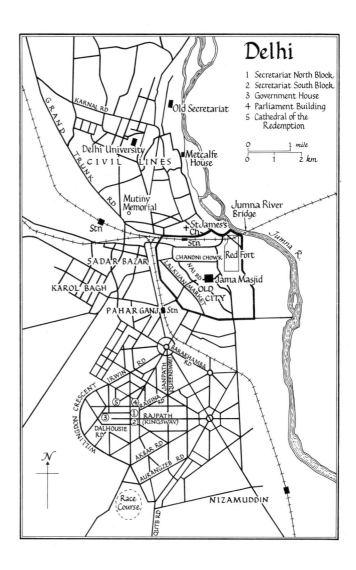

such Indian cities: the Red Fort was a British barracks, and there were many Anglo-Indian institutions within its walls. H. V. Lanchester the town planner, who was brought in as a temporary adviser in the early days of the enterprise, imagined the new city essentially as an extension of the old, and the first rough plan envisaged an imperial Governmental complex directly facing Shahjahanabad and united with it by a highway running through a new gate in its walls directly to its principal mosque, the Jami Masjid. For once the principle of 'shut-upness' would have been abandoned, and the new capital would have been a truly un-segregated city.

It did not happen. Though there were many who wanted New Delhi to be built in predominantly Indian architectural styles – Hardinge himself, the Public

Works Department and many arts and crafts architects both in India and in England – there were few to lobby for racial and social integration. By the time Lutyens, who was to be responsible for the general design of the city, began work in earnest in 1913, it was evident that New Delhi was to be yet another enclave, built in a fundamentally European fashion, and firmly separated by plan as by manner from the existing city of the indigenes. The axial road to Shahjahanabad petered out – it entailed demolishing too many houses, they said, and also conservationists objected to rupturing the city wall – and the Acropolis of the new capital, the Viceroy's House and the Secretariat, was turned away from the old city to face the river. The pattern became familiar after all. New Delhi and Old acquired separate identities, the new becoming in effect the Civil Lines to the old: even the dead land created by the British around Shahjahanabad was left clearly detectable, and over the ridge to the west, here as everywhere, not too near but not too far the British built New Delhi's military cantonment.

It was hardly a radical scheme, and Lutyens was later to be attacked, too, for his failure to achieve a renaissance of Indian arts and crafts in the course of the great construction. But at least New Delhi turned out to be majestically spacious of style, Civil Lines to end them all, if only because it was a twentieth-century city, geared to the car, the bus or at least the ubiquitous bicycle, the telephone rather than the chitty. It had sixty miles of main streets, sixty miles of service roads. Kingsway, its ceremonial central axis, was two miles long, and twice as wide as the Champs Elysées. Huge, to the pedestrian apparently interminable, green spaces divided one quarter from another; immense traffic circles had to be crossed, enormous ornamental ponds circumvented, whole suburbs of bungalows to be passed through.

The city in its final form was roughly hexagonal in shape, and was focused upon three climactic points. In the west was the Governmental centre, Lutyens's Viceroy's House, Baker's Secretariat and Legislature buildings; in the east was the ceremonial plaza and junction of roads around the Arch of India; in the north was a shopping and commercial centre, Connaught Circus, built as a circular colonnade by the Government architect Robert Tor Russell. These three foci were linked by two main highways, Kingsway running east to west, Queensway north to south, and by an elaborate mesh of dead straight roads which frequently met in traffic roundabouts: while the originally planned main axis, from the Acropolis to Shahjahanabad, did at least run on a mathematical alignment north-eastward towards the Jami Masjid, though it never got further than Connaught Circus.

All around was a garden city. Lutyens had been the chief designer of Hampstead Garden City in England, and he applied many of its lessons here. New Delhi was entirely a Government town. Ordinary folk had no place there, and the Indian populace at large was excluded. Housing within the enclave was strictly hierarchical. There were palaces for the Viceroy and the Commander-in-Chief, the second most powerful man in India. Palaces too, though lesser ones, like the houses of the Boyars in St. Petersburg, for the chiefs of the Native States, surrounded by a princely park closed to the public. Then in decreasing order of domestic grandeur came a whole roster of bungalows, a catalogue of the form, ranging from fine Tuscan-pillared villas with five or six acres for Chief Secretaries or High Court judges to four-rooms-and-a-verandah for an Assistant Chief Controller of Stores, or terraced huts for Indian peons. You could tell by a family's address where they stood in the line of official precedence (which recognized sixty-one rungs on the ladder); caste was as carefully honoured in the disposition of these houses as ever it was among the Hindus.

All the roads were beautifully planted with trees, as far as possible a different tree for each street, and their names were scrupulously chosen. If more than seventy of them remembered British sovereigns, generals and satraps, nine recalled previous rulers of Delhi, Tughluq to Jaisingh. You could go via Curzon Road and Asoka Road to get to Queen Victoria Road. Cornwallis Road ran parallel to Aurangzeb Road. King Edward Road was around the corner from Akbar Road, and if you followed Parliament Street over Connaught Circus into Minto Road it would take you in the end to the Ajmeri Gate of Shahjahanabad, the capital of the Great Moguls, where the Red Fort glowered still above the river, and the bazaars of Chandni Chouk seethed and clattered as ever they did.

It was fine enough, but it failed. 'It is really a great event in the history of the world and of architecture', Baker wrote to Lutyens. 'It would only be possible now under a despotism . . . Hurrah for despotism!' But the truth was that by 1919, when work on New Delhi began to reach fruition, the despotism was consciously weakening. Even Lutyens and Baker must sometimes have wondered, as they watched their city develop, for how long it would remain an imperial capital, and how many years it would be before an Indian Head of State sat in the Durbar Room of the Viceroy's House: and this half-cock, unsure feeling they unwittingly symbolized themselves, for disagreeing about the gradient of Kingsway as it approached the climax of the Viceroy's House, they so arranged matters that at the most important moment of the whole approach, as the road drew near to the Secretariat buildings, most of the palace momentarily but disconcertingly disappeared from view, leaving only its dome showing above the tarmac. Baker said it did not matter. Lutyens called it his Bakerloo.

New Delhi was an anomaly – too late for arrogance, too soon for regrets, too uncertain to get its gradients right. Its very name was flaccid. Lutyens had suggested Georgebad, or Marypore, or in testier moments Oozapore or New Belhi, but in fact New Delhi struck about the right note of diminished flair. The city lacked both the insolence of conquest and the generosity of concession, and by its deliberate separateness it perpetuated invidious old comparisons: in the 1930s some 65,000 people lived in the thirty-three square miles of New Delhi, some

Simla.

350,000 in the seven square miles of Shahjahanabad; the death-rate in the Old City varied from thirty to forty-seven per thousand, while in New Delhi it was nine.

New Delhi came to life well enough in its moments of ceremony, when the great processions moved along Kingsway with the proper lurching of elephants, flutter of pennants, beat of drums, and reverberation of armoured cars. But when nothing in particular was happening, when it was just another bureaucratic day in the capital, the clerks scratching away in Baker's pavilions, the Viceroy bored and overworked in his study over the Mogul gardens, the deputies arguing incessantly within the heavy rotunda of the Assembly, then there seemed something wearisome, colourless, even a little drab to the imperial immensities of the place.

True to its times

And in this, New Delhi was true to its times. Calcutta, Madras, Bombay, Lahore, paradoxical Simla and the sweet hill-stations had come into being in the full flush of imperial enterprise and success, commercial, military, political, even social, when the soldiers of the Raj were storming from triumph to triumph across India, the merchants grew richer every day, the formidable administrators of empire knew exactly what they wanted, and even the memsahibs in their bungalows, homesick and frustrated though they might be, felt they were performing God's will beneath the *punkahs*.

New Delhi was a figure of a different age. The British Empire had already lost its assurance, when this capital was built. Tragedy had saddened it, the 'too heavy burden', as Matthew Arnold had called it long before, had weakened its will. The tautness had gone, and the punch, and the conviction of right and purpose, and much of the arrogance, so that these streets too, skilfully though they were planned and lovingly executed, lacked fizz or astonishment – lacked imperialness, in fact.

For the idea of empire, like the idea of war, depended for its style as for its success upon effrontery: in dangerous enterprises of this kind, as Clausewitz had written, 'the worst errors are caused by a spirit of benevolence'.

8 · Envoi

Styles without shadows

'In 2000 years', wrote Herbert Baker to Edwin Lutyens once, 'there must be an Imperial Lutyens tradition in Indian architecture': but within a few years of the demise of the British Empire in India, nearly all its architectural traditions were dead too. The bungalow, bungalla, banggolo, bungle-oh outlived the Empire as it had pre-dated it: but all the devious adaptations, hybrids and devices of the imperial architects, from the Palladian to the Lutyenesque, were abandoned as soon as the Somerset Light Infantry had marched off through the Gateway of India. They were styles without shadows, and the indigenous architects of India, coming into their own once more, threw themselves immediately into the international modernist movement, and put up concrete blocks and curtain-walling everywhere. Nobody ever built, nor ever will, another Victoria Terminus, a second Viceroy's House, a High Court like Henry Irwin's at Madras or an esplanade like Darjeeling's Mall. Almost all the buildings described in this book went up within 150 years: the British had come, the British went, and architecturally there was an end to it.

Reflections

Nor can it really be claimed that an Anglo-Indian taste caught on anywhere else, like chinoiserie, or the Egyptian motifs that were popular in the West in the nineteenth century. It is true that in Georgian and Regency times some buildings were erected in England in a frisky combination of Muslim, Hindu and Gothick – the Prince Regent's Brighton Pavilion, Sezincote House in Gloucestershire, the domed house that Warren Hastings built for himself at Daylesford in the Cotswolds – and Sir Osbert Sitwell once suggested that in these a British imperial style might 'lie dormant'. It never, however, awoke, and few English landowners were much inspired, either, by John Loudon's design for an 'Indian Cottage', which he published in his *Encyclopedia* in 1833 – it was a two-roomed bungalow with a

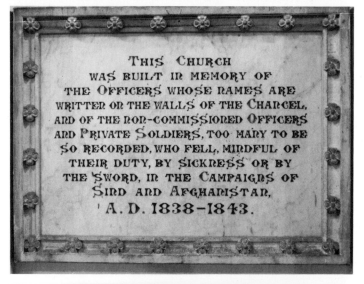

In part of a general Plan
Ordered by the GOVERNOR GENERAL and COUNCIL
28th of January 1784.
For the perpetual prevention of Famine
In these Provinces
THIS GRANARY
Was erected by CAPTAIN JOHN GARSTIN Engineer
Compleated on the 20th of July 1786
First filled and publickly closed by

Plaques: on John Garstin's famous 'Gola', or granary, in Patna; in the Afghan Church, Bombay; and, loveliest of all, on Rose Aylmer's tomb in the South Park Street Cemetery, Calcutta. Walter Savage Landor wrote this brief but graceful poem to the beautiful young woman, whom he glimpsed briefly before she died.

THIS CHURCH
WAS BUILT IN MEMORY OF
THE OFFICERS WHOSE NAMES ARE
WRITTEN ON THE WALLS OF THE CHANCEL,
AND OF THE NON-COMMISSIONED OFFICERS
AND PRIVATE SOLDIERS, TOO MANY TO BE
SO RECORDED, WHO FELL, MINDFUL OF
THEIR DUTY, BY SICKNESS OR BY
THE SWORD, IN THE CAMPAIGNS OF
SIND AND AFGHANISTAN,
A.D. 1838–1843.

WITH EVERY VIRTUE EVERY GRACE
ROSE AYLMER ALL WERE THINE.

ROSE AYLMER, WHOM THESE WAKEFUL EYES
MAY WEEP, BUT NEVER SEE.
A NIGHT OF MEMORIES AND OF SIGHS
I CONSECRATE TO THEE

verandah, a dome and a central ornamental chimney, done in an oriental Gothick and suggested as suitable for a childless estate labourer and his wife. As for the more pretentious mongrel styles of Victorian times, those prodigies of suggestive synthesis, they were never attempted at all outside the frontiers of India.

Architectural reflections of the Raj, nevertheless, did show here and there around the world. To the east, for example, the city of Singapore grew up in the image of Calcutta under the influence of a Director of Public Works, G. D. Coleman, who had gone there from India, and who graced the infant port with a lovely series of Tank Square public buildings, Chowringhee godowns, and even a proxy South Park Street Cemetery. To the west the port of Aden, on the Arabian peninsula, was built as an outpost of the Raj, and looked like it, since every category of Anglo-Indian architecture was translated there, club, cantonment, Government House and all. Scattered throughout the British Empire, Hong Kong to Caribbean, were the military forms of the Raj: the verandah'd barrack-block, so inescapable a part of the Indian scene, was thought as suitable for Aldershot as for Rawalpindi, while high in the Blue Mountains of Jamaica Newcastle Barracks faithfully followed the guide-lines for health and happiness laid down on behalf of his soldiers by C. J. Napier far away.

And in England, the way things went was tellingly represented, in architectural language, by the succession of buildings which housed the London headquarters of the Indian connection. The first permanent office of the Honourable East India Company, occupied in the seventeenth century, was a wooden-fronted house on Leadenhall Street in the City, with an open balcony, a coat of arms, a big painted fresco of ships at sea and the wooden figure of a merchant poised on top, the whole looking somewhat like a squashed or fattened grandfather clock. The next office, built on the same site in the eighteenth century, was a grand Palladian palace, rusticated below, balustraded above, with a portico of six Ionic columns, a huge pediment containing an effigy of George III in Roman costume defending the Commerce of the East, and a crowning figure of Britannia sitting on a lion and supported by Europe on a horse and Asia on a camel.

The Company died, the Crown took over, and in the nineteenth century Sir Gilbert Scott built the India Office overlooking St. James's Park, the subject of a famous architectural controversy, gloomy, enormous, unexpectedly enlivened by a tower at the corner and decorated all over with images of Governors-General, Indian cities, racial types and loyal feudatories. And finally, as the Empire began its retreat and India advanced towards independent nationhood, Sir Herbert Baker and his associate A. T. Scott built, in 1930, India House in the Aldwych, in a part of London that had become almost an Imperial Quarter. This was thick with Indian allusions, sculptural and ornamental, and was decorated by Indian artists especially trained in Europe: but as, over the years, its grey stone darkened, and it turned into the office of the Indian High Commissioner, so it became merged in the mass of the great city, and most passers-by today, like most London guide-books, do not notice it at all.

The testimony

Not much to show, it might be thought, for so long, potent and profitable a relationship: but in India itself things are very different. If the independent Indians have sensibly abandoned Anglo-Indian building traditions, they have not destroyed the Anglo-Indian heritage. Most of the buildings recorded in this book stand there still, shabbier perhaps than they were in their great days, but still generally used for the same purposes (though Gandhi wanted to turn the Vice-roy's House into a hospital).

The anonymous mansions of the Calcutta nabobs may be fading away, but all the public buildings survive, Forbes's Mint to Emerson's Victoria Memorial. The towers of Indo-Saracenia still float over the Madras waterfront; the Gola pre-serves its echoes; Bombay remains, in the judgement of Mr Gavin Stamp, 'the best Victorian Gothic city in the world'. The tremendous railway termini, the hill-stations, the Government Houses, the cantonments, the racecourses, the churches, the Lawrence Memorial Asylum, the Lansdowne Bridge, a hundred clubs and ten thousand bungalows are there for the inspection still – the richest of all imperial mementoes, on the grandest of imperial scales.

Lofty or modest, elegant or preposterous, they are testimony to a great historical adventure, and to the passage through these improbable landscapes of a remarkable people: testimony in fact to a brutal virtue, like it or not.

TREFAN MORYS, 1983

Sleeping lion, Fort William, Calcutta. Empire's farewell.

A BRIEF BIBLIOGRAPHY

The bibliography of Anglo-India is vast, but there are very few books specifically about what the British built in their Indian Empire. The following handful of titles, some less specific than others, have all been published since its dissolution:

Barr, Pat, and Desmond, Ray, *Simla* (London, 1978)
Bence-Jones, Mark, *Palaces of the Raj* (London, 1973)
Berridge, P. S. A., *Couplings to the Khyber* (Newton Abbot, 1969)
Bristow, Robert, *Cochin Saga* (London, 1959)

Irving, Robert Grant, *Indian Summer: Lutyens, Baker and Imperial Delhi* (London, 1981)

King, Anthony D., *Colonial Urban Development* (London, 1976)

Mitra, Asok, *Delhi, Capital City* (New Delhi, 1970)
Moorhouse, Geoffrey, *Calcutta* (London, 1971)
Moraes, Dom, *Bombay* (Amsterdam, 1979)

Nilsson, Sten, *European Architecture in India, 1750–1850* (London, 1968)
—— *The New Capitals of India, Pakistan and Bangladesh* (Copenhagen, 1973)

Panter-Downes, Mollie, *Ooty Preserved* (London, 1967)
Pott, Janet, *Old Bungalows in Bangalore* (London, 1977)

Satow, Michael, and Desmond, Ray, *Railways of the Raj* (London, 1980)

Tindall, Gillian, *City of Gold: The Biography of Bombay* (London, 1982)

Wilkinson, Theo, *Two Monsoons* (London, 1976).

In addition the essays and papers of Mrs Mildred Archer and Mr Gavin Stamp are essential material for the student, while dear old Murray's *Handbook for Travellers*, now in its twenty-second edition, continues to be, as it has been since 1859, the best practical guide to the constructions of British India.

INDEX

Page references in **bold type** refer to plates and/or captions